The Relevance of Liberalism

Studies of the Research Institute on International Change, Columbia University

Zbigniew Brzezinski, series editor

Zbigniew Brzezinski is Herbert Lehman Professor of Government and director of the Research Institute on International Change at Columbia University, where he has taught since 1960. In January 1977, Dr. Brzezinski obtained a leave to serve in the Carter administration as assistant to the president for national security affairs.

Other Titles in This Series

Radicalism in the Contemporary Age, Volume 1
Sources of Contemporary Radicalism
Seweryn Bialer and Sophia Sluzar, editors

Radicalism in the Contemporary Age, Volume 2
Radical Visions of the Future
Seweryn Bialer and Sophia Sluzar, editors

Radicalism in the Contemporary Age, Volume 3
Strategies and Impact of Contemporary Radicalism
Seweryn Bialer and Sophia Sluzar, editors

Asia's Nuclear Future
William H. Overholt, editor

The Relevance of Liberalism

edited by the staff of the Research
Institute on International Change

This volume is the outgrowth of a conference organized in January 1976 by the Research Institute on International Change. The conference represented an important aspect of the institute's research focus on value changes in the world and their impact on international affairs.

The papers and discussion included here touch on a wide range of topics: the development of liberalism as a historical phenomenon, the social and economic conditions that sustain liberal institutions and values, the various elements of liberalism as a system of ideas, the relationship between liberalism and democracy, liberalism's claims to universal validity, the relationship between liberalism and socialism, and the polarization in liberal thinking. They are a fair expression of viewpoints concerning the relevance of liberalism in the contemporary world. They also affirm basic liberal values, an affirmation best summed up in a quotation from Charles Frankel: "To put it crudely, what does liberalism have going for it? It has that very large part of humanity behind it which distrusts zealotry, that is rational enough always to try to hedge its bets if it can, that knows that the people in charge of society have to be watched, but that prefers homely pleasures and joys to the ecstasies of revolution and sudden death."

This study was prepared and edited by the staff of the Research Institute on International Change: Zbigniew Brzezinski, director; Seweryn Bialer, acting director; Sophia Sluzar, assistant director; and Robert Nurick, conference rapporteur.

The Relevance
of Liberalism

CONTRIBUTORS

ROBERT BARTLEY   CHARLES FRANKEL

IRVING HOWE   MICHAEL MANDELBAUM

GIOVANNI SARTORI   EDWARD SHILS

PREFACE BY ZBIGNIEW BRZEZINSKI

edited by the staff of the

Research Institute
on International Change

Zbigniew Brzezinski, Director
Seweryn Bialer, Acting Director
Sophia Sluzar, Assistant Director
Robert Nurick, Conference Rapporteur

WESTVIEW PRESS
BOULDER, COLORADO

A Westview Special Study

Published in 1978 in the United States of America by
 Westview Press, Inc.
 5500 Central Avenue
 Boulder, Colorado 80301
 Frederick A. Praeger, Publisher and Editorial Director

Library of Congress Cataloging in Publication Data
Main entry under title:
Columbia University. Research Institute on International Change.
    The relevance of liberalism.
    (Studies of the Research Institute on International Change,
Columbia University)
    "Product of a conference held at the Research Institute on
International Change on January 21, 1976."
    1. Liberalism—Congresses. I. Title. II. Series: Columbia University.
Research Institute on International Change. Studies of the Research
Institute on International Change, Columbia University.
JC571.C633 1977   320.5'1   77-8202
ISBN 0-89158-134-0

Printed and bound in the United States of America

Contents

Preface

This volume is the product of a conference held at the Research Institute on International Change on 21 January 1976. The subject of the conference, the relevance of liberalism in the contemporary world, represents one aspect of the institute's research focus on changes in values and the impact of these changes on international affairs. This focus reflects the belief that we are living in a time when the sudden expansion in popular political consciousness is altering fundamentally the ways in which politics is perceived, in which political values are translated into political action, and in which political movements and moods transcend state boundaries and thus have worldwide repercussions. Together these changes may result in profound discontinuities in political behavior, in social institutions, and in the basic values around which institutions and procedures are shaped.

The conference, and this book based on it, took liberalism as its subject for examination. Liberalism is one of the key organizing principles which has dominated the world since the time of the Industrial Revolution. It seemed important to examine liberalism from the historical perspective as a system of ideas and to identify its components—cultural, economic, and political.

The overall theme of the discussion was the continuing viability of liberalism. In this connection, questions were posed about the following issues: are specific social and economic conditions necessary to sustain liberalism; does it have universal applicability or was it a phenomenon limited to the Western world at a specific stage of its social and economic existence; what was the interaction between liberalism and democracy; what is its relationship to socialism, another organizing principle claiming universal validity; what are the prospects of liberalism should its influence contract to a small area or even to one country, such as the United States?

Four of the chapters in this volume—those by Giovanni Sartori, Irving Howe, Robert Bartley, and Charles Frankel—were prepared as papers for the conference. Edward Shils was unable to attend the conference but expressed the desire to write a chapter on the trends and attitudes in American liberalism today. The concluding chapter, by Michael Mandelbaum, deals with the future prospects of liberalism. I wish to express my thanks to the authors. At the same time, I would like to thank the principal commentators at the conference for their introductory remarks which initiated such a lively discussion of the issues before the conference. They were Edward Banfield, Harvard University; Donald Fraser, U.S. Congress (Minnesota); Andrew Hacker, City University of New York, Queens; Robert Heilbroner, New School for Social Research; and Richard Lowenthal, professor emeritus, Free University of Berlin.

The other participants at the conference were Seweryn Bialer, Columbia University (and the Research Institute on International Change [R.I.I.C.]); W. Theodore deBary, Columbia University; Midge Decter, *Commentary*; Alexander Erlich, Columbia University; Max Frankel, Columbia University; Richard Gardner, Columbia University; Mary Cronin, *Time*; Walter Goodman, *New York Times*; Stanley Heginbothan, Columbia University (and R.I.I.C.); Erik Hoffmann,

State University of New York at Albany (and R.I.I.C.); Peter Katzenstein, Cornell University; Ira Katznelson, University of Chicago; Mark Kesselman, Columbia University; Robbin Laird, Columbia University (R.I.I.C.); Juan Linz, Yale University; Charles Maier, Duke University; Ernest Nagel, Columbia University; Robert Nurick, Columbia University (R.I.I.C.); William Odom, West Point (and R.I.I.C.); William Overholt, Hudson Institute (and R.I.I.C.); Herbert Passin, Columbia University; Harvey Picker, Columbia University; Norman Podhoretz, *Commentary*; Stanley Rothman, Smith College; Joseph Rothschild, Columbia University; William Rusher, *National Review*; Robert Sharlet, Union College (and R.I.I.C.); Marshall Shulman, Columbia University; Allan Silver, Columbia University; Sophia Sluzar, Columbia University (R.I.I.C.); Sidney Tarrow, Cornell University; Ernest van den Haag, New York University and New School for Social Research; Donald Zagoria, City University of New York, Hunter (and R.I.I.C.).

The organization of the conference was a collective effort of the institute. For their assistance in preparing the manuscript for publication, I would like to thank Barbara Falgoust Williams, Susan Gewirth, Richard Snyder, and Pamela Squires.

Zbigniew Brzezinski

The Contributors

Robert L. Bartley is editor of the editorial page of *The Wall Street Journal,* for which he has written extensively on contemporary economic and political issues. He is a member of the American Society of Newspaper Editors and of the American Political Science Association.

Charles Frankel is Old Dominion Professor of Philosophy and Public Affairs at Columbia University. He has served as assistant secretary of state for education and cultural affairs (1965-67), chairman of the United States delegation at the UNESCO General Conference (1966), and a member of the Board of Directors of the New York State Civil Liberties Union (1960-65). His publications include *The Faith of Reason* (1948), *The Case for Modern Man* (1956), *The Democratic Prospect* (1962), *The Pleasures of Philosophy* (1972), and *Controversies and Decisions* (editor, 1976).

Irving Howe is Distinguished Professor of English at the City University of New York. Coeditor of *Dissent,* he is the author of many books, among them *World of Our Fathers, Politics and the Novel, Decline of the New,* and *A World More Attractive.*

Michael Mandelbaum is assistant professor of government and research associate in the Program for Science and International Affairs at Harvard University. In 1976-77 he was a Rockefeller Fellow in the humanities and visiting research associate of the Research Institute on International Change at Columbia University.

Giovanni Sartori, currently professor of political science at Stanford University and editor of the *Rivista Italiana di Scienza Politica,* was professor of political science at the University of Florence from 1960 to 1976 and has been visiting professor at Harvard and Yale universities. His major publications in English are *Democratic Theory* (1962) and *Parties and Party Systems—A Framework for Analysis* (1976).

Edward Shils is professor of sociology and social thought at the University of Chicago, fellow of Peterhouse College, Cambridge, and founder and editor of *Minerva.* His most recent works include *The Intellectuals and the Powers* (1972) and *Center and Periphery: Essays in Macrosociology* (1975).

The Relevance of Liberalism

1

The Relevance of Liberalism in Retrospect

Giovanni Sartori

If one compares the label "liberalism" with its neighbors—democracy, socialism, and communism—liberalism has one winning claim: it is the most unsettled and misapprehended term in the whole string. We all speak of democracy (in the singular), thereby implying that this concept can be given a core meaning. But most writings on liberalism end up speaking of liberalisms (in the plural),[1] often declare the singular form intractable, and surely are at their worst when attempting a synthesis[2] or when searching for an all-embracing, rarefied meaning.[3] Even more interesting, while all the writings on democracy (the thing) say "democracy," much of the literature on liberalism (the thing) does not employ the word. We say "Lockeian liberalism," but Locke himself did not. We declare Montesquieu a classic of liberalism, but this is not how Montesquieu perceived himself. Likewise, much of the literature on the *American Mind*[4] actually describes what Europeans would call the American brand of liberalism, but is not presented, by its authors, under this focus.[5] And, perhaps, the distinction between the thing and the word offers the best thread for introducing my topic.

The thing was conceived and constructed some two centuries before it was named. For the name liberalism was apparently invented in Spain in 1810—both too late and at a wrong moment. Too late because "liberalism" was coined when liberalism had already delivered its major message, and because the acceleration of history had already begun to shorten time, thereby affording insufficient time for the name to take hold, stabilize itself, and establish its rank. One of the resulting paradoxes was that while the Germans began to speak of "liberalism" when their liberalism—*à l'avant garde* during the Enlightenment[6]—was on the wane, at the other extreme Americans never really adopted "liberalism" as the distinctive label for the constitution and the polity they had constructed. The United States was first perceived as a republic, and subsequently as a democracy, flying as it were over the head of "liberalism" (the name). Thus "liberalism" has not even lent its name to a national party; and the term liberal has always been used, in the United States, in one of its sectarian senses, for reformist, progressive, and/or radical groups.

The overall paradox of this is that while an unnamed liberalism has represented, between the seventeenth and twentieth centuries, the most fundamental experience of the Western political man, "liberalism" as the rightful denomination for this experience has been applied in most countries only for a few decades; and even in England, which represents the most notable exception to this generalization, the word became popular when the liberal experiment was departing from its Lockeian course and extraneous influences--notably German idealism--were muddling its image. Thus England can well illustrate my second point, namely that to the misfortune of having been baptized too late one must add the misfortune of having been baptized at a wrong moment.

When the word arrived in England from Spain, the novelty was not *political liberalism* but *economic liberism*. (I purposely emphasize a difference—the difference between a political system and an economic system—that has not entered, as I am about to explain, into English.) And economic "liberism" coincided with the first industrial revolution—which is also to say with capital accumulation paid for by ruthless exploitation. The first coincidence inextricably confused the central feature of liberalism, the constitutionalization of politics, with one of its possible, but not necessary, corollaries—as if the lineage of Locke, Blackstone, and Montesquieu, intrinsically political thinkers, lay in economics, in Adam Smith, Ricardo, Cobden, and the Manchester gospel. And the second coincidence goes a long way toward explaining the lasting disaffection, if not hostility, to liberalism of the working classes. Even though capital accumulation has ever since exacted heavy tolls (in Socialist and Communist countries as well), yet the first association of "capitalist exploitation" was not with "liberism" but with "liberalism" as an undivided whole. Hence, the newborn label was easily exposed to the negative value connotations which were soon put forward by the early "Socialists" (the word was used first in England, not in France, by the Owenists) and which have been subsequently hammered to no end in all the Marxist literature. Now, it is a pretty safe guess that if "liberalism" had not been coined in 1810 but either a hundred years earlier or later, it would have never occurred to us to use one and the same name for political *and* economic freedom.[7]

Let it be added that while classical liberalism—rooted as it was in the natural law doctrine—was endowed with an ethical flavor, little of this flavor survived in the English philosophy of the time, namely, in the hands of the utilitarians and specifically of Bentham—a thoroughgoing rationalist bent upon the felicific calculus. The retort to this is that the central figure of nineteenth century English liberalism is John Stuart Mill—not his father James Mill, and even less Bentham.[8] Nonetheless when John Stuart Mill wrote his celebrated essay *On Liberty,* an additional element had complicated the picture: democracy. That is to say, J. S. Mill's referent was not liberalism *per se* but liberal democracy—so much so that his major preoccupation was germane to Tocqueville's preoccupation: the tyranny of the majority "over opinion."[9] The issue was further complicated by the fact that the following generations (Thomas Hill Green and Leonard Hobhouse) embraced and disseminated an idealistic "organic" version of liberalism whose highly abstract metaphysics simply did not fit into the language, let alone the tradition, of English philosophy; and the subsequent combination of Mill and Spencer left "the theory of liberalism in a state of unintelligible confusion."[10] The Spencer-Darwin-type confusion made little headway in continental Europe (but mightily crossed the Atlantic). Conversely, the idealistic, and indeed Hegelian, version of liberalism hardly struck roots in the English soil and even less in the American soils, but did confuse many European minds and did travel surprisingly well from Germany to Italy.[11]

The misfortune of having been baptized both too late and at a wrong moment can be highlighted—leaving England—from a more general angle. History proceeds via elementary oppositions and polarizations. Before the entry of "liberalism," the opposition had long been between monarchy and republic. As the republics materialized they lost much of their magic, and—as we see very clearly in Tocqueville—the new opposition might well have been between liberalism and democracy. But this opposition was already shattered by the 1848 revolutions. At least in France, already in 1848 a third major protagonist (and antagonist) had shown its force—"socialism"—and called for a new two-front realignment. An immediate consequence was that, in Europe, liberals and democrats had to converge and merge somewhat too fast, out of necessity rather than out of clear thinking. Let it be recalled that in the aftermath of the 1848 revolutions two entirely different (but hardly well distinguished) conceptions of democracy were at stake: on the one hand the preliberal "democracy of the ancients" (rejuvenated by Rousseau), and on the other hand the "democracy of the moderns," which is younger than liberalism, presupposes liberalism, and constitutes its natural implementation.[12] Now, if reference is made not to the Rousseau-type democracy drawn from distant memories (ethymological democracy) but to the liberal democracy that was the daughter of reality and was establishing itself in the United States, then it can be safely asserted that the convergence between liberalism (Lockeian and constitutional liberalism) and democracy was successful, and that the liberal component of this happy marriage has long remained its central element.

However, this victory of liberalism (the thing) was not the victory of "liberalism" (the word). As time went by, and as "socialism" (the word) affirmed itself as *the* ideal which opposed the prose of liberal-democracy, the new polarization became, in the twentieth century, the polarization between "democracy" (tout court) and "socialism." Of course, one can argue that the substance matters more than the name. Yet *nomina numina.* What is unnamed either remains undetected, or tends to be forgotten. As a consequence the notion of liberalism today is associated, at best, with a typically nineteenth century specimen, with something belonging to the past, if not with a wholly obsolete reality. So allow me to make once more the point that the fortune of liberalism (both the word and the thing) would have been, in all likelihood, far greater had the name been invented either earlier or later.

The thread pursued thus far brings out two points that deserve further scrutiny.

First, a major difficulty in assessing the accomplishments and inadequacies of liberalism resides precisely in the fact that some authors speak of the thing with only passing reference to the word, while other authors, following the word, are led astray by its secondary meanings and/or by the party and sectarian uses of the term. This goes to explain the so-called elasticity of liberalism.[13] The question remains: the elasticity *of what?* If this question is not taken seriously, we are easily trapped into a discussion without object. My stand is that liberalism can be traced back to a distinct and

ve historical connotation, provided that we search
r "pure and simple liberalism" (in the singular) and
tnat ⌐1is unraveling is aided by appropriate distinctions.

Second, it is contrary both to the historical evidence and
to the principles of analytic thinking to deal in one blow
with a political system (liberalism) and an economic system
(liberism). That is to say that we must carefully distinguish
liberalism from laissez-faire, market economy. To the real
founding fathers—from Locke to the authors of *The
Federalist Papers* in the United States and from Montesquieu
to Benjamin Constant in France—liberalism meant the rule
of law and the constitutional State, and liberty was *political*
freedom (freedom *from* political oppression), not free
trade, free markets, and (in Spencer's development) the law
of survival of the fittest. Let it be added that since political
liberalism was born long before economic liberism, if it
was able to perform without laissez-faire earlier, it can
conceivably perform without laissez-faire later.

On the other hand, it is true that the liberal state was
conceived in wholesale distrust of state power, and therefore
with the purpose of reducing rather than increasing the
scope and role of the State. Thus, in the nineteenth century
the liberal state was actually constructed as a small state,
if not as a minimal State, and consequently as a do-little
or even do-nothing state.[14] But the liberal state is not characterized by its size nor by its amount of activity; it is
characterized by its structure and thus is, first of all and
above all, a "constitutional state" in the *garantiste* meaning
of the term.[15] Therefore nothing prevents the liberal state
from evolving into a large and even all-interfering state—on
this essential condition: that the more it ceases to be a
minimal state, the more important it becomes that it remain
a constitutional state.

To distinguish is not to separate. The argument is, then,
that it is only after having distinguished between liberalism
and "liberism" that we can appropriately and profitably
discuss how they relate to each other. The answer may well
be (as in the von Hayek and von Mises line of argument) that

the two things optimize one another, that liberalism performs best when implemented by a market economy—and vice versa. And the best counteranswer is not, in my opinion, the one that challenges this argument, but the one that points to the changing needs and priorities of each epoch. We may prefer, for example, distributive justice (despite its costs) to producing more for less. We may believe that a Pareto optimum is really *the* optimum; but we may also pursue Rawls-preferred solutions.[16] However that may be, I am only pointing out that the connection between liberalism and "liberism" can indeed be conceived as being, or having to be, very loose. The question still is: can the two things be entirely disconnected? More fundamentally, and also more precisely put: can the liberal solution to the problem of power cope with, and survive under, any kind of economic system? Since this is an ultimate question, it is tackled best by envisaging extreme instances: either a non-market, Communist type of planned economy or, at the other end, the principle of private property. And since the whole argument begins with and hinges on how liberalism relates historically to what has been vividly called "possessive individualism,"[17] let my first reply simply be: individualism, yes; possession, no—and give my reasons for so replying.

Marxists read back into history a concept of private property that does not belong to the actual fabric of history. The sacredness of property affirmed over the centuries by the natural law theory and so eloquently reiterated in the 1776 Virginia Declaration of Rights[18] shares nothing with the capitalistic notion of property. From Roman times up until the end of the eighteenth century, property meant, all in one and indivisibly, "life, liberty, and estate;" it did not mean "possession" for its own sake or for the sake of unlimited accumulation, let alone " capital accumulation." Even the Leveller writers maintained that freedom is a function of possession. Were they, for this, inconsistent revolutionaries? I would rather say that they made perfect sense. With a bare subsistence economy and endemic exposure

to undifferentiated insecurity, to "own" signified, very simply, to improve life chances: property was "protection"—
indeed the way of removing insecurity from the bare surface
of one's skin. To be sure, even then to "have" implied to
"have power." But the economic power of property had yet
to gain momentum and to be perceived as such. The patri-
monial state (and, from the top, all the way down the feudal
echelon) was not an economic State: it needed resources for
raising armies which were, in turn, its real power base. Up
until the domestication of politics, far beyond mere influence
power meant "force," the force of arms and violence—not
the force of property.

Hence the allegation that liberalism was founded upon a
"possessive market society,"[19] or that it is a superstructure of
a capitalistic-type economy, is simply untrue to the facts.
Liberalism cannot be reduced to economic premises, or pre-
suppositions, even at this most elemental juncture. If property is an economic concept related to an acquisitive society
and to the industrial "multiplication" of production, then
this is not the concept that upholds liberalism. Liberalism
praises and defends the individual[20] and sustains this individual with that "security" that is his property—with a property
as safety that has nothing to share with an economic vision
of life.

Leaving aside the Marxist interpretation of history we may
still wonder, prospectively instead of retrospectively, whether
the liberal solution to the problem of political power can survive under a propertyless, nonmarket type of economic
system. This is a different question, for the fact that political
liberalism historically preceded commercialism, laissez-faire,
and capitalism, bears no conclusive evidence on what the case
may be in industrial and postindustrial societies. Under these
new circumstances, and in the extreme instance under consideration, the essence of the case was grasped in just one
brief sentence by Trotsky: when the state is the sole employ-
er, "he who does not obey does not eat." So the answer
clearly is that the liberal protection of the freedom of the individual becomes baseless under a Communist-type economy.

But let us not interpret this assertion wrongly. The argument is not that political liberalism cannot survive under Communist capitalism (seemingly a paradox, but not really) *because* liberalism is a by-product of market economy and/or of private property. The argument is, instead, that *any* concentration of all power (political and economic) implies that the individual, and whatever individual liberty he may praise, are crushed. The argument is, then, the very old one that subjects become citizens (with rights and a free voice) only within societal structures that disperse power and allow for a variety of intermediary and countervailing powers. We may well dislike market-type structures and mechanisms. The problem remains to replace them without losing sight of the problem. To conclude on the point, the infrastructure that liberalism requires and Communism lacks (for it simply ignores the problem) is a socioeconomic diffusion of power. As I was saying, to distinguish a political from an economic system is not to separate them. Yet their relationship can and should be conceived, at least in principle, flexibly—as a relationship that allows for a wide variety of combinations.

There is a further distinction that has yet to be drawn: the distinction between liberty and liberalism. It can well be asserted that the "elementary desire to be free is the force behind all liberties, old and new."[21] It does *not* follow that this elementary desire is a "natural" one (it must be nurtured)[22] nor that it necessarily leads to the liberal polity, or to the liberal kind of solution. The elementary desire to be free has found its first outlet—within Western culture—in the Greek *eleutheria,* in something that the Romans qualified *licentia* (in opposition to *libertas*),[23] and is more easily projected in what we have come to call anarchy. However that may be, some two thousand years went by before deriving "liberalism" from *libertas* and "liberty." Had the transition been obvious or natural, this enormous time lag would be inexplicable.

The foregoing also alerts us to the difference between philosophical liberalism and the empirical theory and practice of liberalism. This distinction is thin and of little consequence before the so-called (and previously recalled) idealistic revision of liberalism; but of great consequence after Hegel and with respect to what has been named by Cranston *étatiste* liberalism. For instance, Benedetto Croce expounded, between the two world wars, what he proclaimed (and the audience believed to be) *the* Philosophy of Liberalism. However, it was only a philosophy of Liberty (capitalized), of a "pure category of the Spirit," in which nothing was left of the techniques and ways of taming absolute power, that is, of the *quid sui* of liberalism.[24] In Croce's argument, a man is free regardless of whether he is in prison. This can be granted if reference is made to moral freedom, or to the *inner* freedom of man. But the problem of liberalism is *outer* freedom, and precisely that men should not be imprisoned without due process and due cause.

Pulling the threads together, and briefly put, liberalism is—in its basic historical connotation—the theory and practice of the juridical defence, through the constitutional state, of individual liberty. To be sure, this is liberalism *only,* or liberalism *per se,* not liberal-democracy nor democratic liberalism. However, since twentieth century liberalism is a very composite reality with many layers and many ramifications, any orderly understanding requires us to decompose the "compound" and to distinguish, in a preliminary way, between (1) liberalism as such, in its distinctiveness and pure form, and (2) the progeny of liberalism. In turn, the progeny of liberalism has generated, currently, a considerable number of so-called neo- or new liberalisms. For the purposes at hand, however, I need not dwell on the various streams of relatively recent vintage—such as welfare liberalism, social liberalism, and the like. It will be sufficient to follow the main stream: the transformation of "pure liberalism" into democratic liberalism.

This transformation generally receives little attention in the American literature, among other reasons because American liberalism was incorporated *in toto,* and from the outset, in its theory and practice of democracy. Since the United States was not burdened by a medieval past, the transition did not require revolutionary convulsions and occurred fast—so fast, we know, that "liberalism" (as a name) did not even land in the United States in time. The European literature, however, scrutinizes to no end the relationship between liberalism and democracy, whose essence is generally rendered—from Tocqueville to de Ruggiero, Kelsen, and Raymond Aron—as the relationship between liberty and equality.

To be sure, liberalism already includes a number of equalities, just as democracy does enhance additional freedoms. But what the Tocquevilleian line of interpretation brings out is that the two principles involve a different logic. Liberalism as such demands equality of rights and equal laws, but distrusts equalities gratuitously bestowed from above and unequal ways of equalizing. On the other hand, the freedoms of democracy are freedoms *to,* and the democratic mind is largely insensitive to the requisite nature, procedurally speaking, of a freedom *from.* One may equally say that liberalism pivots on the individual, democracy on the society, thereby implying that liberalism has a vertical impetus (in favor of differentiation, unevenness, and eminence) while democracy has a horizontal urge (in the pursuit of cohesion and distributive evenness).

If we leave the Tocquevilleian sphere of principles and descend to the more mundane sphere of deeds, the distinction becomes that liberalism is, above all, the technique of controlling and limiting the state's power, while democracy is the insertion of popular power into the state. It follows that while the major concern of liberalism is the "form" of the state (the *how,* or the method, of rule making), the problem of democracy is the *what* of rule making, that is, the content of norms. And if the elements of liberal-democracy are analyzed in this manner, also the distinction between *political* democracy and democracy in the *social* and/or *economic* senses can be neatly drawn—as follows: that political democracy is the liberal state implemented by the entry of the demos,[25] whereas the social and economic concerns represent the distinctive additions of democracy as such.

This analysis can be pursued at length, and must also account—in reconstructing the whole—for the reciprocal concessions, and indeed for a reciprocal contagion. Thus liberalism has opened itself to "equality of opportunity," while
democracy has absorbed the caveat that power needs to be
watched over. Likewise, the "atomized" nature of liberal
individualism has been corrected, in the course of the marriage, by the exposure to "social democracy" (as distinct
from socialist democracy—that is, in the ethical or humane
sense given to the notion of social democracy by Bryce:
"equality of estimation," equal respect for the next man, regardless of differences in status and wealth). And if one still
wonders whether there is still much point in this exercise, the
reply is that its value is not only retrospective but eminently
prospective. For liberalism and democracy have seemingly
entered, after a long period of fruitful convergence, if not of
welding, a path of divergence.

The first cracks arise when the component elements of
liberal-democracy become too unbalanced, when "more"
democracy is actually pursued at the expense of "less"
liberalism. A good case in point is the steady erosion of constitutionalism brought about by new constitutions that are so
democratic as to lose their *garantiste* reason for being. No
doubt these imbalances can be managed—but under one essential condition: that all the parties perceive the process as
having a head and a tail, and that our concern for extending
the tail is recognized for what it is—an extension, not a be-
heading. This means that the itinerary from liberty to equality stands in that order, that it is a nonreversible itinerary:
nonimpediment, or freedom *from,* necessarily precedes the
freedoms *to* (and participation *in*).[26] The free individual of
liberalism has "voice," and is empowered to "voice for"
equality; whereas equals can well remain unfree, equal in
being voiceless and abused. Let it be stressed that this is
only a *procedural precedence,* a sequencing—not an order
of importance. When this is well understood, we can still
proceed in aggrandizing the tail. But when this is misunderstood—as appears to be more and more the case—then liberal-

democracy breaks down.

We are now in a position to appraise one thing at a time, and in particular to appraise liberalism (*per se*) with respect to (1) its limits, (2) its lasting validity (in principle), and (3) its decline (in fact).

The *limits* are easily summarized. Liberalism is a political solution to the problem so vividly expressed by Rousseau: men are born free and are everywhere in chains. These chains are not, to be sure, only political. But until the political chains are removed, economic (and other) constraints are covered up (or compressed), and lack, so to speak, legs of their own. This does not detract from the fact that liberalism finds its limit in *not* being a global, all-encompassing program. Its overriding problem is the polity.

Having acknowledged the "limits," or the boundedness, how do we pass from here to the "limitation" and, ultimately, to the "inadequacy" of liberalism? These terms switch into one another simply as a function of, and in response to, the "realization" of liberalism in the real world. Had liberalism remained in books and libraries, it would hardly occur to us to declare it inadequate. Had it produced only a "formal" and empty liberty—as we are being deceived into believing[27]—how is it that the masses have powerfully entered politics turning the power of politics to their advantage? Clearly, if we do look at liberalism in the perspective of its limitations and inadequacies, this is because we have changed perspective, because our yardstick is provided by new goals and broader ambitions. This is right—provided that the baby does not drown as we move him into deeper waters.

We are thus required (in order to save the baby) to underline the lasting, and I would even say everlasting, *validity* of liberalism. For liberalism has shown that absolute and arbitrary power can be curbed; it has defeated the circularity of despair expressed by the objection, *quis custodiet custodes?*, who controls the controllers; it has liberated man *from* the fear and abuses of the Prince. It is important to add that liberalism is unique in this accomplishment also from another angle. Whether we conceive liberalism as a philosophy, a theory, a doctrine, or an ideology, in any case it is the only *engineering of history* that has not failed us: it encompasses ends *and* means, and its practice does implement its theory. Within its ambit—polity building—liberalism (not Marxism) is a theory with *praxis,* a program that "works," a knowledge suited to and capable of "realization."[28]

Despite its value and unique capability, the *decline,* and indeed the decay of liberalism, is neither surprising nor difficult to explain. "Liberalism" has lost the war of words: much of what survives of liberalism today is not identified as such. One might infer from this that the substance of liberalism is still very much alive; and I would not question the statement that the substance fares better than the name. Nonetheless, a defeat in the war of words does entail a crisis of identity and, in its wake, an ominous loss of force. In the end, if people do not know, when speaking of liberalism, what they are saying, the most likely outcome is that liberalism will be killed unknowingly and by mistake.

Another way of looking at the decay of liberalism relates to the very nature of the fabric of history. Bernard Crick has a splendid sentence to this effect: "Boredom with established truths is a great enemy of free men."[29] If the sentence is related to the acceleration of history, and specifically to what I call the "frenzy of novitism" (be wrong but new, and new at whatever cost), then liberalism is bound to be in disgrace. For liberalism results from a very long process of historical testing, of trial and error, and does epitomize established truths.

The cycle of liberalism might also be considered (*pro tempore,* as implied by the notion of cycle) exhausted, on the basis of the principle that "victory kills." Victory, in history, kills in a very thorough way: not only because men are desiring and, therefore, dissatisfied animals who lose interest in what they already have; not only because reality always deceives; but even more because in victory an "ideal" ceases to be such, thereby leaving a deontological vacancy in want of "another ideal." And the principle that victory kills the winner (which is at odds, I am afraid, with the linear concep-

tion of history and with our projective techniques of fore-
casting) should also be borne in mind with respect to liberal-
democracy—the compound to which I now pass for a final
consideration.

Since liberal-democracy follows liberalism and represents
its expansion, the implication is that it overcomes the admitted "narrowness" of its ancestor. The question turns, therefore, on whether in the process of overcoming the limits of
liberalism we may not overcome liberalism itself. So far, we
still have democracy *within* liberalism. But if the tail eats
the head, then we shall have democracy *without* liberalism
(that is, in my understanding, the perfect Leviathan). It is
here that the issue is joined.

Assuming that the outcome is not left to the force of arms
but to the force of ideas and ideals, then the battle hinges on
keeping alive, defending and reappraising the value of the
liberal ground floor of the edifice. As the imagery implies,
this is not to say that the liberal element matters more—even
though it is the case that the "constraints on which the
liberal has concentrated have become more important; the
constraints he has neglected less important."[30] However, even
if we are involved in adding new floors, the cracks must be
repaired wherever they are. Liberalism needs help for the
simple reason that it really needs it. And in help of liberalism
(*per se*) I venture to offer a concluding consideration of
hope.

Western liberals (in the party or sectarian sense) do not
necessarily descend from liberalism, that is, many people that
call themselves liberals have never understood nor valued
liberalism in its historical connotation and accomplishments.
This is so (I hope to be forgiven for being so repetitive) because the thing and the word have lost sight of each other.
The intellectual sources of many of the literate, present-day
self-styled liberals variously range from Paine, Proudhon, and
Marx, to Burke and Calhoun. And a number of self-styled
liberal parties (think of Latin America) perform as sheer
defenders of vested privileges. But while the Western scene
does not offer—in my diagnosis—much ground for hope, what

I do sense is that a growing number of East European intellectuals are in fact, even if unknowingly, rediscovering liberalism (as such). They are rediscovering, I mean, the political virtues (and, in my interpretation, essence) of liberalism: that unchecked power is insufferable and disastrous; that justices and courts must be truly independent; that constitutions are not merely whatever structure a State happens to have, but a specific *garantiste* structure that actually restrains and constrains the power wielders. This rediscovery will take effort, tears, and time; it may take their lives. But if the Western civility (which either is liberal-democratic or is nothing) manages to survive long enough, then liberal-democracy will be sustained, and eventually rejuvenated, by Eastern liberalism. This may appear a paradoxical conclusion. But the ways of history are paradoxical. Nor need we call upon Hegel's cunningness of Reason to explain why liberalism is so important to people who lack liberty.

Discussion

The discussion touched on a wide range of interrelated issues: the development of liberalism as a historical phenomenon; the social and economic conditions which sustain liberal institutions and values; the various elements (political, economic, and "anthropological") of liberalism as a system of ideas; the relationship between liberalism and democracy; liberalism's claims to universal validity; the problem of liberalism in power; and the import of dissident intellectuals in Eastern Europe for liberal thought and practice.

The session opened with a fairly extensive discussion of the development of liberalism as a historical phenomenon, for it was generally agreed that answers to the critical questions about the relevance of liberalism today require reflections on the shape and structure of what *has* been the liberal world. In the view of one discussant the great merit of the Sartori paper is its stress on the centrality of the *political* concept of liberalism: the protection of individual rights. In his opinion, this has always been the central core of liberalism, and is still relevant today. Nevertheless, he felt it would be a mistake to sever its historical links with economic liberalism—the notion that the pursuit of individual interests will lead to the common good—which was based on the rights of property as the main guarantee against arbitrary power. Original liberalism, he explained, thus contained no doctrine of equality and especially no doctrine of the franchise, which is why there was a conflict between liberalism and democracy. The convergence of the two came only when democrats learned to accept the separation of powers, and liberals learned to accept the universal franchise.

Other speakers took issue with this view, arguing that while it may be valid intellectually to distinguish between liberalism and democracy, the distinction is a dangerous one to make. Not only are the two historically linked, but the latter is impossible without the former, since the whole idea of free participation in societal decision making depends on the free articulation of individual and group interests. Moreover, one speaker added, although it is true that the emergence of liberalism was historically associated with an ascendent bourgeoisie, its unique virtue has been to legitimate counterinterests and counterthrusts from below.

One member of the conference agreed that the Sartori paper is a useful corrective to the "crass Marxism" which simplistically equates liberalism with property. Nevertheless, he pointed out, liberalism did emerge within a particular context, namely the simultaneous development of a mercantile role for the State and, within some States, new modes of social relations based on the free exchange of labor. Although there were profound tensions between the mercantile principles and the principles of free exchange, they were resolved on behalf of laissez-faire and the market mechanism. Now, however, the state is neither a counterliberal nor a countercapitalist force; instead, having politicized many of the relations once handled by the market, it is central to contemporary capitalism. In other words, the liberal system is no longer market capitalism.

In response, it was readily agreed that the context within which liberalism emerged has been crucial to its later development. On the other hand, however, the Italian Republic is an example of how similar conditions could yield quite different results. In other words, historical conditions have been influential, but not deterministic. Similarly, while it is also true that liberalism merged with market mechanisms, it should be emphasized that the market is not only an economic system. More broadly, it is a technique for decision making, and as such remains a valid alternative to bureaucracy (including socialist bureaucracies).

At this point, one participant identified a third element of liberalism, in addition to the political and economic. This is what he would call "anthropological liberalism": the idea of historical and rational optimism, which has grown over time into the belief that liberal values are "natural," even necessary. In his opinion, this is where the problem of "the future of liberalism" lies, for although the relevance of limitations on power is as great as ever, the same cannot be said either for the belief that individual interests and the common good are necessarily complementary, or for liberal philosophical optimism in general.

These remarks turned the discussion to the development of liberalism in England and the United States. To one speaker, the English and American experience gives additional support to the argument that political and economic liberalism cannot easily be separated, for in the Anglo-Saxon tradition at least, the concept of "possession" meant more than simply personal safety. Rather, the notion of accumulation of inequalities was bound up with political liberalism from the very beginning. Similarly, the "anthropological" concept of rational intelligence has always been central to the American liberal creed. What is crucial here, he argued, is that liberalism was originally a "processual" value, which in its emphasis on means and processes served as an antidote to teleological doctrines of ends. However, during the course of the nineteenth century, liberalism itself was transformed into a teleology; it became a substantive value system of a relatively narrow ruling class. It is this transformation, he suggested, which has become the focus for critiques of liberalism. That is, it is not the processual rules of liberalism that are under attack, but its pretense to being a substantive value system. But others responded that liberalism was not merely procedural even to the founding fathers. Early American liberalism, they said, was always infused with skeptical elements, but its emphasis was on procedure within a particular framework of substantive values. Moreover, while it is true that political and economic liberalism (or "liberism") cannot be separated in the American tradition, there are several well-developed theories of constitutionalism (such as in Constant's writings after the French Revolution) which are completely divorced from economic considerations. Finally, they thought it important to distinguish between the pragmatism of American liberalism and the empirical cast of classical liberalism. Constitutionalism was the product of a cautious, "trial and error" attitude, quite different in this respect from the more adventuresome pragmatism which informed American liberalism.

Several speakers noted that the tenor of liberal thought and the attractiveness of liberal ideas have been conditioned to an important degree by the value systems that have opposed them. Thus, one member of the conference emphasized the impact of the historical struggle between liberalism and the Church on the development of liberalism as a skeptical creed. As a more recent example, he gave the experience of fascism, which, though never explicitly antidemocratic, was explicitly and adamantly antiliberal. The European experience with fascism has thus seemed to revindicate and revive liberalism in many parts of the West. Another participant wished to qualify this argument. He agreed that the experience of fascism has, to put it mildly, fostered a renewed appreciation for the protection of individual rights and the dangers of arbitrary power, but pointed out that Italian fascism proclaimed itself as the true liberal philosophy. Italian fascists hated not liberalism but democracy, or rather what they deemed the "false democracy" based on the power of money. This perspective is not surprising; after all, Mussolini was once a Marxist.

These comments were closely related to another issue first raised in Mr. Sartori's paper: the import of intellectual dissidence in Eastern Europe and the USSR for liberal thought and practice. One assessment was that the predominant outlook (and certainly the self-definition) of these intellectuals is closer to social democracy than it is to liberalism. In fact, the issue for the dissidents is not liberalism but democracy; that is, they want to democratize their political systems, but not necessarily to liberalize their socioeconomic systems. Thus, it was argued, it makes sense to call them liberals only if we assume that liberalism has a monopoly on democracy.

The more common view, however, was that the writings of people like Sakharov are indicative of the fact that certain liberal values are being rediscovered and thus rejuvenated by intellectuals in the East. More specifically, the significance of the intellectual dissidents in Eastern Europe lies primarily in their rediscovery of constitutionalism and limitations on power—the original thrust of liberalism. This focus is narrower than either liberal democracy or social democracy, for it reflects their belief that political constraints are the central and overriding problem. True, the East Europeans are concerned with democracy, but in a way they think they have it; what they lack is freedom. Moreover, whatever their self-definitions may be, circumstances are driving these people to increasingly extreme positions, thus effectively obliterating any significant distinctions between liberalism and social democracy in Soviet conditions. In spite of their different ideological views, Sakharov, Medvedev, and even Solzhenitsyn (who clearly has moved away from liberalism in many respects), have been forced into a common liberal position against arbitrary and unjust State power. In this sense, the liberal mode or style has received a great historical vindication.

Another speaker offered a somewhat different perspective, emphasizing that there are in fact many different strands of dissident thought. But from the point of view of liberalism the most important aspect is not so much the varying prescriptive elements, as the common appeal to humane values. This appeal, in his opinion, reflects less a borrowing from the West than a call to what are believed to be the authentic values of Russian culture. Moreover, there is also something to be learned from some nondissident intellectuals who, without rejecting the basic premises of Marxism-Leninism, are nevertheless confronting the problem of the tension between individual rights and the claims of the community. Both groups are relevant; the nature of their concerns indicate that the "crisis of liberalism" would seem to refer less to "liberal values" than to the adequacy of particular social and institutional forms.

One participant commented that the "socialism versus liberalism" debate shows the extent to which nonliberal and even antiliberal ideas have taken hold even within putatively liberal circles. What is the crucial variable which distinguishes them, or distinguishes liberal democracy from social democracy? Is it the attitude towards property? Or is it the belief that institutions are at least to some extent independent of economic conditions? He maintained that the latter would be the liberal position; and although it is certainly possible for a socialist to adopt it, he could not be the kind of socialist for whom the main division in the world would be between socialism and capitalism. Rather, the real dividing line would be between those societies which have autonomous institutions (and reflect autonomous habits of mind), and those which do not. Another speaker took a somewhat different position. He said that while the term "socialism" was not coined by Marx, by about 1870 "socialism" had become intrinsically Marxian; that is, it was distinct from liberal democracy precisely because it was based on a Marxist interpretation of history. From this perspective, "social democracy" is socialism which renounces Marxism, for it refuses to dismiss the institutions of political liberalism as no more than the superstructure of a capitalist economy.

The foregoing observations prompted one member of the

conference to pose two questions, which served as the focus for much of the remainder of the morning's deliberations. First, he asked, to what extent is liberalism a doctrine which makes claims to universal validity, but which in fact is quite parochial? Liberalism did seem to be universally valid so long as Europe and European culture were predominant in the world. But implicit in liberalism is a set of assumptions (about the nature of individuality, about spirituality, about the autonomy of the human being) and certain concepts (especially of law and property) that are not part of the cultures of what is now the articulate and increasingly vital majority of mankind. Secondly, to what extent does liberalism depend for its vitality on having firmly entrenched religious and traditional beliefs as targets to attack? In other words, he was suggesting that liberalism functions best as an ideology of opposition, but quickly becomes vapid when enshrined as the dominant orthodoxy. Thus, for example, the rebellion of the young against liberalism in the 1960s seems very much to have been a reaction against liberalism triumphant, which, having won, was empty.

In response, it was proposed that liberalism is culture-bound in the sense that it has been a manifestation of certain cultural values, especially the values of individualism and individual freedom. Still, it can be considered a universal doctrine in the sense that, within a given cultural context, it has been universal over time. In Western culture liberal ideas can be traced back to the Greeks; liberalism thus has not been associated simply with one class, nor tied to a given socioeconomic matrix. Another speaker remarked that universalism is not a claim that liberals themselves have ever made for liberalism. Rather, they have seen it as dependent on certain social conditions; even during the cold war, American liberals assumed that liberalism could only flourish where these conditions had been established. But this line of reasoning prompted a warning against the fundamental philosophical error of confusing causes with validity. For example, physics is a product of Western culture, but the truth of its statements is not parochial. The same can be said of liberalism: the truth of its values and methods may transcend the limitations of culture even though liberalism itself flourishes only within certain cultural contexts.

Several participants then addressed themselves to the status of liberalism in non-Western areas. One pointed out that, although there are few truly liberal states in the Third World, almost all of them nevertheless assert the universality of liberal values. In this sense, liberal values are more powerful than ever. Similarly, it was reported that in Southeast Asia the questioning of liberal democracy is directed mostly at the specific institutional frameworks associated with it, and not at its underlying premises. In an abstract sense, in other words, liberalism is perhaps the dominant philosophy. But at least one speaker did not find these arguments very convincing, for in his eyes the question is not what they say but what sort of state they establish. There is a big difference between slogans and deeply held values; slogans are superficial, and do not necessarily reflect any real commitment to liberalism.

Another felt that we tend both to exaggerate the extent to which liberalism is entrenched in the history and culture of the West, and to underestimate its influence elsewhere. On the one hand, he asserted, there have in fact been few liberal regimes in the West, and many antiliberal ones. On the other, liberalism outside the West presents itself essentially as three doctrines: limitations on authority, protection of individual rights, and (more subtly) individualism. The difficulty is that these values are often seen as unrealistic, even if they are valued in the long run. For example, in the Third World, limitations on authority often mean weak governments. Similarly, individualism without limits tends to degenerate into egotism and selfishness. This is a major issue even in a country like Japan, which since World War II has clearly been a liberal society—constitutional constraints on absolute power are real, individual rights are highly protected, and the need for individual self-expression is accepted—yet is still struggling to accommodate the rights of individuals with the needs of the community. The tension between the two values is especially significant because traditional Japanese cultural values emphasize the subordination of self to the needs of the collectivity. His point was not that liberal values are of little real consequence, either in Japan or elsewhere. Rather, the problem is how to balance these virtues, and how to institutionalize them. For many countries outside the West, liberal values raise what is at bottom a problem of integration, of diversity and its limits. The nature of the social structure is a crucial factor, for while it is true that attempts to create unity often lead to extreme measures, the existence of pluralism in the structure of society would nevertheless seem to be a precondition for liberalism. In any case, he concluded, liberalism is very much a matter of degree; we therefore need to examine the factors involved with its emergence in specific historical situations.

There was little dispute that liberalism must be examined in its concrete historical settings, or that the core meaning of liberalism has left an imprint on the non-West. But there was also widespread support for the view that this is not the same thing as relevance, and that the key question is which values have been internalized. As one participant put it, all other liberal values are derived from, and depend on, belief in the sanctity of the individual.

Nor was there complete confidence that liberalism has always remained faithful to its original ideals even in the West, and especially in its contemporary American manifestation. For instance, one speaker noted a paradox: although historically associated with a free market, much of what is now considered "liberalism" in the United States no longer opts for free-market solutions, yet advocates complete laissez-faire with respect to morals. To him, this represents a major switch in the liberal ethos. He then identified another confusion in contemporary American liberalism—namely, that on the "quality of life" issues it has become a totalitarian liberal force, willing to employ virtually any and all means to achieve its ends. These "liberals" are not merely processual or skeptical; rather, they are absolutely certain what is right. However, other participants wished to qualify both halves of this equation. First, with respect to economics, they stressed that most liberals call for regulation of the market, not for planning. Second, they detected a possible shift away from laissez-faire attitudes toward morality. As evidence for this shift, one speaker cited the recent Brownmiller book, which evidently impressed upon his students the realization that laissez-faire in morals can unleash bestial forces. But others were not so sanguine about the response to the Brownmiller book. One speaker saw it as an example of what he called the "my favorite crime" theory; that is, everyone has a favorite crime (whether it be Watergate, racial discrimination, or rape) for which they are willing to throw over any civil liberties whatsoever.

One member of the conference maintained that liberalism in its American form has in many respects always been quite different from classical liberalism. At least in its formal, institutional sense, he said, classical liberalism has spread well beyond its original historical base in Western Europe, to areas with very different historical traditions and cultural values. In the twentieth century, meanwhile, the social base of Western liberalism has been changing. In his view, liberalism in the West is now based on the "mass man," who is making increasingly heavy demands and who has adopted various "irrationalizations" of the liberal credo. As a result, these societies have tended to move not only toward dirigiste economics, but eventually dirigiste politics as well. But modern American liberalism represents a special attempt to make concessions to "mass man," and has forsaken classical liberal formulations in the process. What remains, he said, is philosophical and political eclecticism, an approach to social policy that wins elections but solves few problems.

This perspective was echoed in the remarks of another speaker, who focused the remainder of the morning's discussion specifically on the question, is liberalism in crisis? His own assessment was that liberalism has been a system for nations in periods of historical ascendancy. These were not merely optimistic systems, but ones which had the resources, will, and confidence to make things work. Although they were fortified by a successful capitalism, their essential underpinning was a propertied class which produced the guardians of the liberal tradition. But property has taken new forms; and it is no longer the central constituency of liberalism. Thus liberalism has turned to knowledge as a substitute, and men of knowledge have replaced men of property as the social underpinning for liberal systems. But, he argued, whereas the resources of the old property class were real, the resources of this new class are not. What we call "liberal knowledge" is in fact a series of myths—the myths of "theory," of "data," of "science"—which we erroneously assume enable us not only to understand the world but control it as well. If such knowledge does not exist, what then is the real basis, what are the real resources, of contemporary liberalism? His conclusion was that the liberal world is coming apart, that there is no human or social basis on which to revive it, and that no other "ism"—whether conservatism, socialism, or totalitarianism—is likely to succeed it. The West will simply wind down.

However, at least one speaker wondered if we would have this sense of crisis if the Vietnam War had not discredited liberal institutions and liberal knowledge. Although he thought that Vietnam (and now Angola) do seem to be evidence for the failure of knowledge, the economic crisis in the West may perhaps be solvable. Another asked if the dilemmas we have been describing are really those of liberalism *per se*. He noted that there are a whole series of eschatologies describing the end of liberal society: the "Times Square" eschatology (it dissolves in pornography); the "garbage strike" eschatology (it drowns in garbage); and the Marxist eschatology (it is done in by the fiscal crisis of the state). But, he maintained, many of these problems are cyclical, occur in nonliberal societies, and beset noncapitalist states.

The morning session concluded with the observation by one participant that his life seems to have been one long series of inquests into the health of liberalism—a phenomenon which in itself indicates that liberalism has a dogged tendency to persist, in spite of intellectual fashions. Such inquests are not the product of Vietnam or any other issue; instead, they are a product of the liberal tradition itself. The "relevance of liberalism" is a peculiarly liberal question, for it was liberals who first raised the point that a social philosophy should be useful in solving changing social problems. Moreover, he concluded, liberal knowledge *has* been useful. To take one commonplace but important example, life insurance works. Hasn't it improved the situation of human beings, and doesn't it depend on social science? But a pessimist had the last word—that life insurance works mostly for the life insurance companies.

Notes

1. See Maurice Cranston, *Freedom: A New Analysis* (New York: Longman, 1953). D. J. Manning, *Liberalism* (London: Dent & Sons, 1976) disputes Cranston's multiplication of liberalisms (pp. 57-58), but concludes that the "essences of liberalism can no more be defined than can the essence of liberalism as a whole" (pp. 142-43).
2. See the otherwise outstanding study of Guido de Ruggiero, *History of European Liberalism,* trans. R. C. Collingwood (London: Oxford University Press, 1927). The poverty of his synthesis is even more evident in his article "Liberalism" in *Encyclopaedia of the Social Sciences,* vol. 9 (New York: Macmillan, 1933), pp. 435-42.
3. For example, Thomas P. Neill, *The Rise and Decline of Liberalism* (Milwaukee: Bruce Publishing Co., 1953) distinguishes between "ecumenical" liberalism and "sectarian" liberalism, and qualifies the former ("the inborn attitude of a normal civilized Westerner towards life") as "generosity of spirit, or liberality of mind" (pp. 25, 23). Manning speaks of "the symbolic form of the doctrine," perceives it as Newtonian, and condenses the liberal doctrine into three principles: "the principle of balance, the principle of spontaneous generation and circulation, and the principle of uniformity." (See Manning, *Liberalism,* p. 143.) This is somewhat less rarefied, but the Newtonian analogy and "uniformity" strike me as very unconvincing characterizations.
4. I purposely recall the title of Henry Steele Commager's admirable *The American Mind: An Interpretation of American Thought and*

Character since the 1880s (New Haven, Conn.: Yale University Press, 1959), which should be read in conjunction with George Santayana, *Character and Opinion in the United States* (New York: Charles Scribner's Sons, 1921).

5. The point is made, among others, by Louis Hartz, *The Liberal Tradition in America* (New York: Harcourt Brace Jovanovich, 1955), p. 11: "Ironically, 'liberalism' is a stranger in the land of its greatest realization and fulfillment."

6. Reference is made to the natural law school, to Kant, to the early Fichte, and to von Humboldt. The fact that Humboldt's *Ideen zu einem Versuch die Grenzen der Wirksamheim des Staates zu bestimmen,* written in 1791, was published only in 1851, illustrates the paradoxical nature of this development. For a more extensive treatment of this development see John H. Hallowell, *The Decline of Liberalism as an Ideology* (London: Kegan Paul, 1946), especially his analysis of German politico-legal thought.

7. A way of underpinning the difference between political *liberalism* and economic *liberism*, and the correlative difference between political and economic freedoms, is to note that the political projection of laissez-faire economics is "anarchy," not libertas; a difference to which I shall return (see note 23).

8. Note that Bentham—at least the older Bentham—was a "liberal" in the current American sense; nonetheless, he hardly contributed to the theory of liberalism, for "liberty, he thought, is nothing in itself, and is valuable only as a means to happiness." See John P. Plamenatz, *Man and Society,* vol. 2 (New York: McGraw-Hill Book Co., 1963), p. 27. Moreover Bentham advocated a *tabula rasa* of the traditions on which English constitutionalism was actually founded.

9. See the recent edition of John S. Mill, *On Liberty,* with a selection of comments, ed. David Spitz (New York: W. W. Norton, 1975).

10. George H. Sabine, *History of Political Theory* (New York: Holt, Rhinehart and Winston, 1951), p. 724. While I agree with this conclusion, it is noteworthy that Sabine considers Green a central figure of liberalism, while ignoring Constant, Tocqueville, and Lord Acton. Thus Sabine himself does not escape "confusion."

11. The Hegelian version of liberalism can also be detected in de Ruggiero, *European Liberalism,* but finds its major representative in Benedetto Croce. How little Croce's "philosophy of Liberty" has to share with liberalism has been cogently demonstrated by Norberto Bobbio, "B. Croce e il Liberalismo," in his *Politica e Cultura* (Torino: Einaudi, 1955).

12. The distinction between the democracy of the ancients and the democracy of the moderns was forcefully drawn by Constant in a famous speech delivered in 1819. I have long dwelled on this difference in my *Democratic Theory* (Detroit: Wayne State University Press, 1962), especially chapters 12 and 13. There is now a revised edition of this work (Indianapolis: Liberty Press, 1978).

13. For example, Jacob S. Schapiro, *Liberalism: Its Meaning and History* (Princeton, N. J.: D. Van Nostrand Co., 1958), p. 35.

14. A recent, if highly debatable, reformulation of the minimal state theory is Robert Nozick, *Anarchy, State and Utopia* (New York: Basic Books, 1974). I prefer in this connection the argument of Bruno Leoni, *Freedom and the Law* (Princeton, N.J.: D. Van Nostrand Co., 1961) which expands upon the thesis of Friedrich A. von Hayek, *Constitution of Liberty* (Chicago: University of Chicago Press, 1960), chap. 11 and 16.

15. I have emphasized this aspect in "Constitutionalism: A Preliminary Discussion," *American Political Science Review* 56, no. 4 (December 1962). See also Nicola Matteucci, "Dal Costituzionalismo al Liberalismo," in L. Firpo, ed., *Storia delle Idee Politiche Economiche e Sociali*, vol. 2, pp. 13-168.

16. A Pareto-optimum solution is such when at least one person gains and nobody is worse off. Rawls-preferred solutions require us, instead, to give as much as possible to those that have least. Pareto's recommendation is, in substance, that nobody should be damaged and has, therefore, far less distributive mileage than Rawls'. Actually, distributive justice must be, in its means, discriminating and, in this sense, unjust. See Vilfredo Pareto, *Manuel d'Economie Politique* (Paris, 1909); and John Rawls, *A Theory of Justice* (Cambridge, Mass.: Harvard University Press, 1971).

17. See C. B. MacPherson, *The Political Theory of Possessive Individualism* (Oxford: Clarendon Press, 1962), which I take to be the most perceptive interpretation of its kind.

18. "That all men are by nature equally free and independent, and have certain inherent rights . . . namely, the enjoyment of life, and liberty, with the means of acquiring and possessing property, and pursuing and obtaining happiness and safety."

19. C. B. MacPherson, *Possessive Individualism,* pp. 270-71 and *passim.*

20. This is not to say that individualism stands alone, and without qualifications, as the characterizing trait of liberalism. On these grounds Paine, Bentham, and anarchists such as Goodwin also enter the tradition

of liberalism. It seems to me, instead, that these authors are better placed with Rousseau in that they all concur in establishing the principle (inimical to liberal constitutionalism) that democratic power—the will of the people—represents the paramount, if not the sole, foundation of the polity.

21. Ralf Dahrendorf, *The Reith Lectures 1974*, reprinted from "The Listener," 14 November 1974, opening statement.

22. Many civilizations and most traditional societies do not express, or repress (if one prefers) this elementary desire. Here one can also enter the doubt whether the liberal "demand of liberty has ever been made by any but a small minority of highly civilized and self-conscious human beings." Isaiah Berlin, "Two Concepts of Liberty" (1958), now in *Four Essays on Liberty* (London: Oxford University Press, 1969), p. 46. His point is reinforced by the "fear of freedom" argument of Erich Fromm, *Escape from Freedom* (New York: Holt, Rinehart and Winston, 1960).

23. On these concepts the fundamental analysis remains Chaim Wirszubski, *Libertas As a Political Idea at Rome* (Cambridge: Cambridge University Press, 1950).

24. See note 11.

25. It is in this context that Kelsen asserted, somewhat too sweepingly, that "democracy coincides with political liberalism." Hans Kelsen, *General Theory of Law and State,* trans. Anders Wedberg (Cambridge, Mass.: Harvard University Press, 1945), p. 288. In truth, liberalism sought equal rights, not equal ballots.

26. Since this is indeed a sweeping condensation, elsewhere (in *Democratic Theory*, esp. pp. 284-87) I have broken down the trajectory of "complete freedom" into five steps: a) independence (or nonimpediment); b) privacy; c) capacity; d) opportunity; and e) power. But see, for many valuable analyses of the point, Carl J. Friedrich, ed., *Liberty* (New York: Atherton, 1962).

27. Among the recent refutations see Raymond Aron, *Essai sur les Libertés* (Paris: Calmann-Levy, 1964). As Norberto Bobbio pointedly and concisely notes, "Freedom as power to do something interests those fortunate enough to possess it, while freedom as non-restraint interests all men." Bobbio, *Politica e Cultura,* p. 278.

28. I have somewhat expanded this point in "Philosophy, Theory and Science of Politics," *Political Theory* 2, no. 2 (May 1974):133-62, especially 142-43 and 146.

29. Bernard Crick, *In Defense of Politics* (London: Weidenfeld and Nicolson, 1962), p. 11.

30. Cranston, *Freedom: A New Analysis,* p. 81. We should not be misled by the growing impotence of present-day democratic governments; for technology allows, in and by itself, an incommensurable multiplication of the power of power.

2
Socialism and Liberalism: Articles of Conciliation?
Irving Howe

It will surprise none of my readers to learn that after a reasonably diligent search I have not been able to find a serious attempt to bring together systematically the usual socialist criticisms of liberalism. The socialist criticisms of liberalism, though familiar enough in their general features, appear in the literature mainly through occasional passages, unquestioned references, rude dismissals, and, during the last few decades, a few wistful beckonings for reconciliation. What I propose to do here is to construct a synthesis, necessarily open to the charge that it is ahistorical, of the criticisms socialists have traditionally leveled against liberalism, and then to offer some remarks about possible future relations.

Socialists, who are they? And liberalism, what is it? I shall choose here to signify as socialist those thinkers and spokesmen who cannot be faulted as tender toward authoritarian regimes: I shall exclude Communists, Maoists, Castroites, as well as their hybrids, cousins, and reticent wooers. I shall assume that with regard to liberalism there has been

some coherence of outlook among the various shades of
socialist (and Marxist) opinion. But in talking about liberalism I shall be readier to acknowledge the complexities
and confusions of historical actuality. And this is for two
reasons: first, that liberalism is our main interest today; and
second, that since a surplus of variables can paralyze analysis (eight kinds of socialism matched against six of liberalism yield how many combinations/confrontations?), I
would justify taking one's sights from a more or less fixed
position as a way of grasping a range of shifting phenomena.

In the socialist literature, though not there alone, liberalism has taken on at least the following roles and meanings:

1. Especially in Europe, liberalism has signified those
movements and currents of opinion that arose toward the
end of the eighteenth century, seeking to loosen the constraints traditional societies had imposed on the commercial
classes and proposing modes of government in which the
political and economic behavior of individuals would be
subjected to a minimum of regulation. Social life came to
be seen as a field in which an equilibrium of desired goods
could be realized if individuals were left free to pursue their
interests.[1] This, roughly, is what liberalism has signified
in Marxist literature, starting with Marx's articles for
the *Rheinische Zeitung* and extending through the polemics
of Kautsky, Bernstein, and Luxemburg. In short: "classical"
liberalism.

2. Both in Europe and America, liberalism has also been
seen as a system of beliefs stressing such political freedoms
as those specified in the U.S. Bill of Rights. Rising from the
lowlands of interest to the highlands of value, this view of
liberalism proposes a commitment to "formal" freedoms—
speech, assembly, press, etc.—so that in principle, as sometimes in practice, liberalism need have no necessary connection with, or dependence upon, any particular way of
organizing the economy.

3. Especially in twentieth century America but also
in Europe, liberalism has come to signify movements of

social reform seeking to "humanize" industrial-capitalist society, usually on the premise that this could be done sufficiently or satisfactorily without having to resort to radical/socialist measures—in current shorthand: the welfare state. At its best, this social liberalism has also viewed itself as strictly committed to the political liberalism of number 2 above.

4. In America, sometimes to the bewilderment of Europeans, liberalism has repeatedly taken on indigenous traits that render it, at one extreme, virtually asocial and anarchic and, at the other extreme, virtually chiliastic and authoritarian. Perhaps because the assumptions of a liberal polity were so widely shared in nineteenth-century America (the slaveocracy apart), "liberal" as a term of political designation can hardly be found in its writings. When liberalism as a distinctive modern politics or self-designated ideological current begins to emerge in America—first through the high-minded reforming individualism of Edward Godkin, editor of the *Nation* during the 1880s and 1890s, and then through the socialist-nationalist progressivism of Herbert Croly, editor of the *New Republic* when it was founded in 1914—it becomes clear that it cannot escape a heritage of native individualism, utopianism, and "conscience-politics." Nor can it escape the paradisial vision that is deeply lodged in the American imagination, going back to Emerson and Thoreau, and further back, perhaps, to the Puritans. Nor can it escape a heritage of Protestant self-scrutiny, self-reliance, and self-salvation. Consequently American liberalism has a strand of deep if implicit hostility to politics *per se*—a powerful kind of moral absolutism, a celebration of conscience above community, which forms both its glory and its curse.

5. Meanwhile, through the decades, liberalism has encompassed a *Weltanschauung*, a distinctive way of regarding the human situation. Despite some recent attempts to render it profound through a gloomy chiaroscuro, liberalism has customarily been an expression of that view of man which stresses rationality, good nature, optimism, and even

"perfectibility" (whatever that may mean). Whether or not
there is a necessary clash between the Christian and liberal
views of man, and despite some strains of continuity that
may coexist with the differences, there can hardly be any
question that historically, in its effort to gain its own space,
liberalism has emerged as a competitor to traditional religious
outlooks.

2

That there are other significant usages of the term "liberalism" I do not doubt; but for today these should be quite
enough. Let me now schematically note some—by no means
all—of the major socialist criticisms of at least some of these
variants of liberalism:

● The socialist criticism of "classical" liberalism (joined
at points by that of conservative iconoclasts like Carlyle)
seems by now to have been largely absorbed in our political
culture—with the exception of such ideological eccentrics and
utopians as Ayn Rand, Milton Friedman, and the former
president of the United States, Gerald Ford. That the historical conditions of early capitalist society made a mockery of
any notion of free and equal competitors entering into
free and equal exchange, with each employing his gifts and
taking his risks; that large masses of people were excluded
from the very possibility of significant social choice; that
even "liberal" governments never quite practiced the non-
interventionist principles of "classical" liberalism but in
fact were actively engaged in furthering the growth of bourgeois economy; that the notion of "entitlement," with its
premise of some early point of fair beginnings, is mostly
ideological—these have been the kinds of criticisms that
socialists, and especially Marxists, have made of early liberalism.[2] The very world we live in—irreversible if inconvenient, and open to almost every mode of criticism except
nostalgia for the alleged bliss of pure capitalism—testifies
to the cogency of these socialist criticisms.

Yet that is by no means the whole story. One of the strengths of Marxist historiography (I shall come to weaknesses) has been that even while assaulting capitalism it saw the vitality of its early phases, and that even in the course of ridiculing "classical" liberalism as an ideological rationale for bourgeois ascendency, it honored its liberating role in behalf of humanity at large. The early Marx—he who could write that "laws are positive and lucid universal norms in which freedom has attained an impersonal, theoretical existence independent of any arbitrary individual. A statute book is the people's Bible of freedom,"[3] or who could write that "without parties there is no development, without division, no progress"—this early Marx clearly recognized his ties to, or descent from, the liberalism he subjected to attack and sought to "transcend."

Socialists—let us be honest: some socialists—have recognized that in its heroic phase liberalism constituted one of the two or three greatest revolutionary experiences in human history. The very idea of "the self" or "the individual," quintessential to modern thought and sensibility, simply could not have come into being without the fructifying presence of liberalism. The liberalism that appears in eighteenth century Europe promises a dismissal of intolerable restraints; speaks for previously unimagined rights; declares standards of sincerity and candor; offers the vision that each man will have his voice and each voice will be heard. It would be making things too easy (at least for me) to say that socialism emerges unambiguously out of this tradition. Obviously, there have been authoritarian alloys in the socialist metals; but when the socialist imagination is at its most serious, it proposes a dialectical relationship to "classical" liberalism: a refusal, on the one hand, of quasi-Benthamite rationales for laissez-faire economics and a pact in behalf of preserving and enlarging the boundaries of freedom.

• Both in some early efforts at Marxist scholarship and in recent academic revivals, socialists have charged against liberalism that its defenders elevate it to a suprahistorical abstraction, an absolute value presumably untainted by grubby interests or bloodied corruptions, whereas in actuality liberalism, like all other modes of politics, arose as a historically conditioned and thereby contaminated phenomenon, and hence must be regarded as susceptible to historical decay and supercession.

Now, if we see this matter mainly as one of historiography, there is a point to the socialist criticism. No political movement, not even liberalism, likes to have the time of its origins deglamorized, yet there is sufficient reason for subjecting all movements to that chastening procedure. But with regard to a living politics, this criticism is dangerous and has done a share of mischief.

The tendency of some Marxists to regard liberal ideas as mainly or merely epiphenomena of a historical movement always runs the risk of declining into an absolutist relativism, that is, a historicism that acknowledges no fixed point of premise other than its own strategies of deflation. A sophisticated analogue is the "sociology of knowledge"; a vulgar reduction, the habit of speaking about "*mere* bourgeois democracy." This mode of historical analysis ignores the possibility that even movements and currents of thought conditioned by class interests can yield ideas, traditions, methods, customs that will seem of permanent value to future generations. There may not be unimpeded progress in history, but there do seem to be a few permanent conquests. To show that the principles of a liberal polity did not descend from Mount Sinai but arose together with social classes whose dominance we would like to see ended or curtailed is not at all to deny that those liberal principles are precious both to newly ascending classes and humanity at large. To show that the Founding Fathers of the United States represented commercial interests or kept slaves or, when in office, violated some of their own precepts is not at all to diminish the value of the Bill of Rights for people who despise commercial interests, abhor slavery, and propose, if in power, never to violate their own precepts. Criticism of Jefferson's inadequacies is made possible by the adequacy of Jeffersonian principles.

If these remarks seem excessively obvious, we might remember that the history of twentieth-century politics, as also that of the twentieth century intelligentsia, offers scant ground for resting securely in common devotion to liberal values. Quite the contrary! We are living through a century of counterrevolution, one in which the liberal conquests of the nineteenth century, inadequate as these might have been, have been systematically destroyed by left-and-right authoritarian dictatorships. "Vulgar Marxism," with its quick reduction of ideas to ideology and its glib ascription of ideology to interest, has become the mental habit of lazy and half-educated people throughout the world.[4] In general, by now we ought to be extremely wary of all statements featuring the word "really"—as in "Mill's ideas really represent the interests of the British, etc., etc." and "Freud's ideas really reflect the condition of the Viennese, etc., etc." Statements of this kind are, no doubt, unavoidable and sometimes fruitful, but they have too often come to be damaging to both the life of the mind and a polity of freedom.

Insofar, then, as the socialist criticism of liberalism has furthered an element of historical reductionism—unavoidable, I suspect, in the contest of a mass movement—it has weakened the otherwise valid insistence that liberalism be treated as part of mundane history and thereby subject to mundane complications.

• A powerful socialist criticism of liberalism has been that it has detached political thought and practice from the soil of shared, material life, cutting politics off from the interplay of interests, needs, and passions that constitutes the collective life of mankind. A linked criticism has been that liberalism lacks an adequate theory of power, failing to see the deep relationships between political phenomena and alignments of social class. (Kenneth Minogue makes the point vividly: "The adjustment of interest conception [intrinsic to contemporary liberalism] . . . omits the crunch of truncheon on skull which

always lies just in the background of political life. . . . ")[5]
Still another linked criticism, in the line of Rousseau, proposes that modern man is torn apart by a conflict between
the liberal acceptance of bourgeois institutions, which sanction the pursuit of selfish interest without regard to a larger
community, and the liberal doctrine of popular sovereignty,
which implies that the citizen must set aside private interests
and concern himself with the common welfare.

Here, surely, it must be acknowledged that the socialist
criticism—in fairness it has also been made by nonsocialists—
has all but completely conquered, indeed taken effect so
strongly as to become absorbed into the thought even of
those who oppose socialism and/or Marxism. Almost every
sophisticated (and thereby, soon enough, unsophisticated)
analysis of society now takes it for granted that politics must
be closely related to, and more or less seen as a reflection of,
social interest; that society forms a totality in which the various realms of activity, though separable analytically, are
intertwined in reality; that no segment of the population can
be assumed any longer to be mute or passive, and that there
has appeared a major force, the working class, which must be
taken into historical account; and that the rationalism of
most liberal theory, though not (one hopes) simply to be
dismissed, must be complicated by a recognition of motives
and ends in social behavior that are much richer, more complicated, and deeply troubling.[6]

Both in our efforts to understand history and affect politics, there has occurred a "thickening" of our sense of society—indeed the very idea of society, itself largely a nineteenth-century invention, testifies to that "thickening." We
might even say that as a result of Marx there has occurred
a recreation of social reality. (The Christian historian Herbert
Butterfield praises the Marxist approach to history in a vivid
phrase: "it hugs the ground so closely"—which in his judgment does not prevent it from surveying what occurs in the
upper reaches.) It is very hard—though some people manage—still to see politics as a mere exercise for elites, or an
unfolding of first principles; it is very hard still to see politics

apart from its relation to the interaction of classes, levels of productivity, modes of socioeconomic organization, etc. Writing in 1885 about his early work Engels says:

> While I was in Manchester, it was tangibly brought home to me that the economic facts, which have so far played no role or only a contemptible one in the writing of history, are, at least in the modern world, a decisive historical force; that they form the basis of the origination of the present-day class antagonisms; that these class antagonisms, in the countries where they have become fully developed, thanks to large-scale industry, hence especially in England, are in their turn the basis of the formation of political parties and party struggles, and thus of all political history.[7]

If the germs of reductionism can be detected in such a passage, so too can the possibilities for complication and nuance: it all depends on which clause one chooses to stress. These possibilities for complication and nuance were seized only a dozen years later by Emile Durkheim:

> I consider extremely fruitful the idea that social life should be explained, not by the notions of those who participate in it, but by more profound causes which are unperceived by consciousness, and I think also that these causes are to be sought mainly in the manner according to which the associated individuals are grouped.

Anyone wishing to trace the development of modern thought—among other things, from socialism to sociology—could do worse than start with gloss on these passages from Engels and Durkheim.

The "economism," real or apparent, of the Engels passage was followed by a vulgarization in popular Marxist writings, but there is also present in the Marxist tradition another—and for our time crucial—view of the relation between state and society. In his earlier and middle years especially, Marx saw that the state could possess or reach an autonomy of its own, rising "above" classes as a kind of smothering Leviathan. (The state in Louis Napoleon's France, wrote Marx, is "an appalling parasitic body, which enmeshes the body of French society like a net and chokes all its pores."")[8] This perception could be crucial for a reconciliation between socialists and liberals—we shall come back to it.

● Yet, from the vantage point of the late twentieth century, it ought to be possible for socialists to be self-critical enough to admit that the victory over liberalism with regard to such matters as the relationship between politics and society, state and economy, has by no means been an unambiguous one, certainly not a victory to bring unqualified satisfaction. Apart from reductionism, I would raise a point that seems to me increasingly important but for which my own tradition offers an inadequate vocabulary. I have in mind what might be called the body of traditional political wisdom, or the reflections of thoughtful men on the "perennial" problems of politics. To speak of "perennial" problems, I want to insist, is to locate them within a historical continuum rather than to elevate them "above" history.

In its historicist relativizing, its absorption with a particular social circumstance, the socialist tradition has given rather short shrift to this body of traditional political reflection. A pity! Marx might have been unsympathetic to Madison's reflections in *The Federalist Papers* regarding the dynamics of faction in a republic; perhaps he would have seen them as excessively abstract or as a rationale for class interest. Yet both of these criticisms could have been cogent without necessarily undermining the value of what Madison said. The socialist movement has sinned and suffered from its impatience with the accumulated insights of the centuries regarding political life. As a result, despite its prolonged attention to politics and its often brilliant analyses of political strategy (from Marx in the *18th Brumaire* to Trotsky on pre-Hitler Germany), the socialist tradition has lacked, or refused, a theory of politics as an autonomous or at least distinct activity. It has had little or nothing to say about such matters as necessary delimitations of power, the problems of representation, the uses or misuses of a division of authority, the relation between branches of government, etc.

Let me cite a fascinating example. In late 1874 and early

1875 Marx read Bakunin's book *Statism and Anarchy*, made extended extracts and attached to these his own sharply polemical comments. Bakunin was anticipating one of the questions endlessly rehearsed by writers of the nonauthoritarian left: how to prevent the bureaucratization of a "workers' state," whether exworkers raised to power would become corrupted, etc., etc. Bakunin writes that

> universal suffrage—the right of the whole people—to elect its so-called representatives and rulers of the State—this is the last word of the Marxists as well as of the democratic school. And this is a falsehood behind which lurks the despotism of a governing minority. . . . But this minority, say the Marxists, will consist of workers. Yes, indeed, of *ex-workers, who, once they become rulers or representatives of the people, cease to be workers.*

At which point Marx interrupts: "No more than does a manufacturer today cease to be a capitalist on becoming a city councilman." Continues Bakunin: "From that time on they [the ex-workers] represent not the people but themselves and their own claims to govern the people. Those who doubt this know precious little about human nature."[9]

One need not acquiesce in Bakunin's hostility to democratic institutions in order to see that, in his own way, he has hit upon one of the "perennial" problems in political thought —the problem of representation, how the elected representative of a group or class can become corrupted or bureaucratized upon acquiring power. Marx's answer seems to me unsatisfactory: the manufacturer representing his class in a city council, though obviously susceptible to corruption, is not expected to help usher in a new, socialist era, he need only defend particularistic interests—while the worker elected to office in a "worker's state" is burdened, according to the Marxist prescription, with great historical and moral responsibilities, thereby rendering the problems of corruption and bureaucratism all the more acute. Surely Marx was able to understand this!—but what made it hard for him to respond to such matters with sufficient seriousness was a historical method, an ideological bent, a political will.

Yet, hidden within the class analyses of the Marxists there

have remained—a Marxist analysis of Marxism might suggest that there *must* remain—elements of traditional political thinking. Lenin, the one Marxist writer most impatient with talk about "perennial" problems, seems nevertheless to recognize in *State and Revolution* that a theory focusing upon change must also take into account continuity. He writes:

> Men . . . liberated from capitalist exploitation will gradually become accustomed to abide by the elementary rules of social life which have been known from time immemorial and have been set out for thousands of years in all regulations, and they will follow these rules without force, compulsion, subservience, and the special apparatus of compulsion which is known as the state.[10]

One wants to reply: but if there are "elementary rules of social life . . . known from time immemorial," rules which can be fully realized only in a classless society, then it must follow that in earlier, class-dominated societies those rules became manifest in some way, otherwise we could not recognize their existence. There are, then, "perennial" problems of politics, by no means so "elementary" either—considering the fact that they have never been solved, nor seem likely ever to be entirely solved. And these problems cannot be dismissed by references to class or historical contexts, though obviously class or historical contexts give them varying shape and significance. They are problems, it might be acknowledged, that have been discussed with greater depth, because more genuine interest, by conservatives and liberals than by socialists.

The Marxist/socialist criticism of liberalism regarding the relation of politics to society now seems less cogent, or at least requires greater complication, than it did half a century ago. And this for an additional reason: with the growth of the modern industrial state, in both its Western and Eastern versions, politics takes on a new primacy, indeed, a kind of "independence," vis-à-vis the institutions and mechanisms of the economy. In the Communist countries, what happens to the economy, what is done with one or another segment of the working class, how the peasants are treated in the kolkhoz: all stem from political decision. Far from the ruling Party bureaucracy being a mere agency of, or even, as Trotsky believed) a parasite upon, one of the social classes, the Party bureaucracy is the decisive sociopolitical force in the country, akin to, even if not quite like, a ruling class. State and society tend to merge in totalitarian countries, so that traditional discriminations between politics and economics come to seem of little use.

In advanced capitalist countries, the state increasingly takes over crucial functions of the market, while still allowing a considerable measure of autonomy to corporations and private business. These developments have been noted frequently and need not be elaborated here; suffice it to say that insofar as they persist, some of the apparently sealed conclusions from the long debate between liberalism and socialism need to be reopened. The traditional liberal notions of politics cannot, of course, be exhumed, but neither can the traditional socialist objections to them be repeated with confidence. What can be said, tentatively, is that the liberal insistence upon politics as a mode of autonomous human action with "laws" and "rules" of its own has come to have a new persuasiveness and, not least of all, within socialist thought.

● There is a criticism of liberal politics and thought that runs through the whole of socialist literature but, by now, can also be heard at many points to the right and left of liberalism: among "organicist" conservatives, followers of the young Marx, Christian socialists, syndicalists, communitarian New Leftists. This criticism is most often expressed as a defense of the values of community—human fellowship, social grouping —against egotism, competition, private property. Necessarily, it raises questions about the quality of life in bourgeois society: the failure of a common culture, the burdens placed upon the family when people lack alternative spheres of cooperative activity, the breakdown of social discipline that follows from laissez-faire. This criticism also takes a political form: the argument that democracy requires public life, that it cannot be successfully maintained in a society of privatized persons whose interests are confined to their families and businesses, and that public life depends upon a sharing of political and economic goods. Does it not seem likely that some of the ills of American society follow from the situation described in this attack upon classical liberalism?

The idea of economic man is declared to be a libel upon humanity; the vision of extreme individualism, an impoverishment of social possibility, and the kind of life likely to emerge from a society devoted to such ideas, a terrible drop from traditional humanist and Christian standards.

Most thoughtful liberals have by now acknowledged the force of this criticism. Indeed, there is rather little in it that cannot be found in John Stuart Mill's essays on Bentham and Coleridge. In the long run, then, freedom of criticism does seem to yield some benefits: does seem to prompt spokesmen for major political-intellectual outlooks to complicate and modify their thought. Liberal criticism has made a difference in socialism; socialist criticism, in liberalism.

Still, who does not feel the continued poignancy in the yearning for community, which seems so widespread in our time? Who does not respond, in our society, to the cry that life is poor in shared experiences, vital communities, free brother- (sister-) hoods?

Yet precisely the pertinence and power of this attack upon traditional liberalism must leave one somewhat uneasy. For we must remember that we continue to live in a time when the yearning for community has been misshaped into a gross denial of personal integrity, when the desire for the warmth of social bonds—marching together, living together, huddling together, complaining in concert—has helped to betray a portion of the world into the shame of the total state.

One hears, these days, celebrations of the fact that in Communist China large masses of people actively "participate" in the affairs of state. They do. And it is not necessary to believe they always do so as a response to terror or force in order to be persuaded that the kind of "participation" to which they yield themselves is a denial of human freedom.

Let us be a little more cautious, then, in pressing the attack upon liberalism that invokes an image of community—a little more cautious if only because this attack is so easy to press. There is indeed an element of the paltry in the more extreme versions of liberal individualism; but the alienation that has so frequently, and rightly, been deplored in recent decades may have its sources not only in the organization of society but in the condition of mankind. Perhaps it is even to be argued that there is something desirable in recognizing that, finally, nothing can fully protect us from the loneliness of ourselves.

A social animal, yes; but a solitary creature too. Socialists and liberals have some areas of common interest in balancing these two stresses, the communal and the individual, the shared and the alone. It is a balance that will tilt; men and women must be free to tilt it.

● Functioning for a good many decades as an opposition movement, and one, moreover, that could not quite decide whether it wished to be brought into society or preferred to seek a "total" revolutionary transformation, the socialist movement systematically attacked liberalism for timidity, evasiveness, vacillation, "rotten compromise," etc. It charged that liberalism was weak, that it never dared to challenge the socioeconomic power of the bourgeoisie, that it was mired in what Trotsky called "parliamentary cretinism," etc.

The historical impact of this criticism can hardly be overestimated. A major source of the "welfare state," insofar as we have one, has surely been the pressure that socialist movements have exerted upon a liberalism that has long gone past its early elan. Insofar as the socialist criticism served to force liberalism into awareness of and militancy in coping with social injustice, the results have been for the better.

But also—for the worse. For the socialist criticism (as the rise of bolshevism and its various offshoots make clear) contained at least two strands: one that disdained liberalism for its failure to live up to its claims and one that disdained liberalism for its success in living up to its claims. We touch here upon a great intellectual scandal of the age: the tacit

collaboration of right and left in undermining the social and
moral foundations of liberalism. In the decades between the
Paris Commune and World War II both right- and left-wing
intellectuals were gravely mistaken, and morally culpable, in
their easy and contemptuous dismissal of liberalism. That the
society they saw as the tangible embodiment of bourgeois
liberalism required scathing criticism I do not doubt. But
they failed utterly to estimate the limits of what was historically possible in their time, as they failed, even more
importantly, to consider what the consequences might be of
their intemperate attacks upon liberalism. It was all very well
to denounce liberalism as what Ezra Pound called—Lenin
would have agreed—"a mess of mush," but to assault the vulnerable foundations of liberal democracy meant to bring into
play social forces the intellectuals of both right and left
could not foresee. There were, as it turned out, far worse
things in the world than "a mess of mush."

Bourgeois Europe was overripe for social change by the
time of World War I. But the assumptions that such change
required a trampling on liberal values in the name of hierar-
chical order or proletarian dictatorship and that liberal values
were inseparable from cultural decadence and capitalist
economy—these assumptions proved a disaster. In the joyful
brutality of their verbal violence many intellectuals, at both
ends of the political spectrum, did not realize how profound
a stake they had in preserving the norms of liberalism. They
felt free to sneer at liberalism because, in a sense, they remained within its psychological orbit; they could not really
imagine its destruction and took for granted that they would
continue to enjoy its shelter. Even the most authoritarian
among them could not foresee a situation in which *their*
freedom would be destroyed. Dreaming of natural aristocrats
or sublime proletarians, they helped pave the way for maniac
lumpen.

• Still another socialist/radical criticism of liberalism,
familiar from polemics of the thirties but urgently revived
during the last decade by the New Left, is that the structure
of liberties in democratic society rests on a shared acqui-

escence in the continued power of the bourgeoisie; that these liberties survive on condition they not be put to the crucial test of basic social transformation—and that they might well be destroyed by the bourgeoisie or its military agencies if a serious effort were made by a democratically elected government to introduce socialist economic measures. The overthrow of the Allende regime in Chile has been cited as a telling confirmation.

It is an old problem. Marx and Engels suggested that a socialist transition in such countries as England and Holland, with their deep-rooted democratic traditions, might be peaceful. Most other European countries not yet having completed the "bourgeois revolution" by the mid-nineteenth century, it seemed reasonable to the founders of "scientific socialism" that revolutionary methods might be necessary on the continent—though we also know that later, when the German Social Democracy became a mass party, Engels accepted the parliamentary course. The standard Bolshevik gloss would soon be that since the time Marx and Engels had written, the bourgeois state in England and Holland had grown more powerful, developing a traditional apparatus of repression. Thereby, the expectation of peaceful transition had become obsolete.

I think it would be an error to dismiss the Marxist criticism on this point as outmoded or irrelevant. Changes in class rule have in the past rarely come about without one or another quantity of violence, and as I remember hearing and saying in my youth, ruling classes don't just fold up their tents and slink away. By the same token, I now reply to my younger self, past changes in class rule have rarely, if ever, taken place within established democratic societies, hence could not be said to provide a test of the socioeconomic strains democratic societies can be expected to sustain.

To insist that liberalism and/or liberties must collapse under a serious effort to introduce socialist measures signifies (a) an unfortunate concession to those right-wing ideologues who insist that political liberty is inseparable from and could not survive the destruction of private property, or

(b) a vision of socialist transformation so "total" and apocalyptic that the collapse of political liberties in such circumstances could as readily be the work of revolutionary insurgents as of a resistant bourgeoisie. (To concede, after all, that liberalism could not survive a "dictatorship of the proletariat" in the Leninist or Leninist-Stalinist versions is hardly very damaging to the claim that liberalism can coexist with more than one form of economy.)

As for the historical evidence, it seems inconclusive and mixed. A very great deal, perhaps everything, depends on the strength of attachment among a people to democratic values; only a bit less, on the ability of a given society to avoid the kind of economic cataclysms that would put this attachment under excessive strain. If, say, the social democratic governments of Scandinavia and England, ruling with substantial majorities and elected as parties pledged to go considerably beyond welfare-state measures, were to introduce extensive socialist measures, there is not much reason to expect major extralegal efforts to undo their policies.[11] For the tradition of pacific social life and "playing by the rules" seems strong enough in such countries to allow one to envisage a major onslaught against the power of corporations and large businesses without risking the survival of democracy.

(I referred a few sentences back to governments with substantial majorities. It seems reasonable, after all, that a government that squeaks into office with a narrow margin should exercise restraints in any effort to introduce major social change.)

At least in some "advanced" European countries, the problem would not seem to be the bourgeoisie itself—by now a class without an excess of self-confidence. Socialist anxiety as to the ability of a liberal society to absorb major change might more appropriately be directed toward the middle classes and the army, which can no longer be assumed to act (if they ever did) as mere pliant agents and accomplices of the bourgeoisie. It is by no means clear that the Chilean experiences "prove" that a democratic path to socialism is impossible. What it may prove is (a) that a left-wing government trying to maintain democratic norms while introducing major social change must be especially sensitive to the interests and sentiments of the middle class; and (b) that the army, acting out of its own interests and sentiments, can become an independent political force, establishing a dictatorial regime that it might well be a mistake to see as a mere creature of bourgeois restoration.

The role of armies in contemporary politics is a fascinating problem, beyond discussion here. Except for this: in a variety of circumstances, but especially where a mutual weakening of antagonistic classes has occurred, the army (like the state) can take on an unexpected autonomy. Nor is it clear that this follows the traditional Marxist expectation that the army would be employed by the ruling class to save its endangered interests. Even if that was true in Chile, it was not in Peru. And in sharply different ways, it is not true either in Portugal or Greece. In Asian and African countries, the role of the army is evidently that of a makeshift power compensating for the feebleness of all social classes. There is, then, something new here, not quite anticipated in liberal or socialist thought.

The question whether a liberal democratic regime can peacefully sustain major social or socialist changes remains open. If a categorical negative is unwarranted, so too is an easy reassurance. Given the probable configuration of politics in the Western democracies, there is some reason to conclude that even left-socialist regimes staying within democratic limits would have to proceed more cautiously, with greater respect for the multiplicity of group interests, than the usual leftist expectations have allowed. And the anxiety provoked by a possible effort to combine liberal polity with socialist economy remains a genuine anxiety, shared by both liberals and socialists.

● If we confine ourselves to the "advanced" countries, one criticism socialists have come increasingly to make of liberalism is that it fails to extend sufficiently its democratic concerns from the political to the economic realm.[12] Early in the century the distinguished British liberal writer L. T. Hobhouse put the matter elegantly: "Liberty without equality is a name of noble sound and squalid result." I will not linger on this point except to make the following observations.

1. It suggests that the difference between social liberalism and democratic socialism keeps growing smaller, so that at some point it may become no more than incremental. Both traditional liberal thinkers and Marxist theoreticians would deny this; a good many social democrats, in effect, believe it.

2. It leaves aside what in a fuller consideration could not be left aside: that there remain serious liberal criticisms of socialist proposals, for example, that efforts to legislate greater equality of wealth, income, and power in economic life will seriously impair political liberty, and that the statist version of socialism (the only realistic one, say some liberal critics) would bring about a fearful concentration of power.

3. We may be ready to subscribe to the socialist criticism that modern liberalism fails sufficiently to extend its democratic concerns to economic life—for example, the governance of corporations; we may also share the socialist desire for greater participation of the masses in political and economic decisionmaking; but to turn things around, I would largely accept the liberal dislike for schemes involving "mass" or "direct" democracy. Such schemes, insofar as they would brush aside representative institutions (elections, parliaments, etc.) in favor of some sort (but which sort?) of "direct" or "participatory" rule, are likely to end up as hopelessly vague or as prey to demagogic techniques for manipulating those who "participate" in movements, meetings, plebiscites, etc. If the survival of democracy depends on greater popular participation, greater popular participation by no means insures or necessarily entails the survival of democracy. Under modern conditions representative institutions are indispensable to democratic societies; any proposals for "transcending" them, even if they come through socialist goodwill, should be regarded with suspicion.

• There is, finally, the plenitude of attacks directed a-
gainst liberalism along a spectrum of positions ranging from
the reactionary to the revolutionary, most of them chas-
tising its "deeper" failures as a philosophical outlook. So
copious is this literature, there is hardly a need to cite texts
or authorities.

Liberalism, we are told, accepts an egalitarianism that
a day or two spent with open eyes in our mass society
shows to be insupportable—while a sage like Professor Leo
Strauss makes clear the traditional warrants and esoteric
virtues of hierarchy. Liberalism proposes a belief in rational
harmony, the "illusion" (to quote Kenneth Minogue) "of
ultimate agreement" among men, "and perhaps most central of all, the ideal that will and desire can ultimately be
sovereign in human affairs"[13]—while a sage like Professor
Michael Oakeshott tells us that life is muddle, efforts at
rational structuring of our affairs are likely to lead to still
greater muddle, even, perhaps, to tyranny. Liberalism
congeals into the simplistic notion, as Lionel Trilling has
written, "that the life of man can be nicely settled by correct
social organization, or short of that, by the election of
high moral attitudes." Liberalism, focusing obsessively
upon change, distracts us from the essentials of existence
largely beyond the grasp of mere reason or public agency.
Liberalism has a false view of the human situation, refusing
to take into account the irrationalities and aggressions
of our nature. (How can a liberal cope with the realities
of the Hobbesian jungle? What can a good-hearted liberal
make of the Freudian view of the human heart?) Liberalism
ignores or dispatches the tragic sense of life, turning people
away from that suffering which is unavoidable (perhaps
even good?) in our experience. Liberalism replaced the
warming cohesion of traditional communities with a rootless
anonymity. Liberalism cannot cope with the mysteries of
death, as Christianity does through its myth of resurrection,
or existentialism tries to do, through its unblinking gaze into
the void.

What is one to say of these criticisms? That often they

confuse the historical genesis of liberalism, accompanied as it was by excessive claims, with later and more realistic versions of liberalism; that the alleged rootlessness of liberal man, though clearly surrounded with difficulties, also has brought unprecedented freedoms and opportunities, indeed, entire new visions of the personal self; that the increasing stress of modern liberal thought upon a pluralist society indicates at least some recognition of clashing interests, irreconcilable needs, confrontations of class; that a recognition of the irrational and aggressive components of human conduct can become an argument in favor of limitations upon power favored by liberalism; that we may recognize weaknesses and limitations in liberalism as a *Weltanschauung*—indeed, refuse to see it as a *Weltanschauung*—while still fervently believing that a liberal polity allows for the best realization of human diversity and freedom; that there is no necessary conflict between "dark" views of the human condition and an acceptance of the liberal style in public life.

Let us grant, then, some of the criticisms made of liberal afflatus (usually in the past) and liberal smugness (usually in the present) and admit, as well, the probability that insofar as men need religious myths and rites to get through their time on earth, liberalism is not likely to offer enough satisfaction. What needs to be stressed, all the same, is that a commitment to the liberal style in politics does not necessarily imply a commitment to a total world view claiming to include all experience from private fantasy to public authority. (Perhaps we would all be better off to live, for a time, without total world views.)

Toward these and similar exchanges between liberalism and its critics, socialists have shown a very wide range of responses. The more extreme leftist tendencies, verging on the authoritarian and chiliastic, have been tempted to borrow some of the arguments of the right, especially those releasing contempt for the flaccid moderation of liberalism, its alleged failures to confront painful realities of social life and human nature. But for those socialists who largely accept the premises of a liberal polity, there are other problems, notably the disconcerting fact that the bulk of the philosophical-existential criticism directed against liberalism can be brought to bear with equal cogency against social democracy.

3

Unavoidably, this leads to the question: apart from whatever capacity both liberalism and social democracy show for handling our socioeconomic difficulties, how well can they cope with—I choose deliberately a portentous term—the crisis of civilization that many people feel to be encompassing our lives? The crisis of civilization that besets the twentieth century has to do, in part, with a breakdown in the transmission and common acceptance of values—which may also be a way of saying, with residual but powerful yearnings toward transcendence. Insofar as this occurs, there follows a pervasive uncertainty as to the "meanings" and ends of existence. One sign of this crisis is the resurgence in Western society of a strident contempt for the ethic of liberal discourse and the style of rationality. Partly this arises from the mixed failings and successes of the welfare state, but partly from an upswell of ill-understood religious sentiments that are unable to find a proper religious outlet and become twisted into moral-political absolutism, a hunger for total solutions and apocalyptic visions. Impatience with sluggish masses, burning convictions, or righteousness, the suffocations of technological society, the boredom of overcrowded cities, the yearning for transcendent ends beyond the petty limits of group interest, romantic-sinister illusions about the charismatic virtues of dictatorship in underdeveloped countries—all these tempt intellectuals and semiintellectuals into apolitical politics registering an amorphous revulsion from civilization itself.

The customary rationalism of earlier generations of socialists (and liberals too) could hardly grasp such a development. Yet, no matter how distant we may be from the religious outlook, we must ask ourselves whether the malaise of our time isn't partly a consequence of that despairing emptiness which has followed the breakup of traditional religious systems in the nineteenth century; whether the nihilism that sensitive people feel to be seeping through their lives may not itself testify to a kind of inverted religious aspiration; whether the sense of moral disorientation that afflicts us isn't due to the difficulties of keeping alive a high civilization without a sustaining structure of belief.

Perhaps, in honesty, there really is no choice but to live with the uncomfortable aftereffects of this disintegration of religious belief, which has brought not only the positive consequences some of us hoped for but also others that leave us discomfited. In any case, nothing seems more dubious than the impulse I detect these days among rightward-moving intellectuals: a willing of faith in behalf of alleged social-moral benefits. Here, finally, liberals and democratic socialists find themselves in the same boat, even if at opposite ends of it. The Fabian course to which some of us are committed seems to me politically good and perhaps even realistic, but we ought to acknowledge that this course fails to stir the passions or speak to the needs of many people. We ought to acknowledge that between the politics we see as necessary and the expressive-emotional needs that break out recurrently in Western society there are likely to be notable gaps. I think, by way of homely instance, of a remark made to me a few years ago by a very decent and intelligent liberal professor: "But the politics of social democracy [he might also have said liberalism] are so boring!" It is a troubling remark, and one that may help explain why cultivated people of liberal training can be drawn to illiberal causes and impulses. We can only worry about this matter, recognizing that it may be one of those instances where virtue entails formidable deficits.

But let me end on a somewhat more hopeful note. Half a century from now, one fact about our time may come to be seen as the most crucial. Whatever the separate or linked failures of liberalism and democratic socialism may be, there have come to us these past twenty and twenty-five years voices from the East superbly reasserting the values of freedom, tolerance, openness of discourse. These men and women have, thus far, "failed"; they have been destroyed, imprisoned, humiliated, isolated. Yet their very appearance signifies an enormous moral triumph for both liberalism and democratic socialism. Beneath the snow, the seed has lived.

Notes

1. The philosophical underpinning is provided by Kant: "everyone is entitled to seek happiness in whatever manner seems best to him, provided that he does not interfere with the freedom of others to strike toward the same objective, which can coexist with the freedom of everyone else under a conceivable general law."
2. In *Capital,* 1, chap. 6 ("The Buying and Selling of Labor-Power"), Marx applies his powers of sarcasm to such assumptions of "classical" liberalism: "The sphere of circulation and exchange of commodities within which labor is bought and sold was in reality a paradise of innate human rights—governed entirely by freedom, equality, property, and Bentham! Freedom! Because the buyers and sellers of a commodity, such as labor-power, are constrained only according to their own free will. They enter into a contract as free and legally equal free agents. The contract is the final result in which their common free will is given common legal expression. Equality! Because their relationships with one another are purely those of the owners of commodities and they exchange like for like. Property! Because each individual makes use only of what belongs to him. Bentham! Because each of the two thinks only of himself. The only power that holds them together and establishes a relationship between them is their egotism, personal advantage, and private interest. And precisely because each individual thinks of himself and never of anyone else, they all work toward their mutual advantage, the general good and common interest, in accordance with a preestablished harmony of things or under the auspices of a cunning knowing providence."
3. See Karl Marx, "The Proceedings of the Sixth Rhenish Parliament," first published in *Rheinische Zeitung,* 5-19 May 1842.
4. Occasionally, there are counterinstances suggesting that "vulgar Marxism" may meet with correction from within traditions it has debased. A leader of the Spanish Communist party, one Luis, is quoted in the *New York Times* of 29 October 1975 saying: "We do not renounce a single one of the bourgeois liberties. If the bourgeoisie can dominate in freedom we want to provide more profound, more real

liberties, not less. Socialism can provide the economic base for more complete liberty, without restricting a single aspect of bourgeois liberty." How much credence, if any, to give to this man's claim to democratic belief I do not know; but the fact that he speaks as he does must be regarded as significant.

5. Kenneth Minogue, *The Liberal Mind* (London: Methuen & Co., 1963), p. 150.

6. A word about the role of the working class in socialist thought, as it contrasts with the frequent claims of liberalism to rise "above" mere class interest. Granted the common criticism that Marxism has overestimated the revolutionary potential of the workers; granted that socialist rhetoric has sometimes romanticized the workers. It nevertheless remains that a major historical and moral conquest of the socialist movement, especially in the nineteenth century, was to enable the masses of the lowly—as liberalism only occasionally did, and with nothing like the same passion—to enter the stage of history and acquire a historical consciousness. Few developments in the last two centuries have so decisively helped the consolidation of democratic institutions; few have so painfully been exploited to violate democratic norms. It would be foolish to say that socialism alone should take credit for the entry of "the masses" into political life; but it was the socialists who gave this entry a distinct moral sanction. At its best, socialism enabled the formation of that impressive human type we know as the self-educated worker in the late nineteenth century. That the rise of the working class to articulation and strength could, nevertheless, be exploited for authoritarian ends is surely a major instance of the tragedy of progress.

7. Friedrich Engels, "On the History of the Communist League," in Marx and Engels, *Selected Works,* vol. 2 (Moscow: Foreign Languages Publishing House, 1962), p. 344.

8. Karl Marx, "The Eighteenth Brumaire of Louis Bonaparte," in *The Marx—Engels Reader,* ed. Robert C. Tucker (New York: W. W. Norton & Co., 1972), p. 514.

9. This is an excerpt from Marx's "Conspectus on Bakunin's *Statism and Anarchy,"* published in *Marx-Engels Werke,* vol. 18 (Berlin: Dietz Verlag, 1964), pp. 599-642.

10. Lenin, *State and Revolution,* chap. 5, section 2 ("Transition from Capitalism to Communism).

11. Harold Laski, in his *Parliamentary Government in England* (London: George Allen and Unwin, Ltd., 1938), questioned whether democracy could survive if a Labor government came to power and legislated

a socialist program. In 1945 a Labor government did come to power and legislated, if not a socialist program then a huge welfare-state program decidedly akin to, or at least pointing the way to, socialism. And democracy did not collapse. This does not yet "prove" that Laski was wrong; only that it would be unwise to assume that he was right.
12. A criticism anticipated in general terms by the early Marx: "Political emancipation is indeed a great step forward. It is not, to be sure, the final form of universal human emancipation, but is the final form *within* the prevailing order of things. . . . Where the political state has achieved its full development, man leads a double life, a heavenly and an earthly life, not only in thought or consciousness but in *actuality*. In the *political community* he regards himself as a *communal being;* but in *civil society* he is active as a *private individual,* treats other men as means, reduces himself to a means, and becomes the plaything of alien powers."
13. See Minogue, *The Liberal Mind,* pp. 79-90.

3

Liberalism 1976:
A Conservative Critique
Robert L. Bartley

American liberalism finds itself in disarray both politically and intellectually, but its plight brings no joy to the conservative. At least not to this conservative, if that is what I am. For my kind of conservative has always reserved a place in his heart for establishments, and liberalism has been our establishment. Its confusion is something to regret, indeed a sign of profound social disorder.

A liberal establishment has ordered our political and intellectual lives for the past two generations, and it is far too early to tell what will replace it, if anything. An establishment of course consists of a union of church and state, or in our secular times, of politics and intellect, of power and truth—or at least a persuasive version of truth. American conservatists continue to find this marriage elusive. Socialists are faced with the perplexing question of whether they really want to nationalize the steel industry, and if not what does socialism mean anyway? The new radicalism is essentially an emotional outburst, to be totted up with the Rev. Sun Myung Moon as a symptom of the social disorder. Through sheer inertia liberalism continues to dominate both the academy and the majority political party; perhaps it will yet find a new invigorating spirit.

More likely, I fear, none of these contenders will establish its leadership. That is, what lies ahead is not a new establishment but continued drift. A period of power uninformed by a vision of truth, which means power unsure of itself. Power unsure of itself, perhaps trying to keep its hold through manipulation and repression, but more likely paralyzed by uncertainty about its political and social support. A leaderless, rudderless society is vulnerable to strife at home and, far from incidentally, to foes abroad. Nor can it satisfy man's need for a context in which he can make some sense out of his existence. This is precisely the state of affairs most abhorrent to the conservative mind as I understand it. The enemy is not liberalism but anomie.

From this perspective, which needless to say is not the perspective of all Americans who call themselves conservatives, one must look back wistfully on the liberal establishment forged during the Roosevelt and Truman years. These may not have been men with a sure grip on the spiritual crisis of Western civilization. Inevitably they made mistakes, most spectacularly in the refusal to face the guilt of Alger Hiss, and sometimes lost control of events, as in the ensuing McCarthy period. But for it all they were men sure of themselves, confident of their relations with the society about them, in a position to take the long view, to lead society as well as reflect it.

And lead they did. Their management of the war effort was superior. After the war they conceived and sold the Marshall Plan and later the containment policy. They constructed a successful international monetary system and reduced trade barriers to open a new era in world economics. For all its problems, their domestic economic management did curb the postwar inflation and avoid serious depression. They broke the seventy-five-year logjam on the great brooding issue of American politics, equal rights for Negro citizens.

Predictably these were the accomplishments not of a

narrow faction but of a broad-ranging coalition. Its major elements were the Democratic Party, organized labor and the intellectual world. The coalition drew crucial support from minority elements among the scions of inherited wealth, investment bankers, and Wall Street lawyers. It reached into the Republican Party to include such prominent names as Earl Warren and, arguably, Thomas E. Dewey. All of these elements joined in a vague concensus centered chiefly on tenets of an interventionist foreign policy and ameliorative reform to aid the disadvantaged at home.

Nowhere was the liberal creed more dominant than in the world of ideas. A man of intellect and character would hardly be attracted to the Stalinists and naifs on the left or to the racists on the right. Even conservatives with ideas and character, such as Robert A. Taft, were typically tinged with an isolationism that seemed unrealistic in a shrunken world. So the right wing of intellectuals was marked by, say, Clinton Rossiter. The likes of Walter Lippmann, starting from the conservative view of society, and Reinhold Niebuhr, starting from the conservative view of man, became not only adherents to but pillars of the liberal establishment.

Indeed, it was an appeal to all men of a rationalist temperament that made liberalism the establishment. It stood for reason and moderation in public affairs. Its politics seemed to flow from a reasoned conception of the public interest, not from narrow interest, blind prejudice, or demagogic opportunism. Even those who disagreed with the thrust of liberalism had to concede that it had something intelligent, something reasoned, to say about public affairs.

In short, liberalism had to be taken seriously. The liberals might be seen as mistaken on individual issues, but their views nonetheless had a special claim to public attention. That is, they were an elite with the mark of legitimacy, and as such an element of stability around which other groups could array themselves. In a word, an establishment.

In 1976 liberalism understandably enough still pretends to this status and the advantages it bestows, but the claims grow increasingly hard to believe. It is no longer clear that the liberals themselves believe. Their historical foreign policy prescriptions are mocked by the most divisive and least successful war in at least a century. Their economic prescriptions are mocked by the combination of inflation and unemployment. Their management skills are mocked by the *de facto* bankruptcy of New York City, the nation's most conspicuously liberal metropolis.

Even worse, the elements of the liberal coalition themselves look increasingly like vested interests. Certainly it is hard today to find someone to shed a tear for organized labor, now preoccupied with trade protectionism, long the epitome of narrow interests. Social uplift schemes are increasingly perceived less as ends in themselves than as means of winning elections and building bureaucratic empires. The intellectuals themselves are increasingly seen not as a disinterested party, but as a faction acutely concerned with its own status and power.

*

In trying to discern how this change has come about, it will pay to trace the evolution of the liberal stance on a few salient issues, and it's just as well to start with the liberal establishment's finest hour, the attack on segregation. This of course was a decades-long effort, for that matter one that continues today. But of all its beacons, from President Truman's desegregation of the armed forces to the voting rights provisions of the 1964 Civil Rights Act, the brightest is the Supreme Court ruling in *Brown* v. *Board of Education.* From that moment it was clear that segregation as a legal system was doomed.

But the Brown decision also left a haunted legacy for the liberal creed. For the justices were not content with the ground staked out by the first Justice Harlan in his dissent from *Plessy* v. *Ferguson,* "There is no caste here. Our constitution is color-blind, and neither knows nor tolerates classes among citizens." Faced with *Plessy's* "separate but equal" doctrine, the court in *Brown* inevitably and sensibly ruled that separate is inherently unequal. But the opinion was not content to stop there. Justice Warren wrote that segregation was unconstitutional because it retarded the mental development of black pupils; the opinion cites as evidence a series of social science findings.

This use of social science did not pass unchallenged by legal scholars. A writer in the *Indiana Law Journal* remarked that if a marshaling of the research showed that segregation did not have a detrimental effect, the constitutional rule would have to be reversed. "I would not have the constitutional rights of Negroes—or any other Americans—rest on such flimsy foundation as some of the scientific demonstrations in these records," agreed a writer for the *New York University Law Review*. He did not think that "our fundamental rights rise, fall or change along with the latest fashions of psychological literature."[1]

More significantly, Justice Warren's rule, we can now see, creates far different rights than Justice Harlan's. Justice Harlan would give Negro pupils the right to be treated like white pupils. Justice Warren would give Negro pupils the right to have white pupils in their classrooms. The second rule creates great difficulties, both practical and moral, that have confounded courts in particular and liberals in general.

In the landmark integration case in Richmond, Judge Robert R. Merhig Jr. wrote that an expert witness "rejected the interpretation placed upon the goal of placing 20% to 40% black students in each school as the imposition of a 'fixed racial quota,' and the court so finds. Rather, he saw that ratio as established by the existing demographic proportions in the Richmond area. . . ."

The quotation reflects the tension between the Warren rule and the Harlan rule. The ideal of a color-blind constitution clearly has no room for racial quotas, as Congress and the courts had declared before Judge Merhige wrote. But the Warren rule practically compels them. The courts respond by attacking the English language, defining away the very meaning of the word "quota." What are men of character and intellect to make of the assertion that requiring a certain percentage of a certain race is not a "racial quota"?

Yet the liberal position has followed the same tortuous development. That is not to say that everyone who thinks of himself as a liberal agrees with every twist in this development, which has already reached the point of requiring women's quotas in the hiring of university faculty. But a departure from any twist, including women's quotas, jeopardizes one's liberal credentials in the eyes of other liberals. Nor is this entirely unfair, for a challenge even to women's quotas is a challenge to a consistent core of liberal belief reaching back to *Brown*. The decision's reliance on social science findings created an inner logic that works itself out into today's liberal positions.

That this has done great damage to the liberal cause is evident enough in the political issue of "forced busing." Busing of school children to meet racial quotas is inconvenient and a challenge to other values that have little to do with race. The inconveniences are often not shared by the liberal judges and legislators advocating busing, for they send their children to private or suburban schools. Yet when the liberal establishment finds it cannot persuade people to put their children through this trouble for the sake of Justice Warren's rule—not Justice Harlan's—it sees the reaction as evidence of how deeply racist the people are.

Even more embarrassing, public opinion polls typically find that busing is opposed by a majority of black parents as well as white. Indeed, many blacks have come to recognize the fundamental condescension implicit in the Warren rule, and some of them have reached the point of wanting *their* schools, as other ethnic groups have in the past. Yet the inner logic of Brown, and of today's liberal creed, requires busing and quotas to help the blacks whether they want it or not.

Finally, one should note the liberal reaction to social science research when it challenges rather than supports the Warren rule. As David J. Armour found, you cannot publish research casting doubt on the educational efficacy of busing without making yourself the center of a controversy reaching well beyond normal academic disagreement. Even James T.

Coleman, whose research has long been used by busing advocates, is met with personal abuse when his conclusions go the other way. One critic expressed a widespread reaction, "It's a kind of cop-out, and might become known as the great Coleman cop-out."[2]

Now, one must sympathize with the emotions behind the liberal stance on civil rights. Racism is a huge moral blot on the nation's history, one by no means requited today. Whatever mistakes liberals have made along the way, they broke the logjam. No reasonably sensitive man wants to give aid and comfort to racism, and even after the law was clear, a plainly racist resistance was bitter and prolonged. In particular, the resistance advanced nominally color-blind rules such as "freedom of choice" as a clear subterfuge to perpetuate dual schools. Impatient with the resistance, the courts felt it necessary to attack not the subterfuge but the principle.

It is all so understandable. But consider the huge expense of abandoning Justice Harlan's high ground. Today liberalism is stuck with a position of quotas, which it refuses to acknowledge by their true name. It is using social pressure to block freedom of inquiry on these topics. In the name of blacks, it is insisting on something the majority of blacks does not want. Having rallied support on the moral principle that skin color should be irrelevant, it now finds itself arguing that students should be told by color above all. And if you doubt any of this, the liberals suspect you of racism.

However understandable these positions and this behavior are in the light of history, they can only destroy the special claim to authority that liberalism so recently held. Even if he can find reasons to support the current liberal position, a man of intellect and character must feel uncomfortable with its tortuous development. This development shows anything but the kind of consistency and maturity that convey a legitimacy to be transferred to other issues. This is no way for an establishment to behave.

*

If the evolution of liberal thought is dramatic on issues of civil rights, it is melodramatic on issues of foreign policy. Twenty years ago the principle of an interventionist foreign policy lay at the very heart of the liberal consensus. Today, the liberal position is evolving toward something that looks more and more like old-fashioned isolationism.

The "military-industrial complex" echoes Gerald P. Nye's "merchants of death." Congressional votes against arms aid to Angolan factions echo congressional votes on the first Neutrality Act at the time of Mussolini's invasion of Ethiopia. But this time it is not the Nyes and Lodges and Borahs, but the self-proclaimed liberals who lead the retreat from the world.

Again, not all who proclaim themselves liberals do so. But no matter what his domestic politics, as Senator Henry Jackson so neatly demonstrates, a liberal who has maintained his 1960 attitude on foreign policy and defense will no longer be seen as a liberal by other liberals. The credentials depend on conformity to a changing norm.

This seachange in liberal opinion was caused chiefly if not exclusively by the Vietnam War. What is so often forgotten, or worse, is that Vietnam was very much a liberal war. To consider Vietnam in proper perspective, one must recall the defense debates of the 1950s, in particular liberal dissatisfaction with "massive retaliation" and "brinkmanship." It was barbaric to threaten nuclear holocaust over Quemoy and Matsu, the liberals argued, and more discriminating policies must be found.

In 1960, the liberals won the government and had a chance to implement their ideas. In "A Thousand Days," Arthur Schlesinger Jr. describes "The Occupation of the Pentagon": The United States, for all its splendid capacity to blow up the world, had, it was obvious, an entirely inadequate amount of what McNamara called 'usable power'—military force capable of serving reasonable ends. The president, who was perhaps less surprised, directed him to begin the work of building a military establishment versatile enough to meet the full spectrum of possible threats from guerrilla infiltration to nuclear holocaust."[3]

In particular, the emphasis was on development of a counterinsurgency capability. The president himself read the strategic writings of Mao Tse-tung and Che Guevara, and Mr. Schlesinger tells us, "He used to entertain his wife on country weekends by inventing aphorisms in the manner of Mao's 'Guerrillas must move among the people as fish swim in the sea'."

Presidential support was needed, for the "organization generals" in the Pentagon "looked on the counterinsurgency business as a faddish distraction from the main responsibility of training for conventional assault. The professionals, infatuated with the newest technology and eager to strike major blows, deeply disliked the thought of reversion to the rude weapons, amateur tactics, hard life and marginal effects of guerrilla warfare."

Yet the president could command, especially since a new system of scientific management was giving civilian analysts rational control over the Pentagon. With the backing of Robert Kennedy, Maxwell Taylor, Richard Bissell, Roger Hilsman, and Walt Rostow, a new counterinsurgency capability was developed. "Over the opposition of the Army bureaucracy, which abhorred separate elite commands on principle," the Green Berets were founded.

"There was, to be sure," Mr. Schlesinger recalls, "a faddish aspect to this enthusiasm. Some of its advocates acted as if the delicate arts of blacking one's face and catching sentries by the throat in the night could by themselves eliminate the guerilla threat. The president was under no such illusion. He insisted that the Special Forces be schooled in sanitation, teaching, bridge-building, medical care and the need for economic progress."

"Winning the hearts and minds of the people" was far more melodic to liberal ears than "massive retaliation." Similarly, the new scientific civilians in the Pentagon wanted to use their "versatile military force in a discriminating and

less destructive way. The teaching of military history that
force should be used massively and overwhelmingly rather
than piecemeal was dismissed as an "infatuation" at best and
at worst a taste for brutality. Instead, scientific civilians
argued, the United States should deal with Vietnam by
sending "signals" to Hanoi, stepping up the U.S. commitment by neatly calculated steps until Hanoi understood its
game was up.

One exchange of these two views came in an exchange of
papers in one of the Pentagon's think tanks. One paper was
written by Captain Elmo Zumwalt, later chief of naval
operations. It argued that the United States should stay out
of Vietnam if it could, and use overwhelming air and naval
air and naval power if it couldn't. The paper spelling out the
"signals" approach was written by a young civilian named
Daniel Ellsberg.

Unfortunately, events on the ground yielded neither to
"signals" nor to "hearts and minds." As the 1960s wore on,
events seemed to deteriorate, though the extent of deterioration was at issue. It seemed minor to official intelligence,
and to a few journalists, notably Marguerite Higgins.[4] But as
Buddhist demonstrations and suicides continued, a sense of
crisis took hold. In particular, this impression was advanced
by the press reports of David Halberstam, Neil Sheehan, and
Malcolm Browne.

The theme of these reports was that the "hearts and minds
of the people" were not being and could not be won by the
authoritarian government of Ngo Dinh Diem. Within the
American government, a group headed by Averell Harriman,
Roger Hilsman, and Henry Cabot Lodge came to see Diem's
replacement as the key to winning the war. Others, including
Vice-President Johnson, opposed this idea, but in time it won
out. The United States encouraged and ultimately, by assur-
ing the plotters that U.S. aid to the war effort would continue, sanctioned the coup against Diem.

This act precipitated further military deterioration. More
importantly, it sealed the commitment of the United States
to the Vietnamese war. Professor Morton Kaplan puts it

neatly, "I know of no more decisive commitment a nation can make than to bring down the president of a friendly country in order to win a war." After this, both morally and in terms of world power politics, the United States could scarcely walk away from Vietnam without a major effort to salvage the situation it had created. The coup took place in the first week of November 1963. By the end of the month John F. Kennedy was dead, and President Lyndon Johnson inherited the aftermath.

Now, this observation is not intended to exonerate everything that happened in Vietnam after 1963. Obviously there are a great many different foreign policy lessons to be learned from so agonizing an experience as Vietnam. The policy of containment was no doubt applied too automatically, with the support of both liberals and conservatives. The will of the North Vietnamese was consistently underestimated, and so on.

But there is no little danger of learning the wrong lessons. The liberal critique of Vietnam is damaging the liberal cause —first because the critique is often directed in a particularly personal way precisely at the liberal establishment itself, at "The Best and the Brightest"; and second because it is so laden with guilt that it becomes a sort of anti-Americanism, as if the United States created the war and pursued it for base purposes. The American people, those an American establishment would lead, know better.

Any critique of Vietnam would be painful, but why has the liberal critique become so cramped and self-destructive? Consider for a moment the thinkers and writers who have been most influential in shaping this post-Vietnam sensibility. Would not a succinct list read: David Halberstam, Neil Sheehan, Roger Hilsman, Daniel Ellsberg?

The hidden agenda of these writers is to exonerate the scientific-civilian conduct of the war in general and the Diem coup in particular. The best and the brightest held up for blame by Mr. Halberstam include everyone connected with the war, with the exceptions of Averell Harriman, Roger Hilsman, and Henry Cabot Lodge. (And David Halberstam, who in 1964 could write, "I believe that Vietnam is a legitimate part of that global commitment. A strategic country in a key area, it is perhaps one of only five or six nations in the world that is truly vital to U.S. interests.")[5]

Mr. Ellsberg, who in 1962 was advocating the war, later decided that the leaders who acted on his and similar advice were cynical, that "the big domino was always the White House." And when he leaked the Pentagon Papers to Neil Sheehan, he no doubt knew how that vast and ambiguous record would be interpreted. When the *New York Times* first published its accounts of those papers, it started the chronology with February 1964, relating events Mr. Sheehan thought led up to the Tonkin Gulf episode that August. The events of November 1963 were relegated to a later account, after a court decision had temporarily stopped publication, and following the report on the historical origins of the conflict.

Nor is the reading put on the actual papers by Mr. Sheehan and his colleagues the only possible one. Edward Jay Epstein, for example, concludes that the theme of "duplicity" unifying the *Times* accounts was a theme of the *Times,* not of the papers.

"The Pentagon study, however, deserves to be read in its own right," Mr. Epstein adds. "At the root of the problem was a supreme commitment to the infallibility of rational planning. Most of the civilian decisionmakers shared the belief that the United States could compel North Vietnam to modify basic national policies through a well-orchestrated program of pressures that would fall short of all-out warfare, or even 'wider war' in Asia."[6]

It is precisely this lesson that so much of the liberal critique of Vietnam is devoted to obscuring and avoiding. This effort is led by some of those most intimately involved, but it finds a sympathetic audience among a far wider section of liberals who shared their sentiments in 1963. Naturally this bent gives the critique an essentially neurotic flavor: don't blame us, blame the military-industrial complex, blame the generals, blame the CIA, blame government secrets, blame the "arrogance of power," blame the "best and the brightest," blame the leaders elected by the American people, blame the political system, blame the people, blame America.

Need it be said that such a critique will not long prove attractive either to men of intellect and character or to an electorate that, whatever its shortcomings, has always displayed a good sense of smell. Such a liberal critique can only destroy the legitimacy upon which an establishment depends.

*

No critique of liberalism would be complete without a few words about liberal ideas on economics. There is a whole group of issues on which someone ought to ask whether the average man prefers the liberal goal of 1960 or of 1976, and precisely who would benefit from the changes. It's tempting, for example, to trace the evolution of the goal of equality of economic opportunity into the goal of equality of result. Or similarly, from lifting poor people over an absolute poverty line to equalizing relative income shares. Or even more deliciously, from the "let's get this country moving again" of 1960 to the "no growth" environmentalism of 1976.

Rather than pick on sitting ducks, though, I will go out on a limb of my own with a prediction. I may of course be wrong, for debate on these issues is at an early stage, and I have already been deeply enough involved to acquire something of a personal stake. But it seems to me that over the next few years we will see an increasing challenge to the very heart of liberal economic thinking, to the Keynesian orthodoxy itself. Liberals will be sorely tempted to behave badly.

The operative idea of this orthodoxy, of course, is that government deficits stimulate a lagging economy. Government spending spreads through the private economy because of the familiar multiplier effect. A significant economic debate is now under way on an issue that might be described in popular language as: But where did the government get the money in the first place?

Analysts at the Federal Reserve Bank of St. Louis have

developed the thesis of "crowding out": that assuming a constant money supply government spending will displace private spending, perhaps by a roughly equivalent amount. If
this is so, it is hard to see any multiplier effect, or any fiscal
stimulus.[7]

The debate is proceeding, but the challenge is not easily
dismissed. The St. Louis analysts offered some empirical evidence in support of their proposition. Econometric models,
for the little in my opinion they are worth, often show that
fiscal measures have a positive multiplier in the short run but
a negative one within, say, a year. Of course, Keynesian economics was not notably successful in ending the Great
Depression before the onset of World War II.

Added to this there is an increasing concern about the adequacy of capital investment. In international comparisons,
there is an extraordinarily strong relationship between economic growth and investment (or since investment equals
savings, between economic growth and savings). The United
States, investment per worker has been declining. There is a
parisons. With a rapidly rising labor force in the United
States, investment per worker has been declining. There is a
spreading conclusion that if we are to maintain our past rate
of economic growth, we must increase our savings and investment.

This concern is intimately related to that of "crowding
out" because government borrowings to finance deficits are
directly competitive with private borrowings to finance
industrial investment. Both must be financed out of savings.
Thus some of us worry that government deficits not only fail
to stimulate the economy, but reduce future growth by reducing investment. This, I am told, was the British Treasury
view Keynes wrote the General Theory to refute.

I take it that nearly everyone agrees that once full employment is reached, government deficits do crowd out private
investment. If resources are already fully employed, the
government can use more of them only if someone else uses
less. The Keynesians argue that if resources are not fully
employed, the deficits will stimulate the economy through

the multiplier, increasing total income and thus total savings. If the policy is successful, the deficits will stimulate enough new savings not only to finance themselves but to provide additional funds for private investment. This assumes, of course, that deficits stimulate in the first place.[8]

Since by early 1975 it was evident that the nation faced three years or more of massive deficits, conservatives began to agitate these issues. The liberal answer came through a Brookings Institution study, "Capital Needs in the Seventies." The study concluded that "we can afford the future, but just barely." Higher investment was needed, but it could be supplied by "a moderate adjustment of fiscal and monetary policies."[9]

This was taken by liberal commentators, and apparently by the Brookings authors themselves, as refutation of an earlier New York Stock Exchange study that talked of a "capital shortage" if we wanted to continue past rates of growth.[10] But upon examination, it became apparent that the chief differences between the two studies was in assumptions of federal finances. The stock exchange assumed government deficits (including off-budget agencies) of some $12.1 billion a year. Brookings had closed the capital gap by the "moderate adjustment" of assuming government *surpluses* averaging $11.5 billion a year in the period 1974–80.[11]

The Brookings assumption is plainly ridiculous, knowing what we aready know about deficits in the early part of the 1974–80 period. Brookings was caught between its own numbers and the Keynesian orthodoxy that prescribed deficits in periods of recession like 1974. When challenged on the assumption in the columns I edit, its economists responded by talking of 1980 as a year in isolation rather than, as the original study had, as the end of a cumulative period; and with semantic confusion about "full employment surpluses," as if capital needs could be met by such hypothetical surpluses rather than the actual ones actually required.

Perhaps this is merely the start of a healthy discussion, but over the next several years the issue of capital formation will be a continuing test for liberal economists. One way to increase savings and capital formation is through tax incentives, which by their nature tend to make the tax system less progressive and are thus opposed by liberals. The other way is to substitute public savings for private savings, which is the recommendation toward which Brookings so haltingly started.

This can be a serious proposal if carried through seriously. Despite its welfare state, Sweden has the highest rate of capital formation in Europe. This is because the Swedes have a supplementary social security system run on the same principles as a private retirement plan, as urged by U.S. conservatives when social security was founded. In effect, the Swedes are taking more in through social security taxes than they have been paying out in benefits, and investing the balance in private securities, that is, making it available for investment by private industry.[12]

I very much doubt that such a system is politically sustainable; in Sweden some of the barriers to use of this money to control private investment decisions are already starting to erode. And so long as the tax incentives do speed economic growth, they meet John Rawls' test of a proposal that ultimately works to the advantage of the lowest income groups. But the difference between British socialism and Swedish socialism is well worth having, and I think serious liberals ought to be thinking about public savings.

If liberals are to start thinking this way, though, something else has to give. For if you consolidate all the accounts, Sweden ran a government surplus year after year from the start of the supplementary system through at least the early 1970s. If you believe in Keynesian multipliers, you should have predicted that the Swedish economy would go through the floor. Or, at least, you have some fancy footwork to do.

It will be fascinating to see how liberals resolve this dilemma in their economic thinking over the next several years. In particular, we will learn a great deal from their attitude toward government surpluses once the economy returns to full employment, at which point everyone seems to concede "crowding out" becomes a reality. Will the liberals then come forward with serious proposals for the kind of spending restraint (or tax increases) that would provide surpluses to turn to private investment?

If not, their current attitudes will be revealed as, well, hypocritical. It would, I should think, be enough to preclude the rebirth of liberalism as an establishment whose attitudes and positions must be given special weight.

*

In the 1960s and 1970s, then, liberalism—or at least its most conspicuous elements—had stumbled into a byway on civil rights, the issue of its greatest historical accomplishment. On its other historical strength, foreign policy, it had not even performed honorably—first leading us into a tragic war, then trying to cover its mistakes by blaming everyone else for the outcome. On economic policy it had developed many faddish offshoots, and its center is now starting to shake.

Inevitably, such mistakes took their toll of the liberals' standing as an establishment, as an elite on which the rest of society could in important aspects rely. The effects of the mistakes could conceivably have been weathered; that is what the legitimacy of an establishment is all about. What was fatal was the liberal reaction to those mistakes.

Far too often the liberals seemed to forsake their own principles, rejecting a color-blind constitution, reversing an interventionist foreign policy, showing a willingness to block freedom of inquiry, refusing to follow their own evidence where it obviously leads. Thus the liberals lost their standing with the rest of society as the one group that must always be taken seriously, as a group that could be trusted, if not necessarily to reach the right conclusions on public policies at least to know how to go about analyzing them—if not to be right, at least to think.

How, the question inevitably arises, did this all come to pass? Without doubt a large part of the answer, perhaps the largest part, is simply that our times are tough on all establishments. The frantic pace of life and instant communications leave no place to hide errors or even disagreements.

Legitimacy, the habit of belief and trust, faces the corrosive test of total scrutiny. This means that no one, least of all political leaders, can afford to take the long view.

If you look beyond this to the elements of the old liberal coalition, you are struck by the decline of the eastern monied establishment to which the liberal establishment owed so much of its success with foreign policy. The world of inherited wealth, prep schools, the Ivy League, and finance has been eroded both by an increasingly rationalized economy and the liberal attack on privilege. One doubts that we will again see the Douglas Dillons, James Forrestals, Dean Achesons, and Bernard Baruchs of the old liberal establishment.

You have to be struck, too, by how little labor has to do with the liberal mistakes cited above. It has no illusions about either racial quotas or foreign governments that keep unions in lockstep. Even in economics, it has backed an investment tax credit, and consistently lobbied for special breaks for *its* industries—understanding the need for investment in those businesses that employ the 25 percent of the work force organized by unions. But increasingly cut off from the mainstream of conspicuous liberalism, labor looks increasingly like a narrow vested interest.

You have to be struck, finally, by the intellectuals, who have now become the mainstream itself. With the spread of education and the increasing demand for communications skills, the intellectuals have become a growing and powerful social class. Society has become so complex it managed only by abstractions, and intellectuals are needed to supply and manipulate them.

Alas, abstractions can also mislead. Indeed, the liberal mistakes of the 1960s and 1970s have been the mistakes of abstractions, the mistakes of intellectuals. Whether in psychological research on the development of the black child, in the military formula of "hearts and minds," in the "fine tuning" of Keynesian economics, in the "community action" programs chronicled by Daniel P. Moynihan, the characteristic mistake has been to press an abstraction further than reality would carry.

It is precisely this type of mistake, moreover, that must be obscured and denied at nearly any cost. For it is not merely a mistake but a threat to the newly emerging class power of intellectuals. If society cannot be centrally managed through the use of abstractions, intellectuals will be less highly regarded and rewarded.

The question of abstractions is a liberal-conservative issue; classically it is *the* liberal-conservative issue. It is Burke versus Rousseau, the "rights of man" versus "the rights of Englishmen." In the French Revolution, Burke saw at work unbridled abstractions, unrooted in history or real interests, and he foresaw years in advance that this would give rise to a Napoleon. We are, or so I hope, learning a similar lesson today.

The old liberal establishment had no pressing need to learn this lesson. Probably even its intellectuals were more rigorous and less faddish, less compelled by abstraction. More importantly, the rest of the coalition was rooted in reality. There were the investment bankers and Wall Street lawyers, with their kind of reality. And always there was labor, with the reality of the workshop and picket line. These roots disciplined the abstractions of the intellectual, while the intellectual disciplined the self-interest of labor.

This balance was lost as intellectuals became increasingly dominant in defining the liberal position. Abstractions were followed too trustingly, and their results defended too passionately. Liberalism departed too far from reality, too far from its own received assumptions, to retain its prestige as an establishment.

If we are somehow to build a new establishment to give some coherence and leadership to our national life, intellectuals will have to play a prominent part in it. Their skills really are crucial in modern society, and in any event someone needs to supply the truth that motivates and disciplines power. Intellectuals have a crucial part to play, but playing it depends on their understanding the error to which they are characteristically prone.

If intellectuals start to understand this, a new establishment can be built. It probably would be built around the conclusion that liberal intellectual abstractions have to be governed by the flywheel of history and concrete interest. Which is to say, it will have to be built on Burke.

Discussion

The Socialist Critique of Liberalism

According to one participant, socialists have at one time or another taken issue with all three elements of the liberal formula: political liberalism (the doctrine of restraints on power), economic liberalism (the doctrine of the free pursuit of self-interest), and anthropological liberalism (the optimistic view of man and his faculties).

The socialist criticism of political liberalism, he continued, is essentially the same as the democratic criticism, namely that for political freedom to be meaningful it must be combined with political equality. This emphasis stems from the conviction of the early socialists that the merger of political freedom and political equality was a precondition for the establishment of social equality, something which liberal society did not inevitably produce. However, with the convergence of liberalism and democracy, this line of criticism seems to have lost some of its force, although not all socialists would agree.

The socialist critique of economic liberalism has taken two forms: first, a denial of the doctrine of economic harmony of interests; and second, a critique of the liberal state. With respect to the first, the main drift of socialist mass movements has been the demand for social equality and social justice, which are seen as requiring major modification, if not the complete transformation, of the liberal economy. This element of the socialist critique has had a great impact, both on extant governments and on nonsocialist political movements. With respect to the second, socialists have argued

that the liberal state is a bourgeois class state, and that the
real task is therefore to wage a class struggle against bourgeois
class rule. The current force of this criticism is somewhat
harder to assess, but it does not seem as powerful as it once
was, at least in the "advanced" liberal societies. The reason,
the speaker suggested, is that the advanced democracies
of the West still have class societies in the sense of unequal
distribution of chances in life, but no longer anything that
can be meaningfully described as class rule.

Socialist critiques of liberalism's anthropological elements
are varied, but tend to center on the liberal glorification of
individual self-interest. One line of criticism is directed at the
anthropological assumption that the "free individual" antedates society—an assumption which lies at the core of the
liberal view of society as a "social contract" of free persons.
To socialists, this is a historical and ideological fiction. Individuals cannot be envisaged as existing apart from society;
and the interests which society must care for are not only
those of the living, but also of future generations. Here, the
socialist and conservative critiques converge. Both believe in
a basic social bond, a sense of community which becomes
atrophied by the pursuit of individual interests. Socialists also
dispute the optimistic liberal notion that the pursuit of self-
interest leads to progress. Such optimism is confirmed by the
enormous development of productive forces in liberal societies, but dissolves in the face of the simultaneous development of awesome forces for destruction. These negative
consequences of the blind pursuit of self-interest make
increased political control and direction of the economic
progress a necessity. Finally, socialists have pointed to the
danger that the free struggle for partial interests within liberal
democracies will lead, not to compromise and harmony, but
to paralysis.

In addition to these other lines of criticism, there is what
he termed the doctrinaire socialist critique, which views
private ownership of the means of production as setting an
absolute limit to democracy and social progress. This is an
argument advanced not only by Communists. It is also made

by Marxist wings of parties generally regarded as social
democratic, which is why it would be inaccurate to say that
social democracy has abandoned Marxism. True, social democratic parties have cut their institutional ties to Marxism, but
they still contain Marxist elements within them.

Taken together, these various socialist criticisms coalesce
into three broad positions: the doctrinaire liberal, who com-
bines the free market with state intervention in the economy;
the doctrinaire Marxist, who calls for the nationalization of
the means of production; and an outlook shared by European
democratic socialists on the one hand and what in the United
States are called "progressive liberals" on the other. What
emerges is not only a relationship of critical antagonism between socialism and liberalism, but also one of mutual influence and common evolution. Democratic socialists see themselves as the heirs as well as the critics of liberalism, which to
them represents a stage in the evolution of the basic values of
Western civilization. Although the concrete institutional
expressions of these values have changed over time, the values
themselves (such as the inalienable rights of the human person, the idea of the voluntary community, the application of
reason to social problems, and the rule of law) have endured.
Of course, this has been a "parochial" continuity in the sense
that it is peculiar to Western social evolution. And yet it is
Western society which, by virtue of its unique dynamism, has
created the entire modern world, with all its achievements
and all its problems and horrors. In his view, for example, the
Third World states would not exist were it not for the effectiveness of liberal arguments in Western societies. In this
sense, the "parochial" values of Western civilization have
universal significance.

Another speaker expressed agreement with much of the
Howe paper, but was concerned about its apologetic attitude
towards liberalism. Apologies would be in order, he said,
from those who deprecate freedom, and who can see no difference between bourgeois democracy and fascism. But such
people owe an apology not only to liberals, but also to Marx,
who saw socialist society as based on the free development

of every individual (a condition he thought impossible to obtain under capitalism). "Vulgar Marxists" have much to answer for, but true socialists need not apologize. However, others felt that some apology to liberalism is still warranted. It is too simple to attribute everything we don't like to "vulgar Marxism," for although we may wish to emphasize other elements, we do have to recognize that "vulgar Marxism" is part of Marxism too. A similar point of view was that both vulgar *and* nonvulgar Marxism are selective, because after all Marxism is at bottom a theory of revolutionary change. The crucial distinction is, then, whether or not one accepts the idea of a transition period, and believes that you can turn democracy on and off. In this sense, the basic dividing line remains centered on the question of "evolution or revolution."

By way of response to these criticisms, it was pointed out that many Marxists today are sensitive to the issue of the transition period, and are aware that there are problems which Marx could not foresee. Thus a great deal of current writing assumes a multisectoral economy rather than all-around regimentation, addresses itself to issues like full employment and wage-push inflation, and argues for the need to go beyond Marx in dealing with the problem of labor relations in the factory. These directions are of great importance, because in spite of their many virtues both American liberalism and democratic socialism have failed to live up to their promises during critical periods. From this perspective, one might well agree with the assessment that much of the radicalism of the 1960s was a reaction against the emptiness of liberalism in power. The task for socialism, then, is to go beyond liberalism and present a viable alternative.

The discussion then turned to the question of the convergence of liberalism and social democracy. One participant pointed out that, in the past, this convergence was largely a matter of partnership in certain social programs; that is, there was a convergence of some ideas and actions. Today, however, they seem to be converging in another respect which is perhaps more important: both seem impotent, and neither one has (or at least believes that it has) the answers to pressing issues. In fact, only American conservatives and sectarian Marxists now seem sure of themselves. Another speaker disputed this assessment. Although social democrats may be uncertain as to the details, he said, they do have a consensus as to the general directions of policy. In particular, they tend to look toward strong international economic institutions, stronger political controls abroad, and different and more stable forms of economic relations with the Third World. But those who believed that liberalism and social democracy are converging in impotence did not find this an impressive program, nor were they convinced that social democrats any longer have faith in their own solutions. There is a great difference between thinking and believing; and at least among intellectuals, they said, there seems to be a great deal of the former, very little of the latter. A somewhat broader view was that the "convergence of impotence" is very much a product of our times and our situation, which is to say that it is no less true of conservatives than of liberals and social democrats. Given the acceleration of history, the magnitude of our problems, and the "frenzy of novelty," we are simply losing control of the world we are creating.

One participant argued that we have made the question of "socialism and liberalism" somewhat easy by equating socialism with European social democracy. In fact, however, there is a great deal of room between social democracy and Soviet totalitarianism. There are many people who call themselves socialists and strongly condemn the Soviet brand of Marxism, but who also deliberately and consciously reject the term "social democrat" and deny that the Scandinavian models are socialist. Thus, the issue is whether liberalism is compatible, not with social democracy, but with this other socialism. And here he detected a basic ambiguity. He quoted a passage written by Harold Laski in the 1930s, which stated that the attainment of power by parliamentary means must be part of a process of radical transformation of government and society, with the strong implication that antidemocratic measures might be necessary. This passage raised what he saw as very serious questions. Is liberalism only accepted instrumentally by many socialists? To what extent are they willing to suspend liberalism for the sake of achieving socialism? He did not mean to imply that these people necessarily have no concern for liberal values. But, in his eyes, these questions do suggest that they would place a higher priority on the achievement of socialism than on the maintenance of liberalism, if they were forced to choose between them.

In response, one speaker concurred that many European socialists reject the social democratic label, but he said that if people like Mario Soares are the examples, then their commitment to democracy is not any the less for it. He also pointed out that the Laski quotation was written at a time when virtually all of the Western intelligentsia was losing faith in democracy, and that Laski himself was not corrected by trade union leaders but by other intellectuals within the British Labor Party. It is true, of course, that there are people within the socialist tradition who take Marxist positions while leaving Marxist solutions open. Further, many of them do cling to the old rhetoric and do refuse to accept social democracy as "real" socialism. But the reality is quite different. Today in Portugal, for example, the Socialist Party is crucial in preventing Communist dictatorship, while Soares relies on the social democrats to help keep liberty alive. European Marxists have learned something from the fate of the Austro-Marxists (who were crushed) and the Italian maximalists (who helped produce a fascist dictatorship). In other words, it is very important to distinguish between intellectual traditions on the one hand, and the history of the particular socialist parties and their specific policies on the other.

Another participant took issue with the "liberalism versus socialism" formulation on different grounds. Referring to southern Europe, he reported that the people there would like to be able to make the choice between liberty and equality. But many of them simply do not see liberalism as the most promising way to achieve the "liberal life"—both freedom from abuse and the freedom to rise on one's own merits. They are therefore likely to choose a form of socialism which, while not Stalinism, is not social democracy either. Thus the real problem is not how to fight totalitarianism, but rather how to maximize the amount of liberty in countries whose future is apt to be more socialist than liberal.

Finally, a warning was issued against minimizing the threat to liberalism, posed not by social democracy but by totalitarian societies. In this view, disagreements on this issue have been glossed over. In fact, for liberals the processual values *are* teleological, which is to say that the struggle with totalitarianism is a religious one. The crisis, then, is not that we have no establishment to help us make sense of our existence, but that we have an establishment which no longer wishes to conduct that struggle.

The Conservative Critique of Liberalism

The discussion of the conservative critique of liberalism began with a summary of the argument presented in Mr. Bartley's paper, which went as follows: it is crucial that there be a cohesive "establishment," a stable, protected elite which can safeguard society from "the enemy"—anomie. The Roosevelt coalition—based on a consensus centering on an interventionist foreign policy and ameliorative reform domestically—was such an establishment. But the basis of this coalition has been upset by a number of factors. One was liberalism's mistakes, compounded by its readiness to forsake its own principles. Another was changes in social structure, especially the emergence of a powerful intellectual class whose characteristic tendency has been to press its abstractions farther than reality could carry them. Because the liberal establishment took the abstractions of intellectuals too seriously, its policy prescriptions became increasingly irrelevant, and eventually it lost society's trust. But a new establishment can be built on Burkean principles, which would insist that abstractions be governed by the "flywheel of history and concrete interest." To one member of the conference this argument presented problems at every step. First of all, he had strong doubts that a new American establishment could or would be Burkean. Intellectuals are not likely to alter their habitual ways of thinking; people who believe it possible to cure social ills by applying some rational system of management will not stop thinking that way simply because it is evident that the application of their system has produced disaster. Instead, they will come up with a new system. Nor are intellectuals any more prone to this error than are businessmen, or most Americans, for that matter. Americans generally believe that social problems are solvable, and any elite which tried to tell them otherwise—that social problems arise from conditions inseparable from social life, that rational management rarely makes things better but often makes things worse, that the centralization of power required must curtail and may destroy liberty, and that therefore we should bear the ills we have—could not make its truth persuasive or hope to gain power. Given these cultural realities an American establishment must be liberal.

Secondly, he felt that Mr. Bartley's impeachment of liberalism was too mild. From the New Deal, to its conduct of World War II, to its postwar foreign policy, to the decisions of the Supreme Court, the mistakes of the liberal establishment have been serious, not trivial or inevitable. Perhaps Mr. Bartley would say that this establishment at least had the supreme virtue of creating public confidence in its rule. The problem with this defense is that the current cynicism and sense of rudderlessness derive as much from the successes as from the failures of liberalism in its "Golden Age." Mr. Bartley's tracing of the Brown decision is a good example; it shows how admirable actions can have unmanageable consequences.

Finally, it is precisely what Mr. Bartley calls the main task of an establishment—to "provide a context in which men can make sense of their existence"—that liberalism cannot do. It cannot because, being liberalism, it is incapable of understanding the limits of social action. As a result, there is a strong tension, if not incompatibility, between the kind of leadership which is now possible in the United States, and successful performance in the long run. In fact, given present conditions, any establishment we have is likely to fall apart before very long. Yet this does not necessarily mean that Mr. Bartley's fear of a rudderless society suffering from anomie is well grounded, because political philosophers are probably of greater effect than political leaders in strengthening or weakening the social bond.

This last statement evoked some disagreement, on the grounds that a cohesive political establishment is still crucial in combating anomie. After all, it was argued, since the United States is by far the largest and most powerful "liberal" country in the world, it should be no surprise that the failure of its establishment to exert some kind of leadership in the world has much to do with the disarray of liberalism in the broader sense. Another participant reported that he is neither comfortable with the idea that no establishment is likely to survive for long, nor satisfied with the critique of the liberal establishment which limits itself to saying that it has failed to live up to what we expect from an establishment. In his view, the liberal establishment was bound to fail. It was bound to fail because it did not strike its own theoretical roots deeply enough into American society, because its proud eclecticism brings short-run results and long-run failures, and most of all, he concluded, because it has not understood the nature of man and thus the proper role and limitations of government.

An alternative hypothesis was that the liberal establishment has failed not because it was liberal and not because it was an establishment, but because it was a WASP establishment. That is, given its socioethnic character, the liberal establishment was inevitably undermined by secular changes in American life, especially the spread of affluence to new centers and the rise of previously excluded groups to leadership. Again, there was disagreement. To one speaker, the disintegration of the liberal establishment has not been the result of its inclusiveness or noninclusiveness, but rather of the nature of the problems it faces, and its apparent inability to find solutions for them. To another, it was not clear that the establishment had disintegrated in the first place. Perhaps the old WASP elite is in disarray, but if so it has been replaced by another one which is just as confident and just as self-righteous. It simply holds different values.

The discussion then turned to an issue that Mr. Bartley had raised in his paper: the tension between accumulation and equality. One participant commented that the differences between liberals and conservatives have often been defined with respect to this issue, the former stressing social transfers, the latter emphasizing the need for accumulation and the difficulty of reconciling more equality with the preservation of liberty. He suggested that the main reason for the cohesion and confidence of the old liberal establishment was that it handled both the task of the right (accumulation) and the task of the left (equality) at the same time. It was able to do so because it worked in a situation of gross underemployment of resources. Now, however, in conditions of scarcity it may be no longer possible to do both things at once. If not, then both the left and the right will have some fundamental choices to make. A related argument was that decisions as to the accumulation and distribution of capital will be crucial, because it is a central fact of economics that growth requires capital accumulation. Given this economic fact of life, there are several possible responses: give up on growth (the faddish answer of the moment); emphasize political control of capital by the state (the socialist response); emphasize control of capital through private persons (the laissez-faire solution); or leave capital to private control, but with state intervention to prevent abuses (the liberal and social democratic answer).

The discussion of the conservative critique of liberalism concluded with a rebuttal to the contention that humanity must learn to bear the ills it has. This assertion was characterized as a common conservative catechism, which is trivial in one sense and profound in another. It is trivial when it is ritualistically invoked as soon as any attempt is made to expand the welfare state, as if mankind were preordained to go no further than capitalist society. On the other hand, it is profound insofar as it warns of unforeseeable consequences of action. This is an important corrective for liberals, but, this speaker remarked, it would be equally appropriate for conservatives to admit that there are unforeseeable consequences of inaction as well. And even as a corrective this catechism is applied selectively; conservatives invoke it against full employment policies, for example, but not against military intervention.

Socialism, Conservatism, and the "Crisis of Liberalism"

The remainder of the discussion centered on what might loosely be called the "crisis of liberalism." It began with some "primitive political questions." Do we expect liberal democracies to endure in this age? Do we expect nonliberal societies to become more liberal? Or, conversely, do we expect the spread of traditional political style and of authoritarian systems? At issue here were the political rather than the intellectual ramifications of these questions. That is, is liberalism a form of polity on the wane or on the upswing, in America and in the world?

The answers of at least one speaker were uniformly pessimistic. First, he detected a contraction of the liberal world, a constriction of those societies which respect individual liberties and establish strong constraints on state power. Second, he thought it very unlikely that presently authoritarian regimes will become liberal in the near future. Third, he could think of no cases in which social democratic regimes had succeeded in implementing a true socialist program; the ones we usually cite have instituted what are essentially social welfare programs instead. Nor do the prospects for several of the presently liberal societies look very bright, especially but not exclusively Italy.

Others were more sanguine. In one view, when we proclaim that "liberalism is dead" we can mean any of a number of things: that liberal institutions function less well than they did in the past; that liberal institutions have fewer proponents than they used to; that liberal institutions are no longer spreading, and may even be shrinking; or that liberal institutions are defended with less ideological vigor. In any of these senses, liberalism is no more "dead" now than it has been in the past 100 or even 200 years. What we may be expressing, then, is disappointment that liberalism has not brought us a millennium. This disappointment may, in fact, be the inevitable product of an intrinsic tension in liberalism between its emphasis on individual freedom on the one hand, and its millenarian impulses on the other. This point was followed up by the suggestion that liberalism is based on the institutionalization of tensions, especially the tensions between equality and freedom, equality and efficiency, and equality and growth. The problem now is how to balance these tensions in an era which has a passion for equality, and in a country which tends toward extremes. (In the words of Michael Novak, "Americans have a sense of sin, but not of original sin.") The question is whether or not we can continue to institutionalize these tensions in the absence of some shared, common values—values which liberalism itself does not seem able to provide.

Grounds for optimism were detected not only in Western Europe—which has recently been witnessing the collapse not of democracies but of dictatorships—but also in the Third World and in Eastern Europe. Although few observers would characterize the present picture in the Third World as bright, it was pointed out that many of these countries were given democratic constitutions in conditions not really conducive to them, and that these conditions may change as the countries develop. Similarly, although the full panoply of liberal institutions may not be appropriate for much of the Third World, this was not taken to mean that liberal policies are necessarily irrelevant there. As one participant counseled, differences of degree should not be overlooked; we should be ready to applaud and support the injection of liberal elements into these societies, even if full-scale liberal democracy seems impossible. Finally, dissident Soviet intellectuals were again pointed to as evidence for the tremendous erosion of belief in Communist solutions and principles. From this point of view, the power of the liberal idea—which consists basically of protection against arbitrary authority—has clearly taken hold among Russian intellectuals, even those who do not call themselves liberals or who profess to be antiliberal.

One speaker argued that the "crisis of liberalism" is very much a crisis of success. In fact, he remarked, there seems to be a standard pattern: successful policies are always interpreted as failures in the end, in the sense that when changes are needed the entire policy tends to be discredited. For example, the Marshall Plan succeeded in its purpose, yet because the achievement of its goals has had some negative side effects, some dismiss it as a mistake. Similarly, the pollution problem is often viewed as a pernicious side effect of technological change and industrial growth. But people forget that water used to be dirty because there was no way to clean it, that the streets were full of cow dung, and that the automobile was the greatest solution to the pollution problem ever invented. The same pattern applies to liberal policies. In both the United States and in the Third World, the task in the beginning was to create effective institutions; but once created they have tended to outrun their original social purposes. The question now is, will gimmicks solve the crisis of success, or only illiberal solutions?

A different perspective was that the "crisis of success" is essentially a question of how to turn ideals, created in opposition, into basic policy, especially when the original target of opposition has lost its force. For example, once the democratic principle of majority rule is enshrined, the next danger becomes the tyranny of the majority. Moreover, success always creates new conditions and new problems; in other words, the "crisis of success" is by no means unique to liberalism. Liberalism's sense of crisis thus reflects a more general problem of disorientation and loss of belief; it is the legacy of a decade of turmoil and uncertainty. In this respect the future of liberalism (or of social democracy) will ultimately depend on its ability to find new solutions.

Another participant presented what he called a "liberal critique of liberalism," namely that those commonly identified, or who identify themselves, as "liberals" in the United

States have reversed their beliefs over the past fifteen years. In economic policy, the 1960 Kennedy campaign theme of "get the country moving again" was applauded by liberals as a call for economic growth. Now, "liberals" tend to be skeptical of its value and utility. Similarly, the liberal foreign policy program of 1960 was active and interventionist, not for any purpose but to check the spread of Communist power and influence in the world. Now, the prevailing sentiment is for withdrawal from these responsibilities. And in social policy, the sacred liberal principle in 1960 was that individuals were to be judged as individuals, and not as members of broad social categories. But today's "liberal" will usually support quotas, affirmative action, and other programs which reflect a conception of social justice as the distribution of rewards in proportion to the strength of any given minority within the society. In his opinion, this "New Liberalism" does not represent merely an adaptation of liberal values, but their complete reversal, and is the main source of liberalism's current crisis. His hope for renewal was that the work of Soviet dissidents will eventually remind us of the viability and nobility of the older liberalism.

A different view, however, was that the problem is less one of changes in liberal values than of a loss of faith in liberalism as relevant to today's world. In 1960, there was an overlap between liberals and social democrats, not only in policy matters but also in their shared optimism that problems could be solved. And there did seem to be some basis for this optimism: the economy was growing, racism was under attack, new initiatives were being developed to rehabilitate the central cities, and American influence and prestige in the Third World seemed high. But fifteen years later all this had been challenged. Economic growth seems both problematical and of ambiguous value, demands have proliferated, the values of secularism and rationality have been called into question, the problems of cities and race no longer seem easily amenable to social engineering, and the Third World is hostile both to liberal ideas and to us. Taken together, these developments have created a crisis of confidence among both intellectuals and the population-at-large. Further, the dissipation of faith in the older liberal certainties has been coincident with a split in the liberal community; some have held on to the faith, others have flirted with the New Left, and still others have taken positions often described as "neoconservative." In general, liberalism seems to have failed, and liberal values appear to be on the way out.

One member of the conference commented that he had expected a discussion of the historical debate between liberty and authority in social systems. Instead, the discussion has focused on issues of the moment. In his opinion, these issues are important but ultimately not very interesting, nor do they seem particularly relevant to the general problem of liberalism and liberal values. He did not expect liberalism to solve all social problems, or prevent society from being boring, or insure that we will win all our wars. What he does expect from liberalism is that it will preserve the "rules of the game" which protect his rights against the claims of authority. It has done so, he said, and therefore no real "crisis of liberalism" exists. The rebuttal to this line of reasoning was to deny that "processual liberalism" and "social liberalism" could be so easily separated. Traditional liberalism, it was maintained, was based on the belief that individual and social interest are complementary, but we have discovered that there are dynamics inherent in liberal processes which move society away from liberal goals. It has been necessary to compensate for them; in this sense forms of state intervention are compatible with liberalism. But we have gone too far. Intervention has led to the proliferation of monopolistic bureaucracies which significantly constrain the range of liberal freedoms of the people subject to their authority. In addition, some speakers argued that "liberty versus authority" is a false dichotomy; in fact, they explained, authority is a consensual relationship between rulers and ruled and thus a prerequisite for freedom. This conception lay at the root of their belief that without informal, consensual relations of authority vested in a stable establishment, we are left only with power, a condition in which liberty cannot survive.

One speaker expressed skepticism that the "liberal establishment" has been truly committed to liberal values. In his view, its public commitment to liberal guarantees and procedures has been reflected neither in its private actions at home nor in its conduct abroad. It has not been a "liberal" establishment in the traditional sense, but rather a "counterpunching" establishment which could succeed because Keynesianism seemed to work. Now, under conditions of scarcity, issues like "accumulation versus equality" have come to the fore, but without the institutional and procedural vehicles necessary for their clear expression. Moreover, while the Right can offer the free market as an institutional alternative, no alternatives seem to be forthcoming from the Left, including the liberal Left.

The afternoon session concluded with two final remarks. Proceeding from the premise that there is no absolute contradiction between capitalism and socialism, and that new forms of social organization are possible, it was argued that the main issue is not whether society is moving in a collectivist direction (for this seems to be happening everywhere), but whether that society can be democratic. This led to the question, has liberalism failed? The answer was said to depend very much on one's time span: ten years gives one perspective, twenty years quite another. Liberalism has had its successes (the Marshall Plan, the victory over Nazism) as well as its failures (Vietnam); it can claim at least some credit for the former, and was not entirely to blame for the latter. But the situation at present is that the first stage of the welfare state is finished. The second stage, which we are now entering, will be a difficult one, because it has more to do with social control and social rule than with specific social reforms. The transition will involve serious struggle between principled conservatives on the one hand, and liberals and social democrats on the other. This is a struggle that should take place, but it should proceed from the recognition that the achievement of liberalism in this country is a political reality, which provides us with the foundation on which to build further.

Notes

1. See the discussion in William B. Lockart et al., *The American Constitution: Cases and Materials* (St. Paul: West Publishing Co., 1967).

2. "Absent Coleman Focus of Parley," *The New York Times*, 3 July 1975.

3. This and the following quotations are from Arthur M. Schlesinger, Jr., *A Thousand Days* (Boston: Houghton Mifflin Co., 1965), chaps. 12 and 13.

4. See Marguerite Higgins, *Our Vietnam Nightmare* (New York: Harper & Row, 1965).

5. David Halberstam, *The Making of a Quagmire* (New York: Random House, 1964), p. 319.

6. Edward Jay Epstein, *Between Fact and Fiction: The Problem of Journalism* (New York: Vintage, 1975), pp. 92-3.

7. A recent discussion of the issue and its literature is Keith M. Carlson and Roger W. Spencer, "Crowding Out and Its Critics," *Federal Reserve Bank of St. Louis Review* 57, no. 12 (December 1975):2-17.

8. For an excellent statement of the Keynesian viewpoint see *Inflation and Unemployment: A Report on the Economy, June 30, 1975* (Congress of the United States, Congressional Budget Office, Washington, D.C.), pp. 57-8.

9. Barry Bosworth, James S. Duesenberry, Andrew S. Carron, *Capital Needs in the Seventies* (Washington, D.C.: Brookings Institution, 1975).

10. *The Capital Needs and Savings Potential of the U.S. Economy* (New York: The New York Stock Exchange, 1974).

11. See the exchange in *The Wall Street Journal*, 8 September 1975, pp. 14 and 15.

12. For an excellent review, see Assar Lindbeck, *Swedish Economic Policy* (Berkeley: University of California Press, 1974).

4

Does Liberalism
Have a Future?

Charles Frankel

"Liberalism" is a word of relatively recent coinage, but liberalism as a political and ethical tendency and a human predicament is much older. And a question which is just as old is whether liberalism has a future.

It has been a favorite question of liberals themselves. In the first prototypical statements of liberalism in the Western tradition—Plato's *Apology* and *Crito*—Socrates, the paradigmatic liberal, delivers his profession of faith while the executioner waits in the wings. The essay which, for a century and more, has inspired most liberals in the English-speaking world, John Stuart Mill's *On Liberty,* is elegiac in tone. The Western intellectual and political stage has had certain characteristic presences on it: the realist who scoffs at liberalism, the radical scornful of it, the liberal apologetic or wistful about it. Take these presences away, still the interplay among them, and a central theme of Western civilization's dialogue with itself disappears: we enter those periods that are called Dark Ages, when this dialogue was not part of men's consciousness. And in this dialogue liberalism usually plays the role of the petitioner, hat in hand, asking to be accepted as a permanent part of the scene.

Today, for example, liberalism is surrounded by problems to which it doesn't have answers, and the inference is drawn that its days are numbered. But conservatism and radicalism are also surrounded by problems to which they don't have answers, yet the same inference is not drawn about them. Conservatism, we assume, will endure in some form whether or not it successfully solves problems. It is a perennial reaction of human beings. Similarly with radicalism. It is Jesus, after all, who says, "If any man come to me, and hate not his father, and mother, and wife, and children, and brethren, and sisters, yes, and his own life also, he cannot be my disciple."[1] It isn't Marxism that keeps radicalism alive, it is radicalism that keeps Marxism alive and that sends new generations in search of the young Marx, the humanist Marx, the ever-renewable Marx. But liberalism, in contrast, is repeatedly viewed as a hothouse flower, an artificial and temporary expedient, a historically bounded phenomenon without deep roots in human nature or in recurrent features of the human scene.

Why does liberalism occupy this curious place in the Western political imagination? No just estimate is possible of the nature of liberalism, of its historical provenance and functions, or of its prospects, I think, without attention to this question. For the question whether liberalism has a future is not peculiarly *our* question, *our* agony, special to our place and time. It has its special contemporary characteristics. But to conceive it as entirely contemporary is, I believe to diminish the values involved in liberalism's survival or disappearance, and to distort even the distinctively contemporary problems which liberalism faces.

It is, indeed, hard to predetermine the answer to the question whether liberalism has a future. For it is to locate it neatly within an historicist framework in which all things (except historicism itself) have their allotted place and time and span of life, and it is to tell us in advance that liberalism is wrong in its central claim about itself—that it is not to be pigeon-holed, that it has a perennial historical utility, and that, though it may well go down in defeat, it will be missed and its message will not be forgotten. It is not just another odd cult that can be consigned to the dustheap of history.

But then why liberalism's uncertainty about itself? We return to our basic question.

The Ambiguities of the Term Liberalism

In approaching anything to do with liberalism there is always an initial and irritating difficulty: what *is* liberalism? How shall we define it?

Twenty-five years ago, Lionel Trilling offered a definition which catches the way in which the word "liberalism" is often used in contemporary discussion: "a ready if mild suspiciousness of the profit motive, a belief in progress, science, social legislation, planning and international co-operation, perhaps especially where Russia was in question."[2] But Professor Trilling also said in the same book in which this definition appeared that liberalism was America's "sole intellectual tradition,"[3]—a statement which, if true, surely implies that "liberalism" signifies something more than a taste for bootleg socialism and fellow traveling. Indeed, Professor Trilling himself conceived the function of the critic of liberalism to be that of recalling liberalism from its self-banalization to "its first essential imagination of variousness and possibility, which implies the awareness of complexity and difficulty," and he built part of his own remarkable achievement as a literary and cultural critic out of playing these different conceptions of liberalism, narrow and broad, in counterpoint against one another.

Moreover, all these conceptions of liberalism—liberalism as diluted radicalism, liberalism as our "sole intellectual tradition," liberalism as the ironic awareness of variousness and complexity—reflect the concerns of literary and intellectual circles. They must be played against another conception which belongs to the mainstream of political life. We may or may not approve of what Justice Holmes, Hubert Humphrey, Senator Jackson, Reinhold Niebuhr, or Jean Monnet represent, and profound differences on many issues separate one from another, but they are all recognizably "liberals" in ways in which Herbert Marcuse, the brothers Buckley, or Aleksander Solzhenitsyn are not.

What, then, does "liberalism" mean? Liberalism is a phenomenon with several dimensions. I believe that we speak of "liberalism" in at least seven different contexts: (1) a "liberal" civilization; (2) "liberal" cultural and moral attitudes; (3) a "liberal" social structure; (4) "liberal" legal-political institutions; (5) "liberal" economic institutions; (6) a "liberal" philosophic outlook; (7) a "liberal" political style.

Liberal Civilization

Probably the broadest use of the term "liberal" is as the description of an image of civilization transmitted to us from Greek antiquity. It is of a civilization that seeks to subject its customs, laws, and modes of belief to conscious explication and criticism, and that regards the development of a capacity to imagine alternatives and to think hypothetically as a treasured goal of education. Obviously, in speaking of such a civilization, we are speaking not of its everyday practice but of its *ideal.* Nor need this ideal be intended for all members of the civilization. A liberal civilization may have neither democratic political forms nor an egalitarian culture. Nevertheless, it is "liberal" if the belief is dominant that those who live and think in a dualistic perspective in which *what is* is distinguished from *what might be* are living human life at its fullest and best.

Plato's *Republic* is an exploration of the conditions for maintaining a liberal civilization so understood. It explicitly rejects a simple, peaceful, stationary society, in which the problems of health, personal morals, and social justice will all be relatively easy to manage, because such a society would offer only "provender for pigs." In its place it proposes a plan for the government of men who, in Socrates' phrase, are in "an inflamed condition." Efforts to associate Plato's *Republic* with totalitarian thought are fundamentally misconceived for this reason. Similarly, Thomas Hobbes favored absolute government, but he did so because he wished to protect liberal civilization and believed that moralistic zealots would destroy it.[4]

Many who do not call themselves liberals are, of course, liberals in this respect—conservatives in the Burkean or Thomistic traditions, for example, and democratic socialists. The question for them is whether the ideals of liberal civilization can be preserved apart from some of the institutional means—legal, economic, educational, sociological—which liberals have employed. But the question for liberals, of course, is whether the means they have employed are now good for the purpose—or ever were. Disagreements over these matters are disagreements within the family. They are different from those that separate the liberal tradition from positions rooted in primitivist or irrationalist models of human felicity.

Liberal Cultural and Moral Attitudes

Although the Athenians developed a liberal ideal of civilization, they were less notably liberal in another sense of the term. "Liberal" and "liberalism" have also stood for a certain way of holding one's ideas, of attaching oneself to one's own culture, and of looking out toward other people, other ideas, and other cultures. The adjective "tolerant" is only the beginning of a description of this attitude. "Liberal" means an active interest in diversity, a cultivated capacity to insert oneself in another mental landscape, to see things from different points of view, and, as a consequence, to see the pathos and limitations in all points of view.

The special modern sense of "culture"—the sense in which we speak of a "cultivated" man or try to produce "liberally educated" people—captures this meaning. "Culture requires liberalism for its foundation," as Santayana said, "and liberalism requires culture for its crown."[5] Culture, in the language of Arnold, brings "sweetness and light." It takes the rough edges, the fanaticism and parochialism out of different points of view; it illuminates and purifies them by subjecting them to discriminating appraisal. Liberal culture, it has been

thought or hoped, is what can save a competitive and individualistic society from anarchy and a democratic culture
from vulgarity.

About this aspect of liberalism Santayana wrote: "The
rightness of liberalism is exactly proportional to the diversity
of human nature, to its vague hold on its ideals. Where this
vagueness and play of variation stop, and they stop not
far below the surface, the sphere of public organization
should begin. It is in the subsoil of uniformity, of tradition,
of dire necessity that human welfare is rooted, together
with wisdom and unaffected art, and the flowers of culture
that do not draw their sap from that soil are only paper
flowers."[6] Liberalism, the paper flower. Still, if we listen
to its critics, it has done extraordinary harm for a paper
flower: it has taught a bottomless relativism, it has been
permissive to the point of being suicidal. Indeed, much
of the criticism of liberalism—and of liberal capitalism—by
radicals and conservatives alike has not been fundamentally
political or economic, but cultural and moral. It has been
that liberalism is anomic, and that it offers no sense of a
civic design that would bring discipline and meaning to
individuals' lives.

Liberal Social Structure

In their origins liberal culture and the liberal ideal of civilization have an aristocratic flavor and a leisure-class bias, and in
abstract principle, they are compatible with highly stratified
and stable societies. In practice, however, such societies
have not usually stimulated liberal attitudes or ideals. An
aristocratic class with a capacity to conceive alternatives
to what exists, and with an active interest in diversity and
novelty, must be a class that has retained its vitality of
imagination. On the whole, however, aristocracies tend
to become stiff with stupidity or, when they remain intelligent, stiff with fear.

Normally, therefore, liberal culture and the aspirations
of liberal civilization have flourished best in societies with
complex and unharmonious combinations of traits. They

retain powerful traditions of aristocratic or patrician liberty, but they are urban, commercial, and usually maritime societies full of people on the make.[7] Social mobility, combined with a sense of increasing wealth, tends to produce in such societies a bullish feeling that almost everybody, over time, is going to do better. In this way the pressures from below for equality and justice, it is believed, can be accommodated without destroying the society's basic structure of liberties.

It is this kind of society that the word "liberal" is often used to describe. Its atmosphere tends to be secular. Its most pronounced interests are personal advancement and the general increase of material wealth. Its preferred means of social selection is free competition in which, in principle, victory goes to the ablest: *les carrières ouvertes aux talents.* And its conception of justice is primarily procedural: what counts is that no individual or group be in a position to stack the deck in its own favor. Liberal societies, accordingly, have a tendency to bear to the left. The effort to keep power distributed in such a way as to make the competition fair usually entails the extending of power to people hitherto excluded. I do not mean that sheer good will produces this effect; it is the maneuverings within liberal society. In nineteenth-century Britain, for example, the landed and industrial interests vied with each other in extending the franchise to the urban and rural proletariats.

Another important characteristic of a liberal social structure, implicit in what has already been said, is its deliberate creation of adversary institutions and roles. For a continuing process of social self-correction to take place, there has to be a guarantee of existence for institutions and people possessing liberties out of the reach of the party in power. A liberal social structure is therefore distinctively marked by the presence within it of *autonomous professions*— lawyers, judges, scholars, journalists—that are presumed to belong to no party but to bear a public responsibility for keeping everyone protected and informed.

This, I hardly need say, is one of the particularly

vulnerable points in the structure of liberal society. The professions possess special liberties, and they are capable of using these liberties as privileges for their own self-aggrandisement. Moreover, the very conception of a profession which serves its political purpose by remaining unpoliticized is hard to put into practice, and hard even for many people to comprehend. It is under concerted attack today, not least in universities, whose central function, in a liberal society, is precisely to propagate a conception of professional vocation. Max Weber's observation, aimed at the churches and their attitude towards industrial capitalism, is equally pertinent to this situation: "It happens nowadays in the civilized countries—a peculiar and, in more than one respect, a serious fact—that the representatives of the highest interests of culture turn their eyes back, and . . . refuse to cooperate in rearing the structure of the future."[8]

It is in the nature of a liberal social structure, however, that it invites attack from all sides. Liberal society is indicted for being materialistic, rationalistic, demystifying. It is condemned for elevating competition to the highest rank among the social virtues. At the same time it is derided for its faith in human reasonableness and tolerance. It displeases aristocrats, who find it mean-spirited; it affronts intellectuals, who cannot find in it the symmetry and unifying rational purpose they find in works of art or philosophy.

Besides, since liberal society institutionalizes self-criticism, the gaps between its theory and its practice cannot be hidden. In theory it offers a free market, in practice a market crisscrossed by monopolies and power plays; in theory it is meritocratic, in practice the people who are at the top, in disturbing numbers, are the beneficiaries of inherited advantages. Its abstract theory is a misleading abridgement of complex facts. Liberal society is composed not only, not mainly, of free individuals entering into free contracts but of families, classes, and transmitting privileges. Not least, the state seems to have a equivocal function, in both theory and practice, in relation to the structure of society. On one side, the critics of liberalism point out, liberal theory holds that the state is different from society. Property relations, family, churches, voluntary associations, etc., all have their own independent existence and their right to such existence. The state's primary function is to respect and preserve their autonomy. But liberal society, with its mobility, its rationalism, its competitive pressures and economic thrust, and with its philosophy of individualism, progressively weakens these other forms of human association. Liberal society then turns to law to shore up what it has weakened, and thus converts these independent associations into creatures dependent on the state. At one end, the minimal state; at the other end, the administrative state, regulating, adjusting, manipulating, creating: the one seems to lead inexorably to the other.

Liberal Legal-Political Institutions

It might be said that liberalism assumes that even in Utopia people won't know that they're in Utopia and will go on struggling with one another. The primary working conception of justice in liberal society, therefore, is procedural: the rules of society, whatever their content, must be laid down in accordance with higher-order rules that define how any authoritative decisions are to be made. And central among these higher-order rules are those defining the conditions under which political authority is to be peacefully transmitted from one group to another. Liberalism, politically speaking, is constitutionalism mediated by elections.

Is there no ethical content to constitutionalism? Is it merely an insistence on rules of the game without regard to results? What, to be specific, is the role of the concept of protected individual rights, which is the most distinctive part of modern liberalism's contribution to the theory and practice of constitutional government? In part, the answer is that the justification for these rights, too, is procedural. They are integral to the scheme of "ordered liberty." A free contest for power and authority cannot take place unless individuals possess guarantees of freedom of speech and press, freedom of association, fair trial and due process. But their justification, of course, cannot be purely procedural. Loyalty to a political game whether one wins or loses in it can only be justified if the game is believed, win or lose, to yield ethically more desirable results than any realistic alternative to it. Indeed, in its day-to-day operations liberal constitutionalism is incomplete except by the use of words like "fair," "equitable," "reasonable," etc., which have moral content and which are indispensable in applying the law and the Constitution to specific cases.

A recurrent tension is present, therefore, in liberal political-legal institutions which is less marked or is absent in polities whose rationale lies in their alleged purposes or substantive accomplishments rather than primarily in their procedures. It is a tension between law and morals, method and results, the duties of law-abiding citizenship and the duties of conscience. Liberal political institutions would not be liberal, I think, if this tension were not present. But it explains why, since the time of Socrates' painful reflections on his duties to the law in *Crito,* the view has been held that there is something inherently artificial and self-destructive in liberalism.

Liberal Economic Institutions

In all the respects in which I have so far discussed liberalism, it antedates the rise of the Manchester School. Indeed, earlier liberal thinkers like Adam Smith, when they advocated a free market, were urging that government actively step into the existing market and rid it of its combinations, monopolies, and privileged positions. They held an affirmative not negative view of the state's role. Laissez-faire is characteristic of liberalism for only a short period of its history.[9] The more constant pattern—I take Smith, Mill, T. H. Green, Woodrow Wilson, and Louis Brandeis as examples—has been to favor policies designed to correct imbalances of economic power. As in politics, the liberal economic game is checks and balances: it is in this primary sense that liberal policies seek "equality." The evil at which liberal reforms have persistently been aimed is caught in Franklin Roosevelt's phrase—"economic royalists."

There is therefore, if I am right, a line of approach to economic matters which differentiates liberalism from both conservatism and radicalism in their present forms. To conservatives, liberals repeatedly overestimate what can be done to correct a social evil by government intervention. Often they produce just the opposite result from that which they intend, as in pushing up the minimum wage and thereby creating a class of chronically unemployed. The liberal mistakenly thinks of government as a problem in social engineering when it is really a problem of ministering to a way of life whose strength lies in its own mysterious and informal methods of self-adjustment. He moves too fast, trusts too much in the quality of his knowledge, places too much faith in good intentions. Society does not move in accordance with anybody's simplistic notions of good and evil.

The radical, in contrast, finds that liberalism does too little, not too much. Injustice is too grave, resources too limited, to make reformism tolerable. Indeed, he takes it that the fundamental assumption of liberalism—that power must be dispersed in society—is, in economic affairs, a recipe for disaster. A modern society's problems require the concerted use of resources to achieve collective purposes, and this is incompatible with liberal institutions, which place vetoes in the hands of every powerful group that would be endangered by such planning.

The "Liberal" Philosophic Outlook

Liberalism as an ideal of civilization holds that discrimination must be made between better and worse. And the openness of a liberal culture to the new and different, its thirst for diversity and singularity in experience, presupposes the existence of a capacity to judge, to sift, to weigh evidence, and, in the end, to resist the meretricious. The logical condition for liberal pluralism is a belief in the supremacy of *critical method.* Otherwise, liberalism has no bounds and therefore no definition even of itself.

Liberalism in culture and morals has traditionally been filled out, therefore, with four principles—in classic eighteenth-century language, "reason," "nature," "progress," and "humanity." This is obviously not the place to discuss how "reason" should be defined. Highly technical matters are involved on which liberal philosophers have disagreed. But until the nineteenth century and the advent of romanticism, liberal philosophers came together in a practical conviction that mankind had at its disposal independent intellectual instruments for testing the credibility of ideas and the legitimacy of social institutions. Nor has this tradition been entirely broken. Whatever their disagreements, nineteenth- and twentieth-century thinkers like Mill, Bertrand Russell, Max Weber, John Dewey, Morris Cohen, all placed fundamental stress on the indispensability to liberal culture and morality of methodical intellectual discipline.

Connected with this belief there has been the conviction—again I speak untechnically—that "nature" has its objective characteristics which it behooves man to understand, and that the methods of reason characteristic of the sciences (for Socrates, geometry; for modern liberals, physics, biology, games theory) have offered progressively better instruments for achieving such understanding. What separates liberalism from conservatism above and beyond everything else, and what protects it, in its own self-image, from radicalism's effort to dismiss it as just another ideology, is its conviction that science is genuinely a method for the progressive improvement of the human understanding. It is this belief that was crucial to the emergence of modern philosophical liberalism in the seventeenth century. It is what separated figures like Spinoza and Locke[10] from sixteenth-century men of merely humanist culture like Erasmus and Montaigne.

So we come to the idea of intellectual progress, and to the liberal belief that such progress, morally and factually, is the most important factor in history. Man seeks the truth;

he sometimes attains it; he should not ever be prevented from engaging in this quest; the sciences increase his chances for success in it; and the consequences of intellectual progress, whether for good or ill, are radical and irreversible. To be sure, intellectual progress may well create problems at a faster rate than it solves them. Even so, intellectual progress is progress, and the liberal ideal of civilization requires us to accept and applaud it.

But what of the oft-repeated point that scientific knowledge obviously isn't wisdom, and that progress in knowledge doesn't imply moral progress? Let us, once again, leap over some of the interesting philosophical technicalities. What eighteenth-century liberals thought, and what most nineteenth- and twentieth-century liberals committed to the centrality of critical method have continued to think, is that progress in knowledge encourages moral progress in a variety of ways: it softens fanaticisms, eliminates superstitions; it encourages less authoritarian methods of child rearing and education; it gives people more powers to defend themselves against deception and exploitation; it broadens people's horizons, so that they are able to comprehend the position of others better and show more humanity towards them. Eighteenth- and nineteenth-century liberalism came together with a very profound moral revolution, evangelical in its origins, to create what we now know as humanitarianism.

Now of course, as is frequently pointed out, in this, the twentieth century, the most "scientific" and "progressive" of centuries, we have had, in the most "enlightened" parts of the world, a holocaust, atomic warfare, corrective labor camps, and the cruelty and indifference of a "dehumanized" world. Yet this does not, I think, defeat liberalism's basic point. Nazism and communism are not triumphs of critical method: they rest on a deliberate assault upon it. And most of the evidence indicates that in the specific senses in which eighteenth- and nineteenth-century liberals were thinking of moral progress, such progress is associated with the progress of knowledge and the growth of education. On the whole, the rearing of children, the workings of the courts and of administrative bodies, the treatment of foreigners, lunatics, criminals, dissenters, women, homosexuals, the poor, have all become gentler, less gratuitously cruel, less cruel, indeed, for the pleasure in the cruelty itself. And the higher people's educational levels, the truer this seems to be. Similarly with other morally progressive developments that are clearly the products of scientific techniques: actuarial tables, social insurance, improvements in nutrition and epidemiology, etc. Easily to dismiss the liberal belief in progress misses most of the point of what liberals have actually believed.

But at this point we must deal with the marriage between liberal philosophy and other points of view often confused with it, particularly the evangelistic humanitarianism to which I have just alluded. No more than other social outlooks, probably less, can liberalism be guarded for its ideological purity. Other movements of thought and sentiment have moved across and through it. The resultant blend has been an odd and precarious one: on one side, the scientifically oriented skeptical liberals, the enemies of what the eighteenth century called "enthusiasm"—Spinoza, Voltaire, Franklin, Diderot, Mill, Holmes; on the other side, the enthusiasts, the revivalists and the romantic idealists—Jonathan Edwards, Emerson, Thoreau, Whitman.

To be a Protestant through and through, certainly to be a Puritan Protestant, is to be—the double meaning is intended—"a disbeliever of the original faith." The purpose of the Protest, of the stripping away of the inessential and external accoutrements of the faith, is to recover the original faith in its first excitement. What is sought is spiritual freshening, a rediscovery of spontaneity, a direct feeling of God's fire, not just an abstract belief in His existence. Accordingly, there have been repeated eruptions in the history of Puritanism, like the eighteenth-century "Great Awakening" led by Jonathan Edwards, in which the hypocrisy of established institutions is denounced and the effort is made to turn passive religious conformity into active religious enlistment. This attitude, secularized and turned into political protest and cultural criticism, is expressed in Emerson's phrase: "The one thing in the world, of value, is the active soul."[11] Emerson was a lapsed minister who had found the established religions, even Unitarianism, too constricting, too purely formal. Dissent itself was the probable sign of individual authenticity, of recovered truth, of divine inspiration. That idea is continuous from John Milton in the seventeenth century to William James, whose treatment of religion is essentially in terms of individual inspiration. It is reflected in some of what John Dewey attempted to do to combat passivity and promote individuality in the schools. Particularly in America, but in Great Britain as well, liberalism as a social movement has been fed by recurrent streams of believers and disbelievers, essentially religious in their provenance, trying to find rebirth for themselves and rebirth—a recovery of the original Idea, a new sincerity, integrity, simplicity—for their societies.[12] What they had sought is, I think, a reenactment in secular society of the experience of resurrection.

Romantic idealism inherits this purpose, takes the more obvious elements of theology out of it, and reads it into the design of history. Each soul is a moment of God's vision. To see into one's soul, to be true to one's own truth, never to be reduced to what external society imposes but always to seek one's uniqueness—this is to add to the world's perpetual discovery of its ever-evolving, ever-unlimited truth. And this is progress—not progress within nature's unchanging structure, or progress mediated by classic reason, but progress that turns nature and reason into human fictions ever new and therefore ever true.

This romantic philosophy is in essence a barely transformed religious radicalism. Its emphasis is on the liberated, the converted, the enlightened, on the freshness of their perceptions and the goodness of their impulses. It is not on the disciplines of method, laws, and social institutions. When eighteenth-century liberals spoke of "contract" it was the business contract that was their model. When Puritan radicals spoke of "contract" it was a covenant of true believers that they had in mind. This is the stream of thought that nineteenth-century American romantic idealism recaptured; it is our native American radicalism, although the habit is to call it "liberalism." It is millennial in its horizons and aspirations, moralistic, distrustful of institutions; it casts the great choices of politics in the classic Puritan terms—principle versus compromise, commitment versus orthodoxy, the nation restored versus the nation corrupt. It lives in uneasy alliance with secular, skeptical liberalism, and with the methods of political democracy that have been the practical setting of this liberalism.

The Liberal Political Style

The blurring of the meaning of liberalism, particularly in recent decades, has obscured what is surely the most obvious and constant characteristic of liberalism over the centuries: I mean its penchant for moderation, its active desire to stand in between conservatives and radicals and to bridge the gap. Liberalism's genius is for mixed constitutions and the relativizing of absolutes. Its repeated function in history has been that of healing and compromise.

Plato proposed a radical reconstruction of Athens based on the application of a single set of consistent principles. Aristotle, no doubt a duller man, pointed out that human needs and circumstances vary and that it is better to create a constitution designed to prevent any principle from being pushed too far. Thomas Aquinas accepted and restated the medieval theory of natural law. Yes, of course, natural law was binding on all—"as far as general first principles are concerned." But "as to more particular cases . . . it remains the same for all only in the majority of cases . . . [and] can admit of exceptions."[13] His philosophy was a heresy for a while, but it brought vitality back to the faith by loosening it up a bit. And the tradition leads from Aquinas through Richard Hooker to John Locke, the father figure of modern liberalism —pious Christian and defender of empirical method, apostle of individual rights and spokesman for corporate and communal rights, defender of a revolution and opponent of revolutions. He is the critic of the radical Puritans who made the first great modern revolution designed to make humankind over: "People are not so easily got out of their old forms, as some are apt to suggest."[14] But he also deals the deathblow to the conservative hope that political authority can ever again be based on patriarchal prerogatives. And as a final example, consider John Stuart Mill's criticism of Bentham's and his father's Philosophic Radicalism—their overdependence on a few narrow first principles, their simple-mindedness about human motivations, their excessive concern for order and plan and efficiency and their relative indifference to liberty. Like Locke's liberalism, Mill's was an effort to heal wounds, to remove sharp dichotomies, to make room for exceptions and for alternate perspectives.

I do not mean to suggest that it is good that liberal philosophies have frequently been glaringly inconsistent philosophies. Still less do I wish to imply that there are no principles in liberalism that a liberal should be reluctant to compromise. One loses one's claim to be a liberal, to my mind, if one is ready to say, for example, that theoretical investigations ought to be stopped because they are socially disturbing. But liberalism is notable for its flexibility and nuances, not the sharpness or economy of its first principles. Plato, Augustine, Hobbes, Pascal, Burke, Dostoyevsky, Sartre, are infinitely easier to lose one's mind over than Aristotle, Aquinas, Locke, or Mill. Liberalism, says its detractors, is for the middling people, the mediocre, the men who, in the contemptuous phrase of that paradigmatic radical, John Knox, are "neither hot nor cold." Well, if one seriously believes that the purpose of history is to provide a stage for heroes, then the detractors are right. Liberalism recognizes that heroes there will be willy-nilly—often even when there's no need for them, and prudent men might do better. But it believes that politics has failed when heroism becomes necessary.

Liberal Strengths, Liberal Weaknesses

Well, what are the prospects and the utility of this complex of beliefs, attitudes, institutions, and tendencies of mind and feeling that we may call "liberalism"? Much of the answer is contained in what I have already said. If I am right, liberalism, for better or for worse, cannot be reduced to a peculiar point of view maintained by a privileged class for a hundred years or so in the North Atlantic corner of the planet. It is not expressive only of special interests and perspectives doomed to die. Like any social outlook, it prospers in some environments and does badly in others. But the interests it expresses, the beliefs it puts forward, the style it represents, all transcend narrow considerations of history, geography, or class. They speak to recurrent experiences and aspirations of some civilized men everywhere.

What then, of the problems that confront liberalism today? They are obviously serious, and they may be fatal, but my own hunch is that they are not. The problems most often mentioned are in any case not the most serious ones. The international environment is distinctly uncongenial to liberal institutions and values but the principal official hostility to liberalism is expressed by governments with very grave problems of their own. Economic pressures like boycotts and international blackmail or terrorism can make life difficult for liberal societies, but not so difficult as to bring them down or require them to become illiberal. The future turns more on the will and self-confidence of liberal societies themselves than on what their troubled adversaries can do against them.

And liberalism, it should not be forgotten, carries its own powerful appeal and rationale. Despite the clichés of cultural relativism, I know of no society whose people in large numbers believe that the bringing up of children is the proper business of the state, or that truth is whatever a political party says it is, or that arbitrary force, imposed in accordance with no known rules, is an acceptable mode of normal governmental behavior. To those who live in societies where liberalism is only a memory or a hope, it doesn't seem like an unrealistic philosophy, or one whose appeal is limited to the idle and the rich.

Similarly, I am not persuaded that the economic problems of the current era, unprecedented though they are, present challenges that will be the death of liberalism. In the case of the United States, it is sometimes said, for example, that the requirements of economic planning in an era of scarcening resources and of disagreements about national priorities will require the further movement of power to the hidden recesses of the executive branch and the intensification of bureaucratic controls cut loose from a democratic framework. But a variety of safeguards against such an eventuality are available. One example is the creation of a national planning board charged with the mission of presenting to the executive, the Congress, and the public alternate plans, based on different conceptions of social priorities and estimates of economic capacity. Such alternate plans could give a structure to public debate, and make it easier for the political decisions related to the development of the economy to be clarified and debated.

To the question whether the limited, incrementalist liberal approach to economic planning is adequate to meet the environmental and resource problems that are foreseeable, the only fair answer, it seems to me, is that no one knows. But we have even less reason to think that totally centralized investment decisions coupled with detailed bureaucratic regulation and what would have to be generous use of the police power is calculated to accomplish anything except to create new troubles sufficient to take people's minds off their older ones.

As for whether a free market, left to itself, could solve all these problems, it seems to me that, in theory, the issue may be debatable, but in practice the market isn't going to be left to itself. The political costs of government inaction in periods of adjustment and readjustment are too severe. And this is true whether the majority of the electorate is conservative or liberal in outlook. To repeat, it may be that liberal institutions will break down under the pressure of economic misfortune. But if they do it will not be because the institutions that replace them will be more competent in dealing with such problems. It will be because they appear to offer solace and surcease from the psychic and institutional strains turned loose by liberalism, and to provide a cure for its political and moral illness.

The Fundamental Contemporary Problems of Liberalism

These, it seems to me—the political and moral problems of liberalism, and an intellectual problem that underlies them— are the gravest problems it faces. I would list them under four headings, and in ascending order of importance: (1) the problem of "social discipline"; (2) the problem of inflationary expectations; (3) the problem of liberalism when it becomes a primary culture; (4) the resurgence of irrationalism.

1. Tocqueville described the process by which "the public thing" tends to become obscured in commercial and egalitarian societies. In such societies, he wrote, "the desire to get rich at any price, the taste for business, the love of gain, the search for well-being and material pleasures are the most common passions. . . . They soon enervate and degrade the entire nation if nothing intervenes to stop them." And what is it, according to Tocqueville, that can stop them? "Only liberty . . . brings passions that are higher and stronger, or furnishes ambition with larger objects than the acquisition of riches, or creates the light that permits the vices and virtues of men to be seen and judged."[15]

A major problem for liberal democratic societies is whether the great collectivities—the corporations, the trade unions, the bureaucracies, the professions, the political parties—are capable of being controlled without recourse either to severely repressive measures or to a policy of constant concessions. Now that Britain has moved very close to the brink, there has begun to emerge a somewhat greater spirit of liberal compromise in the trade unions. Not dissimilar signs can be seen in recent events in New York. But they are still faint signs. All that is plain is what has always been plain about liberalism: that it makes its bet on competition, but assumes also a basic reservoir of good will and shared purpose. The bureaucratization of conflict in contemporary liberal society, not to mention the adoption of confrontationist postures as a kind of proof of liberal authenticity, raise severe dangers for liberalism. Are they manageable? Yes, but not through any magic solution. In the main, it is a problem of will.

2. Closely connected to the problem of social discipline, and aggravating it, is the problem of ascending demands for social benefits and government services. It is easy to be misunderstood when one makes a statement of this kind. In my judgment, government is now doing too little, not too much, to meet some of our very greatest needs, and one of these needs is to redistribute economic power away from the economic royalists of the military-industrial sector. But such a policy is not compatible with the mounting of indefinite numbers of programs that put the government under systemic overload, and allow the nation to fritter its resources away.

In part, the dynamisms of democratic political competition contribute to this cycle of ever more inflated expectations. In part, the cause lies in a kind of broken-backed liberal faith in progress: the benefits we have are good, more will be better, and anyway there aren't any problems that can't be solved. Whatever the causes, the result is to produce liberal institutions so pressed from every side that they are often unable to acomplish even otherwise realistic objectives; and this has aggravated the feelings of resentment, injustice, and inadequacy which are already directed towards these institutions.

3. Both the problems we have just discussed seem to me to involve another: it is the curious position of liberalism in our contemporary culture. Liberalism, I would suggest, has been, through most of its history, a secondary cultural phenomenon. It has been a critique of a received culture, a loosening of its tight reins, a statement to that culture which can be characterized as "yes, but . . ."

Locke, in asserting that government rested on the consent of the governed, did not imagine that he was shifting the relations of women to men or of children to parents. Mill, in arguing that inherited laws and moralities should be brought to the empirical test of utility, did not suppose that he was advocating that people calculate consequences each time they make a moral decision. He took it for granted that they would—and should—be guided by inherited rules for just dealings, and that they would employ the test of utility simply where these rules yielded paradoxical or plainly undesirable results. And Socrates pleaded that he had attempted to promote piety, took pride that he had served his city as a soldier, and refused a chance to escape from prison because he respected his city's laws. "Liberalism" means "liberation"; but for liberals of the past, a minority in cultures governed by illiberal orthodoxies, this "liberation" meant simply release from overwhelming conformities. It did not mean no conformities, and certainly it did not mean a systematic program for overturning inherited mores.

But what happens when, in the dominant intellectual institutions of a society—the universities, the schools, the media of communication, the churches, large parts of the medical and legal professions—liberalism becomes the dominant orthodoxy? One cannot fairly twit liberals for having succeeded. But one can ask them whether it is sensible for them still to regard themselves as a brave minority. And one can ask whether they ought not to perform the critical function with regard to liberalism turned orthodoxy which they have characteristically performed with regard to other orthodoxies.

To take an example, when liberals inhabited repressive cultures that placed severe limits on individual thought and behavior, and when they were faced with people in authority who simply laid down the law and brooked no questions, it was imperative that they point out the limitations in rules and the holes in authority. But in a different culture, a liberal culture, a distinction has to be emphasized between making exceptions to norms and trying to do without norms altogether. Failing that distinction, liberalism collapses into antinomianism. It becomes a parody of itself—a masquerade of liberty unsupported by the classic notions that placed limits on liberal ideas.

4. But this brings us to what I need only mention, for it is thoroughly familiar to all of us. It is the rise of irrationalism, systematic, unapologetic, and welcomed increasingly both in

popular and in high cultural circles. This is the deepest threat to the survival and prosperity of liberal institutions, and it makes the particular business of those of us who take part in discussions such as this—analysts, critics, teachers, political theorists, philosophers—a crucial and decisive business for the future. If irrationalism continues to receive the increasing endorsement of intellectuals and the educated, the fundamental continuities required for the preservation of liberal institutions will be severed.

But let me turn back to the question with which I began. Why does the world so regularly treat liberalism as a point of view apart from all others? Why liberalism's own uncertainty about itself? It is because liberty is heady and disturbing doctrine. It is because reason and moderation are indeed precarious human traits. It is because liberalism is profoundly secular. It rejects the hope for salvation, for a final justice, for an order that will surely reveal the triumph of the ideal. It visits on the classes and the masses alike the fearful burden of individual judgment. And its tendency has been, as both the radical Rousseau and the conservative Burke said, to thwart men's quest for community. In this last respect in particular, I do not think it can be said that liberalism has nothing to learn from other points of view. But "community," as liberals cannot help but remember, has also been an excuse for human oppression. To strike the balance between "com- munity" and the mobile individual is liberalism's great task. Will liberalism survive in the face of all the doubts about it? I think it has not a bad chance, and I believe that the hopes of most of us, including conservatives and democratic socialists, depend on its surviving. What, to put the question crudely, does liberalism really have going for it? It has that very large part of humanity behind it that distrusts zealotry, that is rational enough always to try to hedge its bets if it can, that knows that the people in charge of society have to be watched, but that prefers homely pleasures and joys to the ecstasies of revolution and sudden death.

"Workers of the world unite!" said Marx and Engels. "You have nothing to lose but your chains." Well, they had much else to lose, including their lives, and they didn't lose their chains. Liberalism speaks for some of the highest and rarest human aspirations. For those of us loyal to the liberal ideal of civilization, the liberties it has defended are indispensable. But liberalism's appeal, we should see, is equally to *l'homme moyen sensuel* and to his native skepticism. There are really a great many such people around the globe, and they have shown a remarkable power to resist the pressures on them. This is why I expect liberalism to persist. It speaks for the common sense of the race.

Discussion

The discussion of the future of liberalism revolved around two broad sets of questions: first, what are the major problems with which liberalism will be confronted in the foreseeable future?; and second, what are the implications of these problems for liberal values, liberal institutions, and liberal programs?

Liberalism, Capitalism and the "Limits of Growth"

Consideration of the first question centered on the relationship between liberalism, capitalism, and economic growth, with particular emphasis on the validity and significance of the "limits of growth" scenario. The context for the debate was established at the outset. Liberal societies, in the view of one participant, can accurately be described as "societies of permitted tension," in the sense that instability and changeability are not only allowed, but often encouraged. The paramount and ongoing problem for such societies is defining the limits—that is, setting the conditions under which these tensions can be permitted without jeopardizing the system as a whole. Most important in this respect has been the economic milieu, characterized first by capitalism, and second and more importantly, by a *growing* capitalism and the spread of affluence. Both characteristics have engendered tensions, but up to now they have also established conditions under which tensions could be managed. However, it is doubtful that this can continue to be true for very long. For one thing, we are now entering an epoch of capitalism in which the main danger will no longer be unemployment, but inflation. This prospect is tremendously unnerving to most people, and thus represents a serious threat to the maintenance of liberal capitalism as we have known it. Secondly, it does not seem likely that growth can be maintained for much longer, or that capitalism can be maintained without it. The core problem lies with the force of exponential processes. Although many predictions have been crude in their specifics, they are powerful in their general point that growth will eventually come to a halt because we will run out of resources. Moreover, the increasing leverage of the Third World cannot help but intensify the competition for the resources which still exist.

If this analysis is correct, the speaker asked, then how do you change? His own prognosis was that in industrial societies at least, there is likely to be a drift toward economic planning and control. And while the implications of this drift, and of increasing scarcity, are difficult to foresee, it also seems difficult to be confident that there will not be strong pressures for social control under these conditions. Meanwhile, the tendency in the Third World is increasingly to embrace the authoritarian solutions of "military socialism." In sum, it seems unlikely that liberal societies—societies of "permitted tension"—will flourish in the next twenty-five to fifty years.

These remarks provoked a lively debate. For instance, one member of the conference agreed that growth will be the central issue, but rejected any apocalyptic predictions. In his opinion, the Club of Rome scenario is not merely extravagant, but wrong. It represents the appearance in a new form of the old, tired critique of liberalism, industrialism, and modernity, with the difference that the Marxist element (the internal contradictions of capitalism make it nonviable) has been dropped. In its new version, the critique seems to

combine a conservative distaste for the modern industrial
world with neo-Marxist analyses and solutions. In spite of its
putative scientific basis, it is false, and should be vigorously
combatted. In response it was noted that there are two
aspects to the growth controversy. One is a moral and psychological aspect, expressed in the fear of some people that
we will become sickened by our own affluence. This may be
true, but more interesting is the empirical aspect: where are
we along the exponential curve? Granted, we really don't
know the answer to that question, but we do know that the
curve exists, and that at some point growth stops. The question is, when? This is not only a problem of technological
resourcefulness, but also of competition for resources, especially if the underdeveloped world seeks to accelerate its
rate of growth.

Another speaker also took issue with the "limits to
growth" scenario. He reported that a recently completed
Hudson Institute study of this issue had arrived at very optimistic conclusions for the future supply of resources. These
conclusions hold even on the assumption that no major technological changes take place; if instead you assume ten years
of technological progress, then the prognosis is extremely fa-
vorable indeed. Moreover, he asserted, the prediction of an
intense worldwide competition for resources is both self-
fulfilling and intellectually fallacious. It is self-fulfilling
because if you convince those with resources that they have
a vital interest in not selling them, and convince the industrial
world that it has a vital interest in getting them, then you
produce unnecessary wars. It is intellectually fallacious because simple extrapolations of resource use are spurious, and
because it forgets that the resource curve is rising exponen-
tially as well.

An intermediate position was that there is no persuasive
evidence that growth must stop, but none that any kind of
growth will be possible either. In other words, the "limits
to growth" are qualitative rather than quantitative; we must
learn to grow selectively. From this perspective the question
is not whether liberalism will survive, but whether it can

survive under conditions of selective growth. Will selective growth mean somewhat slower growth? To what extent will selective growth increase conflicts of interest, and thus make liberal decision making more difficult? The mechanism of decision making must be adapted to these questions. One implication would seem to be that selective growth will require planning, not of the Soviet type but certainly involving greater loads on government. Another implication is that there can be no purely national solutions; international mechanisms will be necessary, at least among the advanced industrial countries. But one participant thought this to be an arbitrary conclusion, an expression of preference rather than something dictated by reality. The answer to this comment was that reality dictates that we will reach the limits of specific resources in the relatively near future. These limits may eventually change, but in the meantime we have to take heed of the problem.

Several of the participants questioned, not so much the pessimistic prognosis for growth, as the inferences drawn for the future of capitalism and liberalism. One argued that economic growth is neither an anodyne nor a *sine qua non* of capitalism. It is true, he said, that capitalism has always grown, but erroneous to assume that it *must* grow, for there is no reason to believe that satisfactory profits cannot be generated under conditions of equilibrium. Others addressed themselves to the relationship between growth and distribution. It was suggested, for example, that we follow Mill's notion that the two are (or can be) separate, and that we apply this kind of incremental social intelligence to the growth issue. We can plan no growth, if that is our choice, in the same way the French plan growth. Another speaker argued that slower growth rates in themselves would not necessarily undermine liberalism. The authoritarian danger is rooted not in rationing of resources but in the fact that, in societies with severe inequalities of income, slower growth means much greater social tension. Thus the distribution issue is crucial. But unmanageable tensions can be avoided through a massive and systematic effort to reduce inequalities, by both "leveling up" and restructuring the system of work.

Another speaker raised a related issue: planning versus the price mechanism as alternative ways of allocating scarce resources. He remarked that it is very easy to stop growth if we want to—all we need do is decide to adopt policies which make capital accumulation impossible. This is what worried him about the future of democracy and liberalism, because such policies seem to be of great attractiveness to many liberals. But the only way that the Club of Rome scenario will occur, he said, is if we do not let the price mechanism do its job; if we let it work, it will serve to ration resources. But a participant replied that, if the price mechanism makes the allocation, then the poor are likely to be the major victims, both domestically and internationally. And another maintained that where supply is relatively unresponsive to price (where the supply elasticity is low), reliance on the price mechanism will result in substantial dislocations, strong inflationary pressures, and major redistributive effects. These are problems which we do not know how to manage very well, especially if they accelerate, but they suggest a need for forms of economic management that may be incompatible with at least some liberal norms. Moreover, he pointed out, we know that the ability to respond to the price mechanism is not equally distributed. Clearly, for instance, the United States has the technology to solve its food problems through the price mechanism, but India does not. This does not necessarily mean that we must abandon liberalism and move to a system of total control, but it does mean that some kind of planning will be required, and that we must fashion new structures to preserve liberalism both at home and abroad.

Participants at the conference identified two other problems with which liberalism will have to deal: nationalism, and the use of force in international relations. As one speaker put it, nationalism has become increasingly virulent, may be made more so by economic pressures, and has often been a profoundly illiberal force. The reason is that the impulse

toward unity and cohesion, implicit in so much of nationalism, is relatively easily translated into a totalitarian force.
In this sense, he remarked, totalitarianism is at least in
part a reaction against liberal tension. Another speaker
wished to qualify this argument, which he said has historically been true only of a specific form of totalitarianism,
namely fascism. What is new, however, is that the tensions
of democratic societies have generated a sense of danger
from totalitarianism of the left.

There was also a comment on the incapacity of liberal
thought to deal with the use of force in the world, and
expressions of concern about the dangerous volatility of
American attitudes which results from this incapacity.
Two aspects of the problem were singled out for attention.
First is the global military equilibrium, both facets of which
(strategic relations and the competition in conventional
arms) are becoming increasingly unstable. Second, and
perhaps even more ominous, is nuclear proliferation. The
strong possibility that nuclear weapons will become
accessible not only to other nations but also to terrorist
groups could, it was feared, lead to a tremendous expansion
of police powers—a situation which would in itself pose
a serious challenge to liberalism.

The discussion concluded with the advice that sensible
analysis of the implications of the growth controversy for
the fate of liberalism requires that we make a distinction
between liberalism and capitalism. The two are clearly
entangled, but separate; so when we speak of the "relevance"
of our models, much will depend on whether we refer to
its economic elements or to its social/political elements.
As for the growth issue itself, it should be clear that nobody
really knows the truth. But there is at least plausible evidence
for the view that freewheeling growth is an unlikely prospect.
If this is so, and if intervention is coming, then the next
question is whether or not such changes will be fatal to
liberalism. Here again, we must distinguish among the social,
political, and economic aspects of liberalism; and we can
expect the answer to vary from country to country.

The Future of Liberalism: Models, Programs, and Alternatives

The discussion of the future of liberalism opened with a survey of the principal political issues facing liberals in the Congress. These remarks were prefaced with the observation that the widespread skepticism and cynicism about government presents liberals with a special difficulty on policy issues: how to restore the belief that government can function, when the diversity and magnitude of the problems make uncertainty about government inevitable.

The speaker reported that congressional liberals do share a common perspective on a wide range of issues, though by no means all of them. All Democratic candidates are committed to full employment. Growth has *not* been an issue in this discussion, but most would accept some slackening of growth to attain it. There seems to be little faith in monetary policy as a tool to check inflation or regulate the economy in general, and a cautious attitude toward new federal interventions in social policy. With respect to foreign policy, liberals seem to agree that the United States must deter Soviet aggression, fulfill its responsibilities in Europe, and insure the security of Japan, but beyond this there is little common ground. For instance, there are differences among congressional liberals on the question of human rights abroad and the related issue of U.S. support for repressive regimes, because these questions turn on perceptions of the nature of threats in the world. In general, however, most liberals would opt for greater distance from such regimes. Most conspicuously, there is little clear consensus on American policy toward the Soviet Union, and fairly pronounced differences on the general policy of detente. However, it is clear that the "state of siege" mentality is not shared by most liberals in Congress, as witness their attitude toward the Angola question.

On human rights issues at home, the speaker continued, congressional liberals have always accepted the need to take remedial action against discrimination; hence, they do not tend to see affirmative action as different in principle from past programs. However, one participant objected to this line of reasoning, arguing that there is a great deal of difference between remedial action and quotas. The distinction, he said, is between merit as a criterion and other criteria; the latter perpetuate racial distinctions rather than eliminating them. In response, it was pointed out that a form of discrimination had been implicit in previous liberal programs as well, as embodied in the notion that the victims of discrimination should be given preferential treatment.

But above and beyond the policy issues, the central problem to this speaker was how to discipline democratic society so as to insure its survival. This problem reflects a failure of political leadership, certainly including congressional leadership. For instance, liberals have rejected monetary policy, but so far have been unwilling to commit themselves to the vigorous exercise of fiscal power. In his mind, the most troubling challenge to liberalism lies here: can democratic societies be disciplined enough to do the things that are unpopular, but necessary?

Another discussant expressed the hope that the congressional learning process will not lead to purely reactive policies, especially where foreign policy commitments and the use of monetary policy are concerned. Others agreed, but with respect to foreign policy would emphasize the importance of the international system and the need to bring greater rationality into the way we conduct our affairs, while in economic matters they hoped to see a much greater reliance on fiscal policy. They were not certain that Congress will have the will to use it, but they were convinced that the human costs of excessive reliance on monetary policy have been extraordinarily high.

The discussion of issues before the Congress was followed by a spirited defense of liberalism's continued relevance and vitality. This spokesman noted at the outset that every social outlook has its bastardized version, so it is both unfair and misleading to compare Burkean conservatism, for instance, with cheapened versions of liberalism. Most critics of liberalism do not make clear what kind of liberalism they are talking about. For example, when they say "liberalism is dead," do they mean to predict or advocate the death of parliamentary institutions? Similarly, when they say "liberalism is parochial," do they mean to predict or advocate the death of critical modes of thought? The underlying problem, he said, is that liberalism is often compared with some unexamined alternatives. We need more substance to these alternatives, for while we don't know that incremental liberalism will succeed, we don't know if the others will either. Furthermore, the method of comparing liberalism with unexamined alternatives is really the "politics of despair"; it reflects a nervousness with tension and ambiguity, and a disappointment in the fact that liberalism is not a religion which can provide faith and certainty to its adherents.

He continued by noting that the various aspects of liberalism have certain historical and logical connections. Historically, liberalism has usually been the product of compromises between old and new classes, and has been reinvigorated when it has assimilated new groups into established cultures and institutions. Logically, the liberal emphases—parliamentary institutions, civil liberties, checks and balances, etc.—all come together in the attempt to create conditions in which a certain style of life and thought can flourish. In fact, the emphasis on autonomous institutions for the sake of preserving self-critical methods is the logical core of liberalism. Moreover, liberal methods constitute liberalism's great advantage in dealing with the future: it can account for the major force for change, namely science.

He concluded with two questions, one to radicals and one to conservatives (and Burke). Where, he asked, does liberty fit into the radical scheme of things, or are we simply to trust the good intentions of those in power? And do conservatives really believe that it makes sense, in today's world, to talk about a settled class system and settled authorities?

Other speakers expressed more pessimistic views. One took an historical perspective, pointing out that in 1905 he might well have been optimistic about liberal prospects in countries where liberalism has since died, such as Spain and Eastern Europe. True, Germany, Italy, and Japan have been saved for liberalism in this century, but they have been saved by external forces rather than their own internal dynamics. And another maintained that one cannot evaluate the impact of liberal values simply by reading constitutions or even by looking at institutional structures. What counts, he said, is not the institutions in themselves but the nature of the decision-making processes within them. And here there is a problem of overloads and paralysis; in this sense many liberal institutions have been deteriorating. He emphasized that he was not predicting the death of liberal democracy, but thought it wise policy to listen to the pessimists.

Another participant briefly raised the issue of "irrationalism," a phenomenon to which liberalism has contributed greatly by its profound secularism. As an example, he cited the radicalism of the 1960s, which in his view did not reflect an intellectual preference for irrationality but rather was the outgrowth of a society in which certitudes have systematically been chipped away. His main point, however, was that liberalism is hard to kill because it is so protean. Nevertheless, he felt that the liberalism which puts blind faith in government intervention and the expansion of governmental powers is clearly dead. Similarly, spending as a solution is also under a cloud; the experience of New York has been both traumatic and instructive in this regard.

Nor was there unanimous confidence in the ability of liberalism indefinitely to manage tensions and weather crises. Uneasiness on this score was expressed in three questions: what has been the impact of past crises on the resilience of liberalism, to what extent does liberalism's strength lie in its ability to grow out of tension, and is this crisis different? One member of the conference answered with the remark that liberalism has been in crisis since World War I, that its crises have had a cumulative impact, but that these facts themselves encourage him to believe that liberalism is resilient. On the other hand, he would not assume that it is immortal, and he did agree this crisis is especially severe. This led him back to the growth issue. He agreed with the argument that liberal institutions are nourished by growth; in fact, growth may well be indispensable to their success. He also expressed agreement that the issue is not "growth or no growth" but the direction and objectives of growth, largely because the combination of great affluence and major inequalities that characterizes the advanced industrial societies is demoralizing and delegitimating for liberal institutions. Therefore the objectives of growth will have to be planned, not because the market mechanism is necessarily nonviable economically, but because it is not viable politically. Modern populations simply are not quiescent; they will demand that something at least seem to be done.

Here, too, there was fear that this optimism might be misplaced, because the relevant question is not likely to be "who will solve the problems?" but rather "who will have the power to solve them?" If so, then liberalism will be at a decided disadvantage, because unlike other "isms" it tends to lose power when it cannot produce viable solutions. Nor did this speaker find much comfort in the belief that liberalism will endure because it speaks to the aspirations of civilized men everywhere. To him, the idea that the future of liberalism will consist of expressing, through courageous individuals, certain trancendental values which we all share, is a depressing prospect. He thus thought it crucial to return to the question, can liberalism endure and prosper unless it develops programs of action that are not only concrete and procedurally valid, but compeling as well? The growth issue is a case in point. Nobody really knows the answer to the growth problem, so therefore the key question is not what the facts are, but what the beliefs about the facts are. In other words, power will go to those who can convince *others* about their beliefs, not necessarily to those whose beliefs are most accurate and most useful.

One discussant detected two themes underlying much of

the day's discussion: first, that economic growth in the United States necessarily means greater inequality elsewhere; and second, that liberalism needs a program. The implication would seem to be that the United States has no model to offer the rest of the world, but perhaps we are being a bit too hasty in dismissing it. To give one simple example, liberal society has evidently found a way to extract a great deal of food out of fertile ground—something which most other societies, including the USSR, cannot do. In other words, American liberalism can provide a model for the rest of the world, and a benign model at that. This, combined with a determination to exercise American power responsibly, could constitute a perfectly good liberal program. Another speaker agreed that liberalism had been a responsive and compelling answer to many of the dilemmas of the industrial age in the advanced countries, but was less confident that it constitutes a program for the rest of the world. He did not think that our capacity to increase food production was the same thing as a relevant program, because the dilemmas for these countries are psychological and cultural as well as material. We need a far more differentiated matrix for looking at the Third World; preaching liberty and democracy is not a sufficient answer. Moreover, he concluded, there is a close relationship between the fate of liberalism at home, and our sense of the rest of the world. Liberalism in the United States is based on the twin notions of optimism and universalism, so if the rest of the world seems to defy these notions, then it is bound to have an effect on our own society. Others agreed that we have grounds for concern, but did not believe that the issue is so global as to mean that unless liberalism is on the move everywhere it will collapse. In response it was explained that it is not a matter of one or two countries; rather, it is a question of whether we can survive as a liberal state when we feel like an island of liberalism in a hostile world.

The discussion ended with some final remarks by Mr. Frankel. He expressed agreement with the contention that we are suffering from systemic overload, adding that we will surely *ad hoc* ourselves to death if we continue to pretend that every problem can be solved by specific programs. But, he said, our moral-intellectual crisis has two components. First and foremost is the problem of social discipline: will interest groups be prepared to check themselves? Related to this is the problem of inflationary expectations, promoted both by growth and by bastardized liberalism. But the real issue, he suggested, is whether liberalism can face up to a crisis of self-criticism. As the historical exception to prevailing orthodoxies, liberalism has always presupposed certain stabilities. But when liberalism becomes an orthodoxy, it must learn to raise questions about itself. For if liberal societies collapse, it will not be because of what happens in Thailand or Zaire, but because of a failure of our own will and confidence. In this sense, the crisis of liberalism is very much an intellectual problem, and intellectuals will be crucial in solving it. But it is also very much a problem for political actors. As a rationalist ideology, liberalism is under particular pressure because it is *supposed* to solve problems. In this sense, the future of liberalism depends on political art.

Notes

1. Luke 14:26.
2. Lionel Trilling, *The Liberal Imagination* (New York: Viking Press, 1950), p. 94.
3. Ibid., p. ix.
4. Hobbes' description of what is lost when mankind is thrown back into its "natural condition" is a catalog of the goods of liberal civilization: "In such condition, there is not place for Industry; . . . no Navigation, nor use of the commodities that may be imported by Sea; no commodious Building; no Instruments of moving and removing such things as require much force; no Knowledge of the face of the Earth; no account of time; no Arts; no Letters; no Society. . . ." Hobbes, *Leviathan,* ed. C. B. Macpherson (Baltimore, Md.: Penguin Books, 1968), p. 186.

5. George Santayana, *Soliloquies in England and Later Soliloquies* (New York: Charles Scribner's Sons, 1922), p. 176.

6. Ibid., pp. 177-178.

7. Compare Kenneth Minogue's statement: "Taking a hint from Wittfogel's study of oriental despotism, we may observe that the free societies which we are considering originated out of a combination of feudal and commercial circumstances. . . . Freedom in each case arose out of a compromise of a peculiar kind between an established feudal class and a vigorous commercial one." Minogue, *The Liberal Mind* (London: Metheun and Co., 1963), p. 175.

8. Max Weber, "Capitalism and Rural Society in Germany," in *From Max Weber*, ed. Hans H. Gerth and C. Wright Mills (New York: Oxford University Press, 1946), p. 372.

9. Needless to say, this historical observation says nothing about the intrinsic merits of the view that *laissez-faire* is the keystone of the liberties.

10. This belief in progress has to be put very carefully, which is usually not done by critics of it. Locke, for example, was surely modest in his beliefs about what human reason could accomplish. His most ambitious book was a warning against the intellectual *hubris* of rationalistic philosophers. "I suppose it may be of use to prevail with the busy mind of man to be more cautious in meddling with things exceeding its comprehension, to stop when it is at the utmost extent of its tether, and to sit down in a great ignorance of those things which, upon examination, are found to be beyond the reach of our capacities. . . ." [Locke, *Essay Concerning Human Understanding* (London: J. M. Dent and Sons, 1947), Book 1, chapter 1, p. 2.] But within its proper limits, and guided by an understanding of the proper rules for conducting its inquiries, the mind of man was quite capable of accomplishing useful purposes out of its own resources. "We shall not have much reason to complain of the narrowness of our minds, if we will but employ them about what may be of use to us; for of that they are very capable. . . . The Candle that is set up in us shines bright enough for all our purposes." [Ibid., p. 3]

11. Ralph Waldo Emerson, "The American Scholar," in *English Traits, Representative Men and Other Essays* (London: J. M. Dent and Sons, 1908) p. 297.

12. There are, I believe, parallel movements in other societies—e.g. Jansenism and Jacobinism in France.

13. Saint Thomas Aquinas, *Summa Theologica*, Part 2 (First Part), Qu. 94, Art. 4, conclusion, in *Aquinas: Selected Political Writings*,

ed. A. P. D'Entrèves, trans. J. G. Dawson (Oxford: Basil Blackwell, 1948), p. 125.

14.   John Locke, "The Second Treatise of Government," in *Two Treatises of Government,* revised edition (New York: New American Library, 1965), p. 462.

15.   Tocqueville, *L'Ancien Régime et La Révolution* (Paris: Calmann-Levy, 1928), pp. xi-xii. (My translation.)

5

The Antinomies
of Liberalism

Edward Shils

It is very difficult to assess the merits of liberalism because
it is so ambiguous in its major concepts and so vague in its
boundaries. It is difficult to say what liberals believe not
only because all beliefs are difficult to study, but also because it is so difficult to define and locate "the liberals."
Roman Catholicism was relatively easy to define because
there was an orthodox doctrine, institutionally promulgated
and available in papal declarations. It was possible for a
long time to define and assess Communist policies and
beliefs because they too were promulgated by an authoritative, officially constituted group which claimed the right
to define the orthodoxy.

Liberalism in the United States has been a quite different
matter, since it did not express itself through any one
institution. It is true that since the Wilsonian "new liberalism," one major current of liberalism has been loosely
connected with the Democratic party. There has been
another current of liberalism in the United States which
has in some points of its belief been inclined toward the

Republican party. Nonetheless, it has been one of the features of American liberalism of the past fifty years that it has been free of strict organizational loyalties.

There is in addition a very deep cleavage within liberalism which also makes it difficult to define any single liberal doctrine and to locate its proponents. Liberalism has evolved from being critical of the authority of the state and recommending private and voluntary action into a set of beliefs which remains critical of authority in nearly all forms but which at the same time supports an extremely comprehensive and penetrating extension of governmental action. The adherents of these more recently emerged beliefs have become the chief bearers of the name of liberalism but they too are very heterogeneous in their composition and they share many beliefs with the liberalism from which they have departed.

The task of locating the object of our reflections would be easier if there were a comprehensive and well-defined conservative position in the United States acknowledged by its adversaries to be more than a justification of the prerogatives of the very wealthy. The liberals who are critical of the extension of governmental action are not conservatives, although in this rejection of the prevailing type of liberalism they have become mixed up with the tiny numbers of intellectual conservatives. Conservatism in the United States--patriotic appreciation of one's own country, respect for familial obligations, an expectation of religious piety and observance, a high regard for the virtues of manliness and womanliness, an attachment to locality, a belief that the burden of proof lies on those who seek innovation, and a corresponding respect for traditional ways of thinking and acting, the acceptance of a hierarchy of deference and authority, and a certain inclination toward pessimism regarding the abatement of man's earthly troubles by large-scale rational contrivances--has hardly any defenders among intellectuals and not many more among politicians. This type of conservatism in any inarticulate form is probably relatively common in what used to be called the working and lower-middle classes but it does not have many spokesmen among those who address larger audiences. There also used to be a type of conservatism which put forth "Darwinian" arguments in defense of private business enterprise; this scarcely exists anymore.

This being so, the prevalent collectivistic type of liberalism shades off into a neighboring liberalism which sometimes and wrongly calls itself "conservatism"—and which is in fact a root and branch sort of liberalism. The result is that it has been difficult to see what the various strands of liberalism have in common, and to recognize that there are respectable viewpoints in social and political outlooks that are not liberal. The situation is different on the perimeter of liberalism. The collectivistic liberalism now prevailing in the United States has socialistic revolutionary radicalism as another neighbor. There is substantive affinity between collectivistic liberalism and the socialistic and revolutionary radicalism but it is not as great as the sympathy of sentiment which inclines the former towards the latter.

The two types of liberalism have common traditions but their common traditions do not exhaustively describe either of them. They share a common individualism, but their traditions of individualism branch off from each other; one emphasizes more the rationally acting individual and the other more the affectively sensitive and expressive individual; but even this latter type of individualism also allows a considerable place for rational decision. Both set their faces against traditional religious beliefs and institutions although autonomist[1] liberalism does so less than the other; both set themselves against hierarchies of wealth, power, and deference which are inherited and transmitted within families. Both attribute high importance to formal education for the emancipation of the mind from superstition and for the cultivation of rational or the release of affective powers; both also regard formal education as a means of self-improvement and necessary for economic and social progress. Both, since the latter part of the eighteenth century and at least until very recently, appreciated the value of scientific knowledge as a liberation of the mind from illusions and a replacement of the illusions, including traditional religious beliefs, by a truthful understanding of the world; they also both regarded science as closely allied to technology whereby greater material well-being could be attained.

Both types of liberalism are against tradition and inclined toward rationalism. Autonomist liberalism is less antagonistic toward traditional beliefs—although it is certainly not very sympathetic to them. Collectivistic liberalism has not only been less sympathetic to traditional beliefs and institutions; it has also been even more rationalistic and scientific. It is confident that the prospective accomplishments of an aggregation of rational and scientific intelligence has scarcely any limits. It is convinced that a government which draws on the resources of scientific knowledge could improve its performance and thus make itself more useful in the promotion of the common welfare. Both affirm the possibility of improving social institutions through rational action; they have both tended to believe in the desirability of gradual and piecemeal improvement rather than in a total and drastic resolution of all problems. Both affirm the desirability and possibility of improving the material standard of living and the working conditions of the mass of the population. Both are concerned about the public good, the good of the entire society. In consequence of their distrustful attitude towards the authority of tradition and of government, both have argued for the toleration of diverse beliefs. Both are rather indifferent and secularist in their attitude toward religion; they require the separation of church and state and the toleration of all religions. Both believed in the rightness of equality before the law and of equality of opportunity. Both believed in the rightness of individual autonomy and collective self-government. Both were pluralistic, believing in the organization of interests and in the legitimacy of the cultivation of diverse ends and values. Both accepted the ineluctibility of conflict in society, and proposed and effected institutional means for their restraint and compromise; neither believed in a natural harmony of interests. Autonomist liberalism became democratic through the extension of the franchise into universal suffrage; with collectivistic liberalism it shared an attachment to representative institutions, to the freedom of expression of political opinion and of political association and the separation of powers. Both acknowledged that restraints on the power of majorities to suppress minorities of religious and political belief and of eccentric private conduct were desirable. These are some beliefs postulated by both "autonomistic" and "collectivistic" liberalism. In the course of the latter part of the nineteenth and through the twentieth century, collectivistic liberalism emerged through a fusion with the authoritarian and philanthropic traditions which were alien to earlier liberalism, and by the consequent shift in the interpretation of the traditions which they had in common.

Liberalism has been a unique phenomenon in the history of mankind. It has drawn on much older traditions which arose in classical antiquity but, as a more or less coherent view about man and society and as a functioning pattern of the organization of society, it is a novel feature of the modern age. In one or another of its forms and in varying degrees it has dominated the thought and policy of Western societies and has almost obliterated conservatism as a realistic alternative. In its latter-day evolution in the form of collectivistic liberalism it is in danger of obliterating itself through an unseen modification of its postulates. In recent years there has been a gradual and unannounced slipping over of collectivistic liberalism toward radicalism. This has been made easier in the United States by the absence of significant large socialist and revolutionary radical organizations with clearly marked organizational and doctrinal boundaries. Unlike the radicalism of fifty or seventy-five years ago, this newer radicalism has become pervasive in the educated classes and in the governing and influential groups which are now dominated by the educated classes.

2

Autonomistic and collectivistic liberalism still have much in common, but the differences have now become rather considerable and the tension between them acute. The set of beliefs which now constitutes the dominant collectivistic liberalism in the United States is itself a heterogeneous complex which has become something quite different from what it was and even inimical to those original ideas. Its main present constituents are: first, a demand for far-reaching freedom of expression of opinion, particularly of opinion critical of authority and of established institutional arrangements; second, a demand for control over executive authority by "the people" and by a popularly elected representative legislature and, increasingly, by the judiciary operating with wide discretionary power—that is to say, "participatory" democracy has now become highly prized; third, a concern for the individual's freedom of affective expression from control by authority, private and public; fourth, a desire for a vigorous, comprehensive and far-reaching exercise of authority by the executive branch of government—above all, the central government—for the advancement of the "common welfare"; fifth, a belief in the urgency of realizing these various ends and in the wickedness of those who disagree with this from other than a radical standpoint.

The first constituents derive from a different tradition than the fourth and fifth; in earlier times and in different contexts, these traditions had been generally regarded as antagonistic to each other. Indeed, they are in many ways antithetical to each other. The desire for the freedom of the individual to express himself as the spirit moves him, implies a repugnance towards authority which goes so far as to place in doubt and even to deny the legitimacy of authority, private and public. The affirmation of the desirability of central governmental action on a large scale does not square well with hostility toward authority. The desire to control and restrain authority is not consistent with the demand that governmental authority be extended in order to protect and provide. The desire for substantive benefits through the action of government requires for its realization the enhanced power of the state to assemble and reallocate resources, to regulate and control their distribution and to enforce numerous laws which govern the use of resources; it has entailed also numerous laws and huge staffs for the regulation of productive actions and for the verification of conformity with these regulations. It has implied the exercise of governmental authority to impose patterns of associations which had previously been left to private choice. This has entailed an increase in the size and specialization of the bureaucracy and an attendant increase in the powers exercised by it on a scale beyond the powers of the legislature to control. The implicit reluctance to acknowledge the legitimacy of authority is not congenial to this vast expansion of the powers of government.

In the course of these latter developments, the principle of voluntary private action and organization for self-provision, which was associated with the freedom of action of individuals, has fallen by the wayside. This is so not just because the power of government has itself been so expansive—that is certainly one factor—but also because the demand to annul some of the consequences or to correct some of the insufficiencies of private action has become so clamant, and because federal government has seemed to be the only body capable of providing this annulment and correction. The demand has risen for goods and services not obtainable through the mechanisms of the market and obtainable in the past only through voluntary association and private initiative or, on a small scale, through the state. Welfare services and payments which were once intended for the needy classes have now been extended to the classes once regarded as capable of "paying their way" and under obligation to do so. The powers of the family have been increasingly limited on behalf of the freedom of the individual member and the power of the government. Testamentary freedom and succession, the power of parents over children and the responsibility of parents for children have all been restricted for various reasons which all involve the greater activity of the government.

Private associations abound but they function less to provide gratifications, services, and goods for their members than to urge and threaten the government into their provision. Private business enterprises still exist on a scale not equaled anywhere in the world but these enterprises also have come to demand and to depend on governmental subsidies, guarantees, contracts, and regulations; their legitimacy is not taken for granted or even acknowledged by some tendencies in collectivistic liberalism. In the justification of the "mixed economy," the governmental element enjoys a higher evaluation than the private one. The privately practiced professions exist but, once almost wholly self-regulatory, they too are now increasingly subject to the surveillance and regulation of the government, and this too is widely accepted by collectivistic liberalism. This combination of heightened and multiplied demands, the falling away of voluntarily and privately undertaken provision, and increased reliance on government's providence have engendered a great concentration of power in the state. The bureaucracy has become an organ enjoying a degree of initiative and autonomous action not previously anticipated by any one except persons of Cassandric disposition. Relatively little attention is paid by collectivistic liberals to the control of the bureaucracy. In the United States, there was recently an outburst of collectivistic liberal demand for control over the executive branch by the legislative. The control which was sought, however, was not over the executive as a whole, but over the staff of the president which had come into existence largely because of the difficulty of controlling the civil service. The intellectual and political prosperity of governmentalistic liberalism has left in the shadows the liberalism which distrusted governmental action.

3

Liberalism in the United States has always had greater sympathy for socialism than it had in Europe. Perhaps the absence of large social-democratic parties in the United States meant that persons who would otherwise have supported the socialistic cause found a home in liberal circles. They joined with the humanitarian social reformers, with the improvers of governmental machinery, and with "civil libertarians" to form a coalition such as has not quite existed elsewhere.

The United States did not have a tradition of "statism," the tradition of a strong state, of an intrusively arbitrary central authority such as the countries of continental Europe inherited from the *ancien régime.* Nearly everyone in the United States at one time was opposed in varying measure to

the authority and majesty of the state. When the justifications for slavery ceased and when socialism was the ideal only
of lower-class immigrants, nearly everyone was a liberal although the name itself was not invoked. Those who would
have liked to respect the authority of the state were deterred
by its corruption and vulgarity, and thus became critics of
the existing system of politics and government. By virtue of
this they were regarded sympathetically by philanthropic
reformers and those who did not want the power of the state
to expand. The effort to improve the probity and efficiency
of government proceeded from a distrust of government as it
was; those who disliked the existing personnel and machinery
of government came to be considered by some to be liberals
because they were critical of what existed. The desire to
make government more efficient and less costly was indeed
one tradition of liberalism when it was coupled with the intention to restrict the radius of governmental inquisitiveness
and intrusiveness. Although support for the increased efficiency of government did not necessarily make its proponents into liberals, these reformers were moulded into a
loose coalition with liberals who opposed the government on
other, more fundamental grounds; they were all critics of
existing practices and institutions, they were all reformers in
one way or another, and hence they counted as "liberals."

There were also those "philanthropic" reformers who
wanted government to do more for the welfare of the mass of
the poor, the immigrants, the weak and unprotected. These
persons were not liberals in the same sense as those who were
critical of the expanded action of the state; they were not opposed to state action but they were in favor of the improvement of the moral and effective quality of governments.
They were also usually friendly towards civil liberties because
it was the critics of existing social conditions whose civil
liberties were being restricted. Among these critics fell moderate socialists and trade unionists with a large "social" perspective. The latter were certainly not liberals in the traditional sense, but since they were in favor of the civil liberties, they too came into the loose fold of the liberal coalition.

This coalition had been in process of formation since late

in the nineteenth century but it became animated in the
1920s. Under the stress of the great depression in the 1930s
it became consolidated. The philanthropic, reformatory element was brought into prominence by the visible distress of
the unemployed. The civil libertarian element had already
grown large in the 1920s in response to the "Palmer raids,"
the publicity of the Lusk Committee of the New York State
legislature, and the Sacco and Vanzetti case, all coming after
the suppression of *The Masses* and the trial of its editors
during the First World War. The chief protégés of the civil
libertarians tended to be radicals of socialistic inclinations.
The protectors acquired the tincture of the protected.

The Russian revolutions of 1905 and 1917 were significant
factors in this collectivistic turn of American liberalism. The
sympathies of many educated Americans had been drawn to
Russian opposition to the tsarist regime ever since Tolstoy,
Turgenev, and Chekhov had aroused their appreciation. The
revolution of 1905 seemed to be an outcropping of this
movement and the two revolutions of 1917 even more so.
Not many American liberals were critical of the Bolshevik
phase of the revolution. Only "reactionaries," fearful of
Bolshevist determination to abolish capitalism, argued that
it would destroy political liberty as well as private property,
family life, and Christianity. Their arguments were so crudely
put that they deepened the suspicions of Americans towards
the autonomist liberalism which supported private business
enterprise; in fact, these arguments had the contrary effect
of reinforcing the appreciation of the Bolshevik revolution as
the fulfillment of the aspirations of a philanthropic liberalism
concerned for intellectual and artistic freedom of expression.
The gap between the two main types of liberalism was
widened and autonomist liberalism became narrow in its
explicit concerns. It became preoccupied with the protection
of the autonomy of the economic order.

On the other side of the gap, the Soviet Union in its reality
and its transfigured and derivative versions became a touch-
stone for American collectivist liberalism. That is why a
repressive regime which called itself socialist usually had the

support of American collectivistic liberals. It is also the reason for the persistence and pervasiveness of the simpleminded distinction between "Left" and "Right" and the disposition to think that the "Left" is always right and the "Right" is always wrong.

The movement towards collectivistic liberalism in the United States was influenced, too, by quite similar developments in Great Britain in the course of which Benthamism—which aimed at the greatest happiness of the greatest number—turned from individual freedom to the use of an efficient government as a means of increasing the general happiness. If the proper and chief end of man was happiness, then the means by which happiness was attained was only of instrumental and hence of secondary significance. From this standpoint, freedom of initiative and action in the political, economic, and cultural spheres became less important, once it was thought that the end of happiness could be effectively attained by the action of the government. Fabian socialism did not pretend to be liberal—it acknowledged that it was utilitarian. Nonetheless, it was widely esteemed by American collectivist liberals in the 1920s; the writings of the Webbs and R. H. Tawney's *The Acquisitive Society* were among the favorite books of liberal intellectuals of the 1920s. The more preponderant the socialistic philanthropic element in liberalism became, the more its bearers turned against individual initiative and enterprise, and towards the expanded action of a more efficient government. Nonetheless they did not swerve in their devotion to civil liberties, particularly those of radicals and literary men whose works were under ban for moral improprieties.

In the time of the administration of Franklin Roosevelt the liberal outlook moved toward an unqualified affirmation of far-reaching regulatory and initiatory actions by the central government. There was a growing confidence in the capacity of the central government to accomplish not only most of what had previously been accomplished by private and voluntary action, but to accomplish much more than private and voluntary action had ever attempted. In their eagerness to bring about increased material well-being, which had been one of the concerns of the older types of liberalism, liberals turned away from the precepts of that type of liberalism which asserted that government should do only those things that could not be done by private and voluntary action, as well as from the wide-ranging distrust of authority which had been common to all types of liberalism.

This modification of belief became more pronounced when the mechanism of the market and the ethic of individual initiative, self-help, saving, and ambition were shown to be of no avail for many persons. The depression of the 1930s brought collectivist liberalism nearer to its full flowering. Keynesian economics, which was disparaged by many socialistic and radical critics of the capitalist system as a means of saving capitalism, strengthened the foundation of collectivistic liberalism which was very critical of capitalism but not ready to replace it by socialism. Keynesianism raised the standing of government; it showed the dependence of the market on governmental action.

The Second World War increased the confidence in the capacity of government to accomplish things on a scale not conceived in earlier times. The successes of the American government in production, in organizing supplies, and in moving soldiers over a worldwide front of military operations, and in its organization of scientific and technological research for the development of the atomic bomb and radar, raised the credit of government to new heights. There was no turning back from this point. The collectivist liberals saw their faith in government tested and vindicated; they became confident of government and did not fear it. It seemed entirely possible to combine an omnicompetent government with public liberties without endangering the latter.[2]

The "discovery of poverty" at the end of the 1950s led further along the same path. The source of this was both humanitarian compassion and the resurgence of the temporarily suppressed animosity of the literary wing of the collectivistic liberal intellectuals against American society. The compassion but not the animosity had been latent in liberalism; the latter had been nourished by a long-existent tradition of bohemian literary culture admixed with a general sympathy for socialism. This had little to do with liberalism in its earlier form, but as liberalism moved towards collectivistic liberalism, its adherents found a congenial companionship there. In the United States for most of the 1950s, the combination of fear of McCarthyism, the discredit of the Soviet Union, the prosperity of American society, and the full employment of intellectuals had led to a pronounced recession of radicalism. The release of radicals from the burden of admiration of the Soviet Union occurred as a result of the events of 1956 in Poland and Hungary. The Anglo-French military action in Suez aroused the slumbering radicalism of French and British intellectuals. These events induced the birth of the "New Left." The tradition of radicalism was thus resuscitated. In the United States the first result of this rebirth of radicalism was the "rediscovery of poverty." Shortly after the rediscovery of "the poor" came a new awareness of the unhappy plight of the Negro part of American society.

In the United States, liberals were usually opposed to discrimination before the law and to the allocation of opportunities on the basis of religion and race. They were sympathetic with immigrants when these were inequitably treated; they disliked the maltreatment of Negroes. Nonetheless, except for the few who were involved in the National Association for the Advancement of Colored People and the National Urban League, white liberals, including the collectivist liberals, were not greatly exercised about the discriminatory activities against Negroes. Until the 1950s they disapproved of the disfranchisement of Negroes in the southern United States but did not become very concerned about gaining the franchise for them; they opposed restrictive covenants in northern cities but this was a minor and not a nationally prominent issue.

The situation changed in the course of the 1960s, and this change had important consequences for the subsequent evolution of the beliefs of American liberals during this period. In a way the white liberal experience of "the black experience" became as important as the liberals' interpretation of the Bolshevik revolution.

The movement of blacks for civil rights was, of course, a movement to realize the liberal ideals of equality of opportunity, of equality before the law, of the operation of the market mechanism without regard to ethnic qualities and the right of the citizen to affect the exercise of authority through representative institutions. It was liberal to demand equality before the law, it was liberal to demand equality of opportunity to take one's chances in the market, it was liberal to demand the right to vote and to hold office, to demand the freedom to political opinion, assembly, association, and petition. The civil rights movement was a movement to realize the traditional ideals of liberalism. The civil rights movement sought to establish the Negro as a citizen by virtue of his existence within the civil community. The idea of citizenship is one of the major ideas of liberalism; its extension to the entire adult population is one of the areas where the liberalism of privacy and autonomy and collectivistic liberalism are identical and it is crucial to both.

Liberalism, even collectivistic liberalism, lost credit on the intellectual plane when the riots of blacks in black districts engaged public attention. Black intellectuals and black political agitators denounced the insufficiency and the "failure" of liberalism. They counseled violence or at least praised it with overtones of recommendation; in this they were eagerly joined by white intellectuals who ordinarily passed as "liberals" but who now took to fancying themselves as "revolutionaries." The demand was no longer for freedom and rights within a preponderantly white society but for withdrawal from that society. Nothing could have been less like liberalism, which postulated the value of civility. The demand for secession was associated with the equally illiberal praise of violence and the explicit denunciation of many of the institutional arrangements that were basic to liberalism.

Collectivistic liberalism lurched further toward radicalism in its next phase. This was the war in Indochina. For various reasons and causes which cannot be entered into here, authority in the United States in the second half of the 1960s experienced an unprecedented buffeting. The vulnerability of authority disclosed by the assassination of President Kennedy and his brother and Martin Luther King, the incapacity to prevent the riots in the Negro districts of the large cities, the inability to bring the war in Indochina to a successful conclusion, the feebleness of university and college administrators and teachers in the face of the student agitation—all these showed authority to be inept and indecisive and even cowardly. In fact authority was collectivistic liberal in most cases, and it was dominated and paralyzed by its own convictions. The result was a desertion of liberalism, a going over to radicalism which was in point of fact only collectivistic liberalism writ large. The major transformation from liberty to libertinism and perversity, from civility to emancipation, from the welfare state to the omnicompetent and ubiquitous state, from equality of opportunity to equality of rewards, from "careers open to talent" to vehemence against "elitism" were products of these years.

The blacks and "the poor" were amalgamated to provide the justification for a vehement attack on the liberal traditions of American society. The attack was carried out mainly by collectivistic liberals, some of whom became more radical in their censure of the limited capacities of traditional liberalism, above all for its failure to bring about a degree of equality which neither liberalism had previously sought. This alliance of collectivistic liberalism and radicalism cast "elitism" and traditional liberalism in the role of the enemy.

4

What was there in that loose constellation of beliefs called "liberalism" which permitted such transformations? Whenever American liberalism has confined itself to political concerns, it has for the most part placed the freedom of the individual and the values cultivated privately by individuals above the claims and standing of government. But when "the economic problem" and the "social problem" became the dominant concerns of liberals, a fissure occurred. When the "economic" and "social" problems came to the forefront of the field of liberal attention, the appreciation of individual freedom suffered and the state which had been distrusted was given the vital tasks of curbing the power of individuals and making up for their inadequacies.

The split in the ranks of liberals, which had been visible since the last decades of the nineteenth century, became more marked after the First World War. One section had remained faithful to the older liberal tradition that emphasized political freedom, individual initiative, and the rule of law, and to the belief that the market was the most efficient and beneficient mechanism through which individual initiative and decision could work. Adherents to this strand of liberalism also believed in the efficacy of hard work as a moral virtue and thought that professional politicians were by and large a meddlesome and shoddy lot. These liberals came to be called "conservatives" or "reactionaries" or at best and derisively "Adam Smith liberals" or "laissez-faire liberals" by other liberals. No distinction was made between liberals who had a vision of social order and of the human mind in which reason and liberty were central, and those persons who were preoccupied almost exclusively by their attachment to private property and private enterprise and who wanted not only an unintrusive government which acted as a "night watchman" but one which would also stand guard against the importation of goods of foreign manufacture and against radical criticsm and subversive activities. The numbers of the autonomist liberals did not increase proportionately to the increase in the size and prominence of the educated class. As the latter grew, it provided fewer recruits for an articulate autonomist liberalism. Engineers, chemists, accountants tended to be silent adherents of autonomist liberalism. The social sciences, the fundamental natural sciences, and humanistic studies produced a more articulate body of collectivistic liberals. They pressed forward the ideas of collectivistic liberalism; they also gave currency to the identification of autonomist liberalism with narrowly self-serving capitalistic arguments.

The collectivistic liberals took an instrumental attitude toward government to compensate for the deficiencies of the market, defined from a philanthropic point of view. The intervention of government into the operation of the market was not thought by collectivistic liberals to be dangerous to political freedom in any respect as long as it was initiated and controlled by the politically qualified public. Some of the intervention supported by liberals was in fact intended to restore the competitiveness of the market by action against "trusts and combinations." This was another point where autonomist and collectivist liberals remained at one with each other. This action against monopolies was also intended to reinforce the representativeness of representative institutions by impeding the concentration of power in the economic sphere. Some of the philanthropic intervention by government was intended to aid individuals and families which would otherwise fall out of the circle of "respectability"; it was intended to "tide them over" until they could take their place in the market again. As citizens, the "needy" were entitled to support for the period of "neediness"; it was not thought to be a permanent condition. Unemployment insurance was the main instance of this type of philanthropic intervention and it too was a measure on which both kinds of liberals could agree. In these and other respects, collectivistic liberalism remained liberal. Nonetheless it was already launched on a new path with a compelling direction of its own.

There was another type of philanthropic intervention which was not liberal since it was not intended to restore the competitiveness of the market or the capacity of individuals to return to the market. It was directly Christian in inspiration and exclusively philanthropic in intention. It was directed to the care of those incapable of caring for themselves, such as the derelict aged, the parentless child, the deserted mother, the mentally defective, the severely deformed. They were persons who had to be protected in a regime which left so much to private initiative and self-maintenance. This current of philanthropic liberalism was also not intended to be broadened to the point where it would flood the sphere of autonomy; it was intended only to compensate marginally for the limited efficacy of autonomous action in making possible the attainment of earthly happiness. Nevertheless, when Christian philanthropic liberalism became governmental policy, it broke out of these earlier constraints and it lost its visible connection with Christianity.

To the major traditions which have entered into American liberalism from Great Britain there should be added that which came from a different source. American liberalism of British inspiration, embracing devotion to individual liberty, responsibility and initiative, rationalism, belief in the efficacy of the market, and Christian philanthropy, had eschewed recourse to the state except for the maintenance of public order and defense and for treating marginal situations. Private initiative, whether in business or philanthropy, was to prevail in all except marginal situations. But in the period after the Civil War many young Americans went to Germany to study the social sciences, history, and philosophy, and brought back with them some ideas and assumptions about the state that were quite different. The American students of the *Staatswissenschaften* saw the state as something superior to the individuals who constituted it. It was seen to have a value of its own, quite apart from its instrumental uses. For them the state was not to be distrusted; it was to be admired. It was not a supplement or corrective to individual actions that had gone astray or fallen short; it existed in its own right, an initiating creative power.

The situation in the United States at the time seemed to call for such ideas. The state was in disarray; it was corrupt and inefficient. There was no governor to restrain the excesses of successful economic individualism. The message brought back from Germany seemed to provide the ideal solution, especially in combination with American populistic postulates. Populism, which regarded "the people" as the locus of virtue and was in some respects the very antithesis of "statolatry," was very ready to avail itself of a very active state in order to control its adversaries, the banks and railways. The corruption of government which the muckrakers exposed was interpreted in the circles influenced by their German mentors as evidence of the need to repair and elevate the state and to animate it for high purposes. The action of the state, directed by this high calling, would thus serve the interests of "the people." Neither "statolatry" nor populism was liberal but, in the United States, they became amalgamated into liberalism.

Scientism was another tributary tradition which flowed into the making of collectivistic liberalism. American liberalism, with its dislike of traditional authorities, had always been strongly disposed towards science, both as a replacement of religion and for its practical utility. What was new, however, was the belief that scientific methods and scientific knowledge could provide the basis for social engineering on a massive scale.

This belief—that the application of science could "solve" social problems—affected a wide range of academic disciplines, and turned them into fortresses and arsenals of reform. The emerging discipline of political science, with its strong Germanic imprint, was thought of as the science which could purify, elevate, and strengthen the state, thereby permitting it to do what its own nature and the condition of American society required. Institutional economics, similarly nurtured from a German seed, also contributed mightily to the shift from autonomist to collectivistic liberalism. Sociologists were also eager to contribute to the progress of their society; they were reformers to a man—except Sumner. They were concerned with "social conditions," meaning poverty and demoralization. Even W. I. Thomas, the most profound sociologist of his time, moved in that direction. The natural sciences were less involved with the state; their beneficences went to industry, agriculture and medicine, and for a long time they expected little from government other than a modest contribution. (As a matter of fact, the contribution of the government to the development of science in agriculture was great.) Anthropology and psychology also tended to remain outside the circle; they persisted in the line of the natural scientists and the technologists. Still, the scientistic view that science should and could contribute to social well-being was strong, and flowed smoothly into the notion that government should become the chief instrument for ensuring the social welfare.

The reforming sociologists and the political scientists shared many liberal attitudes. In particular, both grounded their hopes for effectiveness on a pillar of traditional liberalism, namely the freedom of an enquiring and critical press. The organs of opinion would report on "social problems" and disclose "social conditions" in need of reform; they were not expected to examine those conditions which were not so deplorable and which were neither so newsworthy nor so demanding of academic and journalistic attention. Free inquiry would illuminate public opinion; legislators would be impelled to act on the basis of meticulously gathered facts. It was the journalists and social scientists who were to bring the issues before the public and thence to the politicians.

This is indeed what happened. From sociology and political science, the involvement spread into the teaching of law, and from there exerted a penetrating influence on educated public opinion and then on the judiciary and on the legislation of social policy. Roscoe Pound significantly called his doctrine "sociological jurisprudence." Institutional economics also entered into jurisprudence and, supported by what these learned lawyers thought to be social science, turned the law into an organ of collectivistic liberalism.

5

As events outside the boundaries of the United States achieved prominence in liberal attention, the foreign policy of the government became increasingly important as an object of contention. The attitude and action of the government toward the Soviet Union, toward "socialism" in other countries, toward the colonial policies of Western European countries, and toward the regimes of the Third World has become a primary interest of collectivistic liberalism. In consequence of this, the divergence between autonomistic liberalism and collectivistic liberalism has become wider.

By its traditions, liberalism has been universalistic in the direction of its attention. It was not fortuitous that Bentham was ready to write constitutions for countries everywhere. Liberalism has always been concerned with what has been happening in other parts of the world; the improvements in means of transportation and communication and the growth of scholarly and journalistic knowledge about all corners of

the earth have fostered this disposition. Autonomist liberalism, especially during its period of formation, had a profound
sense of the affinity of European humanity and the other
parts of the human race. The moral relativism and the con-
comitant disparagement of Christianity which characterized
some currents of European liberalism, particularly in France
and Great Britain, were closely related to this readiness to
see all of humanity as one. The growth of anthropological
and oriental studies further opened the awareness of European liberalism of the rest of mankind.

However, liberalism has not only been universalist in its
range of attention; it has also been "internationalist"—the
word itself seems to have been coined by Bentham. There
have been isolationist currents and moments in American
collectivistic liberalism but they have never been dominant.
For the past four decades, American liberalism has been internationalist. Liberalism generally has sought peace between
states, it has disparaged the martial virtues—in its autonomist
liberal phase, it also praised the mercantile virtues that were
contrasted with the martial ones. For a long time liberalism
was against tariffs and in favor of free trade. In its more collectivistic phase, especially in its alliance with trade unions,
its attitude towards free trade has been somewhat more
ambiguous. But it is against war, except when the war is on
behalf of principles and especially when it is veiled as a civil
war fought on behalf of a collectivistic liberal principle. It is
certainly against nationalism in its own society; it wishes the
foreign policy of its own government to be internationalist,
and moreover to be internationalist in accordance with moral
principles such as national self-determination, democracy,
and populism.

Opposed though it has been to "chauvinism," "jingoism,"
and nationalism under whatever name at home, liberalism,
and especially collectivistic liberalism, has been greatly exercised on behalf of the right of national self-determination in
other countries. At one time, its proponents thought that the
realization of the right of collective self-determination
brought with it the advancement of the rights of individuals

to education, enlightenment, and public liberties. Liberalism, especially in its collectivistic variant, has been consistently sympathetic with the nationalism of colonized peoples and of newly established states, even where this was accompanied by the suppression of public liberties.

Liberals—persons who desired freedom in their own societies—were once critical of tyranny abroad as well as in their own countries. So it was in the nineteenth century and the beginning of the twentieth century. A great change occurred after the Bolshevik revolution of 1917. Throughout the 1920s, collectivist liberals in the United States accepted the Soviet Union as a country in which their ideals of individual freedom and welfare were being realized. This was probably less true of liberals in Europe, including the United Kingdom. There, liberals were more concerned with political freedom and less with humanitarian ends; and the social democrats, who incorporated a considerable measure of political liberalism into their outlook, were reinforced in their dislike of Bolshevism by their awareness of the fate of social democrats under the Soviet regime and of the vehemence with which Communists denounced social democracy.

Why did the American liberals come to the support of the Soviet Union in the 1920s, even though they were not Communists? (I am thinking here largely of the contributors and sympathetic readers of *The Nation* and *The New Republic* although there were many more sympathizers than these.) They supported the Soviet Union because they associated "revolution" with the improvement of the conditions of "the poor" and with freedom of the arts and freedom of opinion. They supported it, too, because "reactionaries"—the supporters of private business—opposed it. The Soviet Union was after all the one place where capitalism had been abolished; the attachment of the collectivistic liberals in the United States to the Soviet Union for such a long time shows how hostile to capitalism they have been—even though within the United States they have reconciled themselves to its hobbled existence. They refused to believe about the USSR what more detached students of the subject told them, because they distrusted the "reactionary" press and found it nearly impossible to believe that revolution and freedom were not identical.

As many collectivistic liberals came under Communist influence in the 1930s, they also began explicitly to relegate political freedom to a secondary position. Fascism and National Socialism became their main enemies; and they were, of course, hostile to imperialism, an attitude consistent with their traditional views. With respect to the Soviet Union, however, they fell into a more self-contradictory position. On the one hand they opposed imperialism and tyranny in the name of democratic or collective self-determination and of individual freedom in politics, in the arts, and in intellectual activities. On the other, they were attached to the Soviet Union. They reconciled these contradictory attitudes by denying the evidence of Soviet tyranny, or by explaining it away as a temporary measure, or by asserting that the Soviet Union was genuinely democratic but in a new way which was unappreciated in liberal-democratic countries.

There was another aspect of the Soviet Union which attracted American collectivistic liberals. The Soviet Union was a "planned economy," indeed even a "planned society." At a time when the United States was suffering from unemployment, the Soviet Union was portrayed as "the land without unemployment." This great accomplishment was alleged to be a result of central planning; this was contrasted with the chaos of "a laissez-faire economic system," with all its unhappy accompaniments. The New Deal was seen as a step, faltering and insufficient, in the right direction. "Planning" was held forth as an ideal towards which the United States should move. After the Second World War, the idea of comprehensive planning diminished in the publicly expressed affection of collectivistic liberals, but a strong subterranean attachment remained. There is still a clandestine love of planning. It is after all a logical necessity. If one believes in the powers of reason and of scientific knowledge, in progress towards ever higher targets or "goals," in collective self-determination, as well as in the limitless competence of government which proceeds in accordance with rationality and scientific knowledge, then one must be in favor of planning. However tarnished the image of the Soviet Union has become, it still retains the credit of being "planned."

For these very diverse reasons, the Soviet Union in its foreign policy was credited by a substantial fraction of collectivistic liberals with being generally on the right side. Liberals were temporarily swept loose from this position during the period of the Molotov-Ribbentrop agreement, and again after the Second World War. The assumption of Soviet virtue was eroded for a time during the cold war, when patriotism became stronger than usual among American liberals. The Americans for Democratic Action supported the policy of the Democratic administration which followed the war, although many collectivistic liberals also supported the Progressive Party of Henry Wallace and the fellow travelers who espoused the traditional pro-Soviet policy of so many American collectivistic liberals during most of the period after the Russian revolutions.

The tendency of American liberals to view foreign policy from a moral standpoint, to combine a high evaluation of freedom with the demand for the material well-being of the mass of the population by means of governmental action in all countries, gave a particularly favored position to the Soviet Union. The tangible evidence of the brutality of Soviet domestic policies in the 1930s—in connection with the collectivization of agriculture and the "purge" of Stalin's opponents and his real and potential rivals—was often denied; and even when it was acknowledged it was, in the main, acknowledged unwillingly, and did not affect the attitudes of many collectivistic liberal intellectuals. Even today some liberals who have acknowledged the brutality of the Soviet regime—partly because of the publication of the works of Solzhenitsyn—still seem to waver in condemning the Soviet Union outright. Some write off Solzhenitsyn as a talented crank in political matters; others accept his evidence, but tend to discount it as the report of an aberration whose repressiveness does not affect the claim to inherent superiority of a "truly" socialistic regime. And of course they are pas-

sionate in their denunciation of the cold war. They denounce
the cold war not because it was conducted in a doctrinaire
fashion by John Foster Dulles but fundamentally because it
was distrustful of the Soviet Union. They seem to think that
socialistic regimes must by their nature realize the ambitions
of collectivistic liberalism. The reports of the brutal repressiveness of socialistic regimes they interpret as exaggerated or
as referring to transient conditions necessitated by the
"needs" of development or of the threat of inimical "capitalist powers." They have added to the traditional liberal view
of the larger world an image inexpungibly impressed on the
recollection of liberals more than a half-century ago by the
Allied intervention in Russia in 1919.

It is a paradox that the Soviet Union, which is one of the
most illiberal of all the regimes of modern times, should hold
the lingering affections of many American collectivistic
liberals who are so devoted to civil, artistic, and intellectual
liberties. When affection for the Soviet Union is renounced,
then it is redirected to some other regime like it. When attachment to all these regimes is renounced or qualified, the
attitude of the collectivistic liberals towards American
foreign policy which underlay their affection for these regimes still endures.

This same attitude finds expression domestically in the
animosity of most collectivistic liberals towards the Federal
Bureau of Investigation and the Central Intelligence Agency,
which they see to a large extent as being directed primarily
against the Soviet Union and its American and foreign
sympathizers. Trotskyites, Maoists, and all the various
combinations come under the protection of this attitude,
which has at its heart the unextinguishable memory of the
Soviet Union as the bearer of the best hopes of humanity.
The emptied ideal still guides their outlook; they might
have renounced their old love but they retain their old
enemies.

6

The radicalism which asserts the failure of liberalism—it
does not generally distinguish the autonomist liberalism from

collectivistic liberalism—considers itself to have broken out of
the confines of liberalism. But it has done so only in the way
in which a neurotic exaggerates and distorts the dispositions
of a person of normal conduct. Radicalism claims to offer
something to mankind which liberalism has failed to offer. It
is in fact only an extension, to the point of corruption, of the
principles contained in liberalism. Radicalism extends the
ends of liberalism to points beyond the intentions of those
who promulgated it and beyond the traditions that have
sustained it. Contrary to the beliefs of radicals that their
program is disjunctively different from that of collectivistic
liberalism, there has been a movement toward a loose approx-
imation between them. A process of transformation has
swept collectivistic liberalism towards radicalism. The transformation has not been announced. It is not even noticed
because—since contemporary radicalism is no longer dominated by a dogmatic Marxian orthodoxy—it has become
easier to pass from liberalism to radicalism. Nonetheless the
central ideas of liberty of expression, equality of opportunity, and individuality have been subjected to reinterpretations
which have moved them away from liberalism. Collectivistic
liberalism has become thereby radically different from what
it was.

Liberty of expression has until relatively recently meant
the liberty of expression, in an intellectual form, of a substantive belief. It meant the liberty of expression of an argument that was intended to justify the belief and to convince
others. It meant the liberty of expression of scientific ideas,
moral ideals, political ideals and programs, and religious
ideas; it meant the liberty of publishing literary works. The
argument for the liberty of expression has always presupposed the seriousness of intention, and the intellectual and
aesthetic character, of the works and activities to be protected. Liberty of expression was not intended simply to be
the expression of an affective state, unless it was given an
intellectual or literary form. Liberty of expression did not
mean the liberty of expression as such, without regard to
content; the content was expected to be something *serious* in

the Durkheimian sense. The content was expected to be a belief regarding a problem of society, a problem of the proper conduct of authority, or of the church, or of the individual; it was expected to be a belief about the earth or the cosmos. These were the matters which the right to freedom of expression was intended to open to public view.

Traditional liberalism tended to be puritanical regarding affective expression and particularly regarding erotic matters. At various points, its principles contained implications of freedom of affective expression, but these were not developed. What is specifically collectivistic in collectivistic liberalism does not logically require the extension of the freedom of expression into the sphere of affective and erotic expression. But in the course of the nineteenth century, philanthropy and idealistic individualism became fused with the romantic idea of individuality as the cultivation and development of the emotions. Autonomist individualism spurned this alliance. The entry of bohemian radicalism accentuated this tendency in collectivistic liberalism.

Still, in the nineteenth century and in the early twentieth century literary works which would now be called pornographic were not at issue for either of the currents of liberalism, even though they were already becoming quite widely separated from each other. The writing and publication of pornography and blasphemy and the public performances of sexual actions for purposes of public entertainment or for the sheer pleasure of performing them in public were not regarded by the liberal political theorists of the eighteenth and nineteenth centuries as falling within the class of the actions whose freedom they were attempting to establish. The arguments on behalf of works that were soon recognized as literary classics, such as *Madame Bovary, Fleurs du Mal,* and *Leaves of Grass,* which were prosecuted for offense to public morals, did not extend to the justification of pornography nor to the performance of sexual acts in public. The idea that avowedly pornographic works should be protected by the right to freedom of expression apparently did not occur to the political philosophers who argued for a regime of intellectual freedom. They lived in a tradition which simply did not acknowledge the legitimacy of such works; they accepted that tradition. It is only recently, when the tradition of literary and artistic seriousness has faded and when any sort of posturing and self-exhibition has come to be regarded as art, that pornography has been placed under the protection of the right to the freedom of expression. The protection of the liberty of authors like James Joyce and D. H. Lawrence has been extended to works of pornography and acts of public indecency.

The liberal defenders of pornography have extended liberalism to justify actions and works that were not intended to enjoy the benefits of a liberal regime. They have done so effectively, to the extent that any proposal for the censorship of pornograhic works and of acts of public indecency is avoided by liberals for fear that they would thereby show themselves to be illiberal. After all, should not any affective states and erotic impulses be as expressible as scientific or religious or moral beliefs or as political aspirations? According to this radicalized liberalism, whatever can be expressed must be provided with the guaranteed liberty of its expression. Liberty of expression has become distorted into a doctrine of emancipation from the restraints of social institutions, cultural traditions, and interior inhibitions. The criticism of the repression exercised by public and ecclesiastical authority over the expression of beliefs and opinions in an intellectual or artistic form has been extended to the rejection of restraints of any kind.

A similar process has occurred when the argument for equality of opportunity was jostled and forced aside by the ideal of the equality of rewards. Classical liberalism in its autonomist branch was at first egalitarian in two very specific senses: it insisted on equality before the law and on equality of opportunity. It was ambivalent about equality of the franchise and it moved very cautiously in that direction. It accepted that there were inequalities of nature, propensities and talents among individuals, and it was concerned for *la carrière ouverte aux talents*. Abilities should be rewarded commensurately to their magnitude and application.

Liberals of both major types have in principle always been opposed to the privilege of unearned, superior rewards and opportunities; they have disapproved of competitive advantages which have not been won by achievement and talent but acquired through birth. They had therefore to regard educational qualification and educational achievement as better criteria for occupational appointment and promotion than familial and ethnic connections. They both regarded the education of the natural talents as the best means of undoing the injustice of the familial transmission of wealth and status.

Liberals were concerned to see that the cultivation and training of these natural talents were not impeded by inherited wealth or any other institutionally sustained privilege based on affiliation or biological descent. Yet liberalism in the nineteenth and even through much of the twentieth centuries accepted that human beings within any particular society, however successfully that society had realized the program of liberalism, would be inegalitarian in the distribution of deference. It would be less inegalitarian than the societies of the *ancien régime,* and it would maintain a floor of dignity below which human beings would not be degraded. Nonetheless, since there would be differences in excellence of achievement and differences in excellence of moral character, there would inevitably be differences in deference.

It has not appeared to be a great step to pass from equality of opportunity to equality of results—after all, both were about equality! What good is an equality which ends up in inequality? Equality is a term sufficiently ambiguous to allow diverse constructions to be laid upon it without a sense of inconsistency or of departure from its "true" meaning. To pass from disapproval of differences in deference derived from differences in the status of ancestors, to the disapproval of differences in status derived from differences in achievement or in moral merit, is not a great step either. Might it not be argued that the qualities which foster achievement or moral merit are not themselves the product of the individual's achievement or moral merit? They might be inherited genetically, although few equalitarians would argue that; or, they might be results of luck or chance, or they might be the results of hidden privileges. Hence, equality of opportunity is only another way of guaranteeing the continued existence of inequality. As a result, it has not appeared to be a great step to pass from the removal of present and actual inferiorities to compensation for inferiorities inherited from the past. If past ancestral advantages were to be obliterated, it has not seemed inconsistent to argue that past ancestral disadvantages should be compensated. Nor has it been any more of a strain to pass from the disapprobation of unearned or inherited superiority of position to the denunciation of earned superiority, of superiority of accomplishment, together with the institutions which make superior accomplishment possible.

Insisting on the desirability of equality of opportunity, liberals have insisted particularly on the opportunity to become educated. This was regarded as of the first importance because it was the way in which abilities were trained and tested. This is why liberals pressed for the extension of educational provision and for universal and free primary and secondary education; in the United States they also supported the provision of higher education by the states so that the offspring of poorer families could attend. This high evaluation of education has, in an increasingly bureaucratic and governmentally dominated society, become adulterated by an excess of confidence in educational certification, as a precondition of admission to a widening range of occupations. There have been two by-products of this. One is the deprecation of the development of talents through experience, and the other is the willingness to accept the simulacrum of education represented by a diploma or a degree and an increased indifference toward the intellectual substance of education. Both of these unwholesome occurrences may be attributed to liberalism and above all to collectivistic liberalism. They are the price that has been paid for the elimination of familial descent and affiliations as qualifications for deference and opportunity.

Education has become the chosen instrument of the radical equalitarianism that has been insinuated into collectivistic liberalism. There were many reasons for the liberal reformers' desire to widen access to education. Through it, economic and cultural benefits would accrue to the individual as well as to society by incorporating new generations into a common national culture and a common civilization, and by promoting a sense of civility. It was also regarded as just that those who were especially talented should have the opportunity to develop the talents with which they were endowed; this was integral to the belief that if these especially talented young persons were successful in the use of those talents they should be rewarded correspondingly and more amply than those with poorer talents, less developed talents, or less fruitfully applied talents. This was thought to be beneficial not only to the talented individual but also to the society that would be improved by superior accomplishments, whether in the economic, artistic, intellectual, or civil spheres.

Some liberal writers occasionally referred to the injustice of the unequal distribution of native endowment. They did not make anything of it, in contrast with early socialist writers who regarded it as an argument against remuneration in accordance with performance and who argued that "needs" should be the criterion for remuneration. Liberals have been opposed in principle to the inheritance of advantages such as titles, ranks, offices, and powers, but they did nonetheless admit the existence of differences in genetic endowment, and they accepted them.

There was however a significant difference between these two types of hereditary transmission. In the one, which classical liberalism allowed and which autonomist liberalism still allows, the superior reward was conferred in acknowledgement of an actual achievement, presumably made possible by superior endowment and by corresponding effort. In the other, there was no achievement. There was thus a rationale in the liberal acceptance of differences in the quality of genetic endowment. Nonetheless, this difference has not been tolerated by the radical criticism, and it has been increasingly rejected by collectivistic liberalism. Beginning with the denial of genetic differences between class, ethnic, or racial aggregates, the denial has now been extended to a reluctance to acknowledge the existence of individual differences within such aggregates. Where such differences between individuals are admitted, it is argued that they should not be provided with correspondingly different opportunities, for example, different kinds of schools in which superior endowment could be cultivated so as to lead to superior achievement. The result is a shift of collectivistic liberalism from acknowledgement of superior achievement made possible by superior hereditary endowment, to the radical stress on the injustice of any superiority of genetic endowment and any prospective advantages which might be conferred by it. Achievement has come thus to be disregarded and disparaged as an important criterion by which human beings are to be assessed.

One of the most striking manifestations of this self-transformation of collectivistic liberalism is the allocation of opportunities by "quotas" for particular ethnic groups—by "targets," as it is sometimes evasively put. It sets aside the accomplishments in the prior utilization of opportunity which have resulted in differences in standing and begins the race again. It is as if in a one mile race, the differences between the runners are cancelled after a quarter mile, after a half mile, and after three-quarters of a mile, and all the runners are forced to begin again from the same starting line. Even those runners who fell out of the race earlier are enticed into returning to the race and their past failures are cancelled. At the end, according to this policy, the prizes are equally distributed to all the runners, the poor ones receiving prizes as good as the superior ones. This is, of course, never done in athletics, but this is the policy which collectivistic liberalism recommends in the allocation of opportunities for higher education. American collectivistic liberalism in its latter-day desire for substantive equality has replaced one primordial qualification by another. Kinship descent and affiliation are replaced by ethnic descent and affiliation. And yet, collectivistic liberalism remains specifically liberal in spirit, in that it persists in treating educational certification as the qualification for reward. In doing so, however, it has ceased to treat educational certification as having any necessary correspondence with the application of talent.

Traditional liberalism was not in favor of equality of income. It was against inequalities of income which arose from contrived, organized, or traditionally or legally protected monopolies. It was in favor of equality of opportunity. But equality of opportunity did not mean that outcomes would be equal any more than the requirement that all competitors in a foot race begin at the same line and moment meant that all must be treated as having run with equal speed and arrived at the finish line at the same moment. Traditional liberalism never doubted that in any society there would be different tasks which were differently assessed, that they would be performed with different degrees of proficiency, and that these differences would and should be differently rewarded in deference and income. Most socialists did not think this way but liberals did. Accordingly, the progressive income tax was first conceived as a means of raising revenue for governmental purposes; these purposes did not include the equalization of income. The progressive income tax was intended only to make the tax burdens commensurate to the ability to pay, which was a way of equalizing responsibilities for the maintenance of government. The introduction of estate or death duties again was not a first intended to equalize income, although it moved in that direction by its attack on the ethical validity of familial continuity over generations and on the freedom of testamentary disposition. Gradually, fiscal policies came to be viewed as appropriate instruments for influencing the distribution of income; those which did not diminish the inequality of the distribution of income were censured. Recently, collectivistic liberal economists have established the equalization of income as a desideratum of public policy. Of course, like the liberal political philosophers of a century and a half ago, who did not mean to assert a justification of pornography, the liberal economists do not really mean a complete equality of income. Nonetheless a path has been taken and a direction has been set. It is everywhere noticeable in the policies of collectivistic liberalism.

Collectivistic liberalism in its newest, radical phase has coined the term "elitism," an ugly coinage to express an ugly attitude. "Elitism" is employed to denounce any institutional arrangement which allows some human beings to perform in a manner more excellent than others. Any belief which asserts the desirability or inevitability or differences in excellence of achievement is similarly denounced. Institutions which offer a superior, more exigent education are denounced as "elitist." Acknowledgement of superiority in science or in business is denounced as "elitist." Training and education which aspire to maintain, inculcate, and demand a high standard of achievement are denounced as "elitist." Praise of and aspiration to observe a tradition of moral excellence are also denounced as "elitist." Collectivistic liberalism seems to be veering towards an apotheosis of mediocrity and even failure; the very term "failure" is regarded as reprehensible. Few indeed have been the collectivistic liberals who stood out against this stampede towards radicalism.

This many-sided transformation of collectivistic liberalism into radicalism has been eased by the complex ambivalence of the foundation of liberalism. In one tendency within the traditional liberal conception of man, liberal ideas were joined to a secularized conception of original sin which took the form of a belief in the egocentric character of human conduct. In the thought of Adam Smith, this egoism was balanced by the operations of the moral sentiments; in Mandeville's, by the transformation of private vices into public benefits; in Bentham's, by the various arrangements for the artificial identification of interests. (All of these views were put forward with the understanding that human actions took place in a realm of scarcity.) On the other side, there was the idea of a natural benevolence and sympathy in human beings which makes them "other-regarding" rather than "self-regarding." This latter idea, coupled with associational psychology, made it possible to conceive of a humanity which, if subjected to proper educative influences, would not sink into the morass of egoism. The addition of an expectation of a state of plenitude, which was alien to liberalism, fortified attachment to this idea of natural benevolence.

Although autonomist liberalism was not attracted to the idea of natural benevolence, the idea was increasingly assimilated into collectivistic liberalism. Education was thought to be a means of cultivating man's rational faculties so that egoism, enlightened by the informed consideration of the consequences of action, would be disciplined and constrained; but it was also thought of as the nurturing of the essential benevolence of the human being. In the right environment, man's natural benevolence and intelligence would come into realization.

The belief in the decisive influence of environment on the development of the mind and character acquired an additional ingredient from a populistic romanticism which saw in ordinary human beings capacities for creativity reserved by a more restrictive, "aristocratic" romanticism for rare geniuses. This has led to the view, which is now widespread among educators, that every human being possesses not the spark of divinity in which radical Protestants believed but the secular equivalent, a spark of genius. Every person has a creative power which the cessation of an artificially maintained scarcity and the right kind of emancipatory education would bring into flower.

7

The rationalism that was characteristic of autonomist liberalism, and the combination of radicalism and expressiveness which became characteristic of collectivistic liberalism, have both been uncongenial to the coherence and continuity of the family and to traditional things. Liberalism has always been distrustful of the family largely because it has represented such a fusion of authority and traditionalism. Liberalism would not accept traditionalism. It offered alternative paths to freedom from the "cake of custom." In autonomist liberalism with its characteristically narrow, puritanical hardheadedness, the path was set by the "genius of hard work";

more sentimentally, collectivistic liberalism has chosen the realization of "creative" or "true individuality," of the "vital self" as the path to its ideal.

Such a "true individuality" can, it was thought, be attained only after the emancipation of the individual from the traditions in which he was born and raised. "Society," "tradition," "culture," suffocate human beings. A person who possesses such true individuality, who is really alive will see the world through his own eyes, experience it with his own senses, not through the senses of those who have gone before him. A person who possesses true individuality will assimilate into himself the fruits of his own experience, which he elaborates into something distinctive and therefore valuable.

This ideal of the vital self has undergone a transformation. Originally the idea was both disciplined and aesthetically aristocratic; it envisioned a life made whole by complete devotion to "work"—whether literary or artistic work, or one's own "life as a work of art." Now, however, the ideal has become more discontinuous and momentary, and the attainment of states of sensation has become the end. Being creative is not an accumulative process, but a series of creations and states of mind. It does not require the development of a "unique life style," as much as it involves trying out all sorts of "life styles" in succession. Thus a radical syllabus of religious education for state schools, prepared by a commission of the Church of England, calls for each pupil to "examine alternative life-stances," none of them to be dogmatically recommended by the teacher; the child would presumably try them all and adopt them as and when he saw fit.

In contrast with major currents of autonomist liberalism, collectivistic liberalism—especially in its educational program and in its increasingly radicalized outlook—thinks that the discovery of our true identity, the creation of a "satisfying life-style," is open equally to everyone. According to this view, individuality entails the exercise of powers of feeling and imagination, which every human being could, under the right circumstances, attain. To be a true individual is to be "alive," to be in contact with and to experience what is vital. "Everyman a king!" "Everyone burning with his own hard gem-like flame!"

This particular extension and self-annulment of collectivistic liberalism into radicalism is even more unsympathetic toward tradition than collectivistic liberalism was in its unextended form. Whereas the latter stressed the value of the rational and reflective assimilation of immediate experience, in its radical variant it has laid the accent more emphatically on the affective side of experience. It has emphasized the need to create and discover the self rather than to develop it through sensation and experience, through discipline and rational reflection on experience, training, etc. The idea of a "search for identity" is something which did not occur in the theories of autonomist and collectivistic liberalism through most of their history. The idea is still alien to autonomist liberalism, which assumed that most normal human beings "know who they are," and thus require no long and arduous search to "discover themselves." The self was formed from what it received from an unacknowledged tradition and from experience, and the superior individual could enrich it by disciplined and discriminatingly assessed experience and by rational reflection. The "self" did not have to be created: it was there and it had to be and could be improved.

In the liberalism of the eighteenth and nineteenth centuries, there was no idea of a "search for identity" in order to fill the "awful sense of emptiness." Critical though it was of the "dead hand of the past," it was not so much in revolt against the past as to think that every human being should "make himself" *de novo*. Even collectivistic liberalism was not so thoroughgoing in its rejection of tradition as to refuse completely the inheritance with which the self begins; it only emphasized the need to go ahead and build on it. Only when it moves towards radicalism and opens itself to the aestheticism of vital expression and sensation which the long alliance of revolution and bohemia brought before it, does it become sympathetic to the belief that the only life worth living is life wholly and freely chosen and created. The notion of choosing one's "life-style" in complete freedom is, of course, an unrealistic fantasy; it does nonetheless form a part of the newer radicalism.

Fragments of this outlook have been taken into American educational doctrine and in some distorted way into educational practice as well. It attributes little importance to the assimilation of the past achievements of the human race, and in this regard it is not much different from the traditional progressive education that has been part of the collectivistic liberal program. It has now become an egocentric irrationalism, destructive of learning and art, and inimical to individuality which builds on tradition and goes forward through the disciplined accumulation of experience and imaginative reflection of it. Not many persons attempt to realize this ideal in an unqualified manner; those who do end in disaster and disillusionment. Nonetheless, the ideal has inserted itself into the idiom of one strand of contemporary radicalism.

The "new sensibility" which underlies the desire for complete freedom and a voice which "shares in every decision which affects itself" has produced a new turning toward plebiscitary democracy. Autonomist liberals had been aware of the noxious inconveniences of plebiscitary democracy ever since the end of the eighteenth century, and consequently had noted a tension between democracy and liberalism. Representative institutions were thought to resolve this tension. However, with the passage of time and the emergence of monstrous totalitarianism, the tension has receded as a subject of concern. After the end of the Second World War, criticism was silenced; repairs were suggested here and there but generally democracy—representative democracy—seemed to have reestablished its good name in the West and not least in the United States.

A new turn was taken however with the resurgence of the new brand of radicalism. The universities and related institutions of science have been the loci of this radicalism. "Participatory democracy," "people's science" are its demands, although what it usually comes down to are places on governing bodies for radical intellectuals who proclaim the imperative of giving a voice to "people" who will look after the interests of "people." Participatory democracy is the companion piece of "antielitism." Prior to the coming together of the "new left" and the student agitation, participatory democracy had never been a part of the program of collectivistic liberalism. Guild socialism was indulged from afar with a marginal sympathy. Despite the great prestige of the Soviet Union, the idea of *soviets* as mechanism of collective self-determination never caught on among collectivistic liberals who were otherwise ready to swallow a great deal of the Soviet mythology. "Industrial democracy" never moved into the center of the concern of collectivistic liberals in the 1920s, when it had a faint and flickering existence as an aspiration but not as a practice. The New Deal, and the National Labor Relations Act which was one of its monuments, did nothing more than offer legal protection for the organization of workers into trade unions for the purpose of collective bargaining.

Since the universities and colleges were the first institutions affected by the movement of the New Left in the United States it was there that the demand for participatory democracy made its first insistent appearance. Once made, it was often readily agreed to. To some extent the alacrity of accommodation to it was simply the result of cowardice and cynicism. But like many of the seepages of the radical outlook into collectivistic liberalism, participatory democracy seemed obviously correct. After all, if democracy was right, then its extension was right. Teachers and administrators were overpowered by the patent truth that if universities and colleges were "communities of scholars," the case for participatory democracy was unanswerable. Democracy had moved forward through the extension of the franchise from property owners to citizens, from adult males to adult females, and from those over twenty-one to those over eighteen. What could be more reasonable therefore than participatory democracy, which was after all nothing more than the more thoroughgoing application of a generally acknowledged principle? (The special claims of youth gave further impetus

174 The Antinomies of Liberalism

to the acceptance, but "juvenolatry" is not a phenomenon unique to collectivistic liberalism; Nazis and Fascists also reserved a special place of prominence for youth.)

There has been no pronounced renascence of the older instruments of direct democracy—neither of the initiative, nor the referendum nor the recall, which were the three favorite recipes of populist reformers of the early part of the present century. Nor have the trade unions in the United States been very demanding for "codetermination." On the other side, tenants associations, welfare-rights associations, public access to the meetings and records of regulatory bodies have been taken into the repertoire of collectivistic liberalism. There is a widespread belief in "responsiveness," which is understood to mean more than the responsibility of elected and appointed officials. The demand for continuous institutional "responsiveness" is another manifestation of the pattern whose dominant theme is the primacy of "feelings"—the belief that desire establishes a right to the desideratum.

Liberalism, both in its autonomistic and its collectivistic variants and especially in the latter, has always had a strong cast of progressivism; it has been especially prone to a belief in the perfectibility of human existence. The education of the rational and the expressive powers of the "person" unencumbered by the baggage of literary and cultural tradition came to be regarded as the indispensable means to this attainment of perfection. Reason in the form of scientific knowledge and the scientific approach would give human beings the knowledge they needed to organize and govern themselves toward this end; the release of the expressive powers, in themselves creative, would itself be an installment or movement toward the ultimate condition of perfection.

With this intellectual tradition, which insisted on the perniciousness of tradition, collectivistic liberalism acquired the basis for further movement into an ultimately anarchistic radicalism. The contradictory combination of unrestricted individual expression, a denial of all authority over the individual, plebiscitary self-government, and rational central planning by an omnicompetent government provided both the ends and the means of progress.

Malthusianism has for a long time been a term of accusation and abuse in the vocabulary of collectivistic liberalism. It has suggested the idea of an ineluctible scarcity and of the inevitable hardness of life. It denied that all human problems are definitively soluble. Collectivistic liberalism, with its belief in the powers of scientific rationality and in the benignly "creative" powers inherent in emotional expression, with its belief in the efficacy of the education of the sentiments and in the exercise of governmental authority as a means of developing and harnessing these for the highest ends of man, was antithetical to the Malthusian conception of man's existence here below. Plenitude such as has been imagined to prevail only in heaven came to be thought of as a realizable condition, under the stimulus to the imagination given by the modern economy and the technology and science on which it increasingly depended.

In its "social gospel," liberal Protestantism had preached the striving for the attainment of the kingdom of God, the kingdom of plenitude, justice and peace on earth; but what it sought in practice were small, piecemeal reforms of particular institutions and practices. The voice of collectivistic liberalism in the early part of the present century was muffled in the traditions of a Christian bourgeois society, the structure and leadership of which seemed almost irrefragable. Although increasingly subject to scrutiny and criticism, the authority of governments and of property owners—like that of military officers, policemen, clergymen, and professors—was still accorded a high degree of legitimacy. Nobody expected them to provide a clear road to the kingdom of God.

As long as collectivistic liberalism was to a large extent dominated directly by practicing politicians or was very dependent on them, it was hampered by the restraints of tradition and the necessity of compromise. However, once the academic intellectual culture of collectivistic liberalism became more influential, the utopian potentiality began to appear more clearly in the lineaments of the collectivistic liberal program. Utopia came within the realm of earthly possibility. Government would be its deliverer.

Traditional radicalism has held itself aloof from government. It did not expect to be invited to join governments as cabinet members nor did it anticipate a large-scale entry of radicals into the civil service. It accepted that governments would rule, would use all the powers to keep the existing social order intact, and would keep secret those matters which concerned them most vitally. Secretiveness was regarded as one of the constitutive vices of existing governments, and radicals showed no interest in obtaining the secrets. Radicals were much more concerned to keep their own secrets from the police under whose scrutiny they knew themselves to be. Radicals benefited by the "exposures" of governmental misdeed by energetic journalists, but they regarded themselves as so far outside the central circle of society that they could not obtain such guarded information themselves.

Liberals, on the other hand, have from the beginning been against the secretiveness of governments. From the Benthamite maxim that "the eye of the public is the virtue of the statesman," through the struggles for the freedom of the press not only to express opinion but also to scrutinize publicly the actions of government, to Woodrow Wilson's declaration for "open covenants, openly arrived at," liberalism has always been in favor of publicity. How else could the iniquitous propensities of government be restrained and its beneficent potential promoted? Liberalism was not however thoroughgoing and it left many traditions intact; one of these was the secrecy of governmental activities having to do with "intelligence." It was ready to accept that the gathering of "intelligence" was essential to the effectiveness of the military and the police, and that the value of such intelligence would be negated by its public disclosure.

After the Second World War, another phenomenon emerged. This was the scientists' movement—mainly those who had worked on the Manhattan Project—which denounced secrecy regarding nuclear weapons. They desired the abolition of secrecy on the grounds that "nature has no secrets" and that the knowledge kept secret would sooner or later come into the possession of rival and potentially inimical states. They said that disclosure of information about the construction of nuclear weapons would have beneficial effects in international politics. The persecutions set loose by Senator McCarthy and like-minded politicians only increased the enmity towards secrecy. The efforts by governmental intelligence services purporting to deal with subversive activities and the development of a new electronic technology of surveillance only raised the opposition of collectivistic liberals against secrecy.

Radicals of the newer dispensation played only a small part in this movement toward the universal transparency of authoritative institutions. It was only partly to protect radicals, and partly to extend the liberal tradition of publicity, that liberals pressed for a legislative guarantee for access to hitherto withheld governmental documents. Radicals themselves contributed very little to it. The Freedom of Information Act was passed in 1966 before the student agitation began to concern itself with the confidentiality of university records, "secret dossiers," etc. By the beginning of the next decade, however, a common front was formed between collectivistic liberalism and radicalism. There was an accumulating insistence on public participation in governing investments, the demand that universities disclose their investments, that students have access to the files of the universities which refer to them, that governmental files be made available to radicals engaged in litigation against the government, that the records of private corporations likewise be made available to litigants and thus, as part of the public record, become accessible to competitors and opponents. The disclosure of the "Pentagon papers" by Dr. Ellsberg and the universal acclamation of his action was greatly aided, of course, by the press with its liberal tradition and with its professional interest. It was, however, more than that. It was accepted as evidence that authority could not be trusted, least of all when it could keep its deliberations secret.

The radical view, which carries further the liberal postulate of man as his own creator, demands that all institutions and all of society become transparent, that all become visible, that walls be torn down, that boundaries be washed away. Man can become his own creator, completely self-determining only in a completely transparent society. A collectivistic liberalism that has slipped its moorings and a new self-confident radicalism form a common front here.

Together with this insistence on transparency or publicity, there has been a marked but ambivalent concern about privacy in the past two decades. On the one hand, the enhancement of the powers of observation through electronic technological inventions, and the promulgation of techniques for the study of behavior, have fostered a new desire to protect the privacy of individuals. But this desire is largely a concern for privacy from the authorities of established institutions in government, business, and universities who have become more curious about their citizens, employees, customers, and pupils. It is a desire for privacy from institutions that have grown so large because so much has been demanded from them. It is a demand for privacy that is at the same time a denial of the legitimacy of established authorities.

On the other hand, however, there has been very much less interest in the private sphere as an area of seclusion from perception by others. This has for many decades been an object of invasion by the press, the popular press at first and later the "quality" press, and this intrusiveness has been justified by appeals to the liberal principle of the freedom of the press. Yet, one of the saints of collectivist liberalism, Louis Brandeis, was also the author of what, for a very long time, was the most elaborate argument for respect for the private sphere and its protection from the invasion of malignant or idle curiosity. His concern in this regard has almost been forgotten.

The romantic bohemian strand in collectivistic liberalism was never very attentive to privacy and particularly the privacy of the erotic sphere. Radicalism of the newer sort, unlike Marxism which was rather Victorian in this respect, has been indifferent to the value of personal privacy, except in the face of institutional authority. The commune has given institutional form to this indifference toward personal privacy. Collectivist liberalism in its latest phase has assimilated this indifference. The rule of publicity has been extended.

The strains of governing a society of indescribable complexity in which multitudinous voices, hitherto silent, have become clamorously demanding, have been very trying. Wants rise faster than resources and capacities to satisfy them. On top of this, scientific knowledge—ranging from scientific knowledge about the structure of the atom to scientific knowledge provided by experts in the surveying of public opinion—has made politicians even more than ever aware of their insufficiencies. Continuous exposure to publicity has the same effect as moral relativism. Neither keeps the center of gravity low enough to keep judgment steady. This misleading appearance of steadiness in policy is the result of the constant pressure of collectivistic liberal opinion.

Moral relativism, at least as a polemical device to weaken the ascendancy of church and state, has long been a device of liberalism. It was never a wholehearted thing adopted without qualifications. It was sort of a moral luxury which did not completely supplant the self-confidence rooted in the acceptance of a secularized variant of Christian belief. Nonetheless it was always there in liberalism and in the increasingly antinomian and antiwestern attitudes of many intellectuals. It has taken a prominent place in collectivistic liberalism. Hence, when faced with the furious criticism which radicalism directed against them, collectivistic liberal intellectuals and politicians had no answer with which they could confidently rebut their critics. Indeed since the radicals were only extending many of the collectivistic liberal arguments, it was difficult for liberals to resist the pressure to move from equality of opportunity towards substantive equality, from the emancipation from tradition by the exercise of reason towards the emancipation from tradition by the expression of emotion and the attainment of "genuine" selfhood, from the prizing of expression of belief toward the freedom of expression of affect, from self-government through representation toward continuous and direct participation, and from the support of the needy towards universal subsidy by government. Collectivist liberals, unsteadily attached to the balance of their values through their commitment to moral relativism, and at the same time facing charges of inconsistency with their own principles and of being "elitist" and self-interested, could not withstand the force of the radical criticism.

Under the fire of radical criticism, collectivistic liberalism also became prone to the loose praise of revolution. Ever since the beginning of the present century it had had a *faiblesse* for revolutions in other countries; revolution was a way for backward countries suffering from aristocracy or foreign rule to enter on the road of progress. The crisis of the late 1960s made the adherents of revolution abroad think sympathetically of revolution in their own country. They found themselves in a position in which the burden of proof lay on them to show that their own "system" could achieve the ends sought by revolutionaries, and they were not confident that they could supply that proof. "Radical chic" was one trivial manifestation of their going over to belief in the rightfulness of revolution. For some time, any public disturbance, any unconstitutional violence which designated itself as "leftist" was accredited by collectivistic liberals. "Revolutionaries" were accorded the sanction of "history"; they came to be regarded as the authentic instrument of the purposes of history. Those who set themselves against this were classified as "rightists." It became fashionable among intellectuals who had, for all they knew, been liberals, to espouse the illiberal revolutionary ideas of radicalism. After all, were not these ideas an extension, a logical and consistent application of liberal ideals which held out the desirability of extending to all members of society the goods and conditions of self-discovery and fulfillment that hitherto only some had possessed? If liberals had been critical of authority, was it not right to go further and to deny its legitimacy? If equality of opportunity was liberal, was it not right for those who did not possess it to commit crimes "in protest" against the society which denied them such opportunities? All these activities coalesced into an image of an anticipated revolution.

For the present, the exhilarated anticipation of a "revolution" in the United States has passed. The affection remains.

For much of the nineteenth century and a part of the twentieth century liberalism could be contrasted with fanaticism. Its belief in progress by small and steady increments and its devotion to rational discussion moderated its demands and its way of expressing them. Its rationalism and its unsympathetic attitude toward tradition did, it is true, make it prone to a doctinaire, schematic application of its principles but fanaticism was in general avoided. This cannot be said equally for the more recent rhetoric of collectivistic liberalism; it has acquired some of the rhetorical decoration as well as the substance of radicalism. Political discourse under conditions of modern democracy and mass communication tends in any case towards hyperbole and the melodramatic. Collectivistic liberal speeches now are well-embellished with ill-defined but no less bitter words of accusation: "racism," "elitism," "fascism," "genocide," "cold warriors," and the like. Such words derive from a Manichaean distinction between the "children of light" and the "children of darkness." They inject an air of commotion into political discourse that is not conducive to the moderation of conflict or to the maintenance of a sense of affinity which reaches across the lines of partisanship.

Collectivistic liberalism in its noisy decline toward radicalism has lost much of its civility. It bespeaks a lack of concern for the whole of society. It has become a crusade on behalf of the "poor" and "minorities" and of its own moral outlook on a scale and a manner which offends the larger interests of society and other sections of the population as much as did the references to "bloated capitalists" of an earlier generation of radicalism. It has become disregardful of the moral outlook of the working and lower-middle classes, which it regards as plainly reactionary for their dislike of the emancipationist views of the collectivistic liberal intellectuals. It

has forgotten that liberty of opinion and liberty of organization were intended to serve the common good, and not just
the good of individuals or the groups into which they formed
themselves.

Contemporary radicalism has absorbed enough of Marxism
to retain the peculiar sectional partisanship of that doctrine.
It speaks of "the workers" rarely, of "the poor" or "the people" far more. Its aim is to change society so that "the poor"
will no longer have to suffer inferiority of status or remuneration; incidentally it is to see to it also that the protectors of
the poor also benefit by ample opportunities, remuneration,
and power. The former is a worthy goal; the latter a repug-
nant self-seeking. But even the former goal is worthy only in
a constellation of other goals, and not as the sole or deter-
mining one.

The assimilation of elements of radicalism into collectivistic liberalism has been rendered easier by changes in
radicalism itself. The cracking of Marxist orthodoxy after
1956 and the crystallization of the New Left released radicals
from their fixation on the "working class" as the destined
agent of revolutionary possibilities. The "working class"
had obviously been heedless of this mission which "history"
had assigned to it. Most radicals had had enough of it. The
"poor" became the stick with which the dog of bourgeois
society could be beaten; they replaced the working class
as the favorite of revolutionary hopes. Collectivistic liberalism—with its inheritance of the old concern with the
"debtor and dependent classes," with the weak, poor, and
friendless—found the "poor" a more congenial category
to which "to devote its solicitude" than the "working class."
The latter was a term with Marxist overtones and hence
was implicitly hostile towards the philanthropic strand
of collectivistic liberalism; the real working class was moreover made up of persons who on the whole looked after
themselves—except when unemployed—and who were
independent in spirit and did not offer so many opportunities
for the services of the welfare-providing state. Among others,
this change reduced a barrier which had hitherto separated

collectivistic liberalism from radicalism.

Another change which has aided radical influence is the common intellectual culture. Contemporary radicalism, although drawing much from Marxism, has also absorbed a lot of contemporary academic social science. The theme of "bureaucratization" as a main feature of contemporary society is of course drawn from Max Weber; words like "lifestyle" come from the same source. The New Left in the United States has been an academic matter. It was supported and given its doctrine by teachers and students and its main activities have occurred in universities and colleges. Collectivistic liberals are to be found mainly among the highly educated; "middle America" might accept the subsidies offered by collectivistic liberalism in power but it does not like its outlook. Furthermore, radicalism no longer has a "special relationship" to aesthetic bohemianism. Liberalism, even collectivistic liberalism, was always more puritanical and traditional in its erotic and aesthetic dispositions than radicalism, which early formed an alliance with aesthetic bohemianism. However, it could be said that Greenwich Village now embraces a large part of the educated class through-out the United States. As a result of these changes, to a far greater extent than was the case a half century ago, collectivistic liberals and radicals share a common culture. The shift from collectivistic liberalism to radicalism was not a drastic conversion; that is why so few of those liberals perceive the change in themselves. If they do call themselves radicals—some do—they think that they are still faithful to their old convictions. They are probably correct.

The instances which I have given of certain ideals of radical ethos—such as free undisciplined expression, of equality of reward, of individuality, and of the attainment of perfection and plenitude—are alien to liberalism as well as hostile to it. So is the idea of a universally active and omnicompetent government. These ideas will destroy liberalism, even collectivistic liberalism, if their temptations are not resisted. Yet it would be incorrect historically and a disservice to the rehabilitation of liberalism to refuse to see the lines of affinity which link both kinds of liberalism, at least in their points of departure, to radicalism. They show the dangers of utopian self-transfiguration which lie in wait for all social and political outlooks when they turn into doctrines and cast off traditional inhibitions.

8

Collectivistic liberalism in the United States has triumphed. Much of its program has been realized; even administrations which purport to be conservative have accepted its accomplishments or have been unable to undo them. It has also triumphed intellectually; those who disagree are thought at best to be eccentrics, at worst, misanthropes—and misogynists. Its demand for the freedom of the individual has been realized far more extensively and intensively than was anticipated or even initially sought. Its demand for governmental regulation and provision has been gratified to a far greater extent than had been believed possible by its earlier proponents. Yet it has recurrently been said by radical intellectuals that liberalism has failed. Many persons who had always regarded themselves as liberals—in the collectivistic, American sense—have agreed. Some did not go so far; they said it was "on trial"—obviously, in a trial in which radicals were judges and prosecutors. It was conceded by collectivistic liberals that if the "system" were found wanting, then it was to be jettisoned and rightly so.

In the 1960s, liberalism was charged with having failed to satisfy the demands of the poor, and the public disorders of that period were, it was said, protests against these failures to eliminate poverty. It was also charged with failure to renounce a foreign policy which entailed the support of reactionary governments against those which were popular, democratic, and socialist.

The radicalization of collectivistic liberalism had reached the point where the liberals regarded it as fashionable to say that liberalism has failed. They seemed to think that they would stand condemned by right-thinking persons if they did not stress the horrible failures of their society. It could hardly have been otherwise when "poverty" was recurrently being redefined by social scientists and social workers so that it was necessary to run faster and faster to remain in the same place.

Can it, however, be said in good faith that liberalism has "failed?" On the contrary, it seems to have succeeded better than its chief competitors.

The late John Plamenatz once enumerated the "rights to which liberals in the West attach great importance." These were "the right to an education which enables you to assess the opportunities (occupations and ways of life) that society offers to its members; the right to choose your occupation provided you have the requisite skills; the right to get the special training needed to acquire these skills, provided you are capable of profiting by it; the right to choose your partner in marriage; the right to be gainfully employed; the right to a minimal standard of living, whether or not you are so employed; the right to privacy, especially in your own home; the right to express and publish your opinions; the right to form or join associations for any purpose that appeals to you and does not invade the rights of others; the right to be tried for alleged offenses, and to have your disputes settled by courts not subject to political pressures; the right to take part in choosing at free elections the persons who make policy at least at the highest level, in the communities or associations you belong to."[3]

If we look at the societies of Western Europe and North America at the beginning of the nineteenth century before liberalism became the belief of those who were active in politics, and the present situation after more than a century and a half of autonomist and collectivistic liberalism as it was incorporated into the programs of various political parties, we will see that much has been achieved in the realization of this "program." If we compare the situation in these countries of Western Europe and North America with the countries like those of Eastern Europe, Asia and Africa where liberalism is denounced as a bourgeois deception and where socialism is offered as a vast improvement, we will see how successful liberalism has been in contrast with its adversaries and self-proclaimed competitors. In some respects liberalism has been more successful than its great nineteenth century proponents intended.

Nonetheless, the success of liberalism—the realization of the ideas of liberalism in the practice of contemporary Western societies—leaves much to be desired from the standpoint of collectivistic liberalism. Some of these deficiencies are indeed indirect results of autonomistic liberalism. Others are results of the excesses of collectivisitic liberalism.

There is too much unemployment of persons who seriously attempt to find jobs and fail to do so. There is still discrimination against blacks simply on grounds of their being black. The large cities of the United States have become an eyesore and a menace. The housing conditions of some parts of the semiskilled and unskilled sections of the working classes are unsatisfactory. The costs of medical care are higher than genuinely ill persons with low incomes can pay. Inflation is a curse to all. Criminality has increased. Some of these defects are the results of collectivistic liberalism; for instance, unemployment is partly a result of minimum wage laws and of government fiscal policies which hamper investment. Inflation is partly a product of the determination to use the powers and resources of government to control the economy and to provide for the poor and weak; the condition of the cities is largely a result of governmental policies promoted by collectivistic liberalism; criminality is in part a function of the liberal restraint on the repressive powers of the police; etc. There are many other features of our society that are unsatisfactory from conservative and autonomist liberal standpoints, but these are not relevant when we are considering the successes of the collectivistic liberal movement of ideas and policies.

All these notwithstanding, the civil, intellectual, and artistic liberty and the material conditions of life for the vast majority of the population are far superior to what they are in regimes which allege that they have gone far beyond collectivistic liberalism. Some of the critics of liberalism are not radicals; they are social democrats. Although they take no pleasure in the actual accomplishments of existing regimes that have been thoroughgoing in their socialism, namely, the regimes of Eastern Europe, they persist nonetheless in holding out socialism as superior to liberalism.

The myth of the universally curative powers of socialism seems almost unexpungible from the human mind in our country. Socialism has certainly not been a success in any country. In the existing socialist–Communist, totalitarian societies—the economies are failures even from their own standpoint, and politically they are, of course, destructive of even the degree of freedom which the mass of the population was able to acquire under the regimes that preceded communism. In the democratic-socialist countries—which remain largely capitalistic in their economies and which are governed by socialist parties, alone or in coalition, like the Federal German Republic, the Netherlands, and the Scandinavian countries—the alleged socialism is in fact collectivistic liberalism and it is supported by capitalistic enterprise. The successful democratic-socialist countries are what they are largely because of the success of autonomistic and collectivistic liberalism and not because of the successes of socialism. The freedom they enjoy is an autonomistic-liberal inheritance; their high standard of living and their elaborate and pervasive welfare services are made possible by the productivity of their capitalist economies.

There is no question that liberalism—both autonomist and collectivist—has succeeded, that communism has failed, and that democratic socialism has not itself been responsible for the successes it enjoys. The absence of public liberties in Communist countries and their amplitude in liberal and democratic socialist countries is surely evidence of that. The condition of intellectual life in science, scholarship, and literature is evidence of it. The condition of economic well-being of the mass of the population is evidence of it. So real is the success of the liberal societies that those which are as diametrically different from them as the authoritarian and oligarchical societies of Asia, Eastern Europe, and Africa, insist that they too provide for the liberty and material well-being of their peoples, or that they will do so as soon as it is feasible. Thoughtful democratic socialists admit that their socialist forerunners went much too far in disparaging the achievements of liberalism as a transient, historical phenomenon, or as the by-product of a class interest. In Eastern Europe, courageous persons testify to the value of liberty at great risk to themselves. Even the most extreme terrorists allege that they are commiting their desperate deeds in order to establish regimes that will provide the freedom and material well-being possessed by liberal societies. This is evidence that despite the denunciations of liberalism, its accomplishments are so great and impressive that even its enemies claim its merits for themselves. Their hypocrisy is the compliment which vice pays to virtue.

Nonetheless, the achievements of collectivistic liberalism are not generally esteemed in countries where they have been most marked. They are disparaged or denied. The deficiencies of their liberal societies preoccupy the minds of many intellectuals. Autonomist liberals who call themselves "conservatives" (which they are not) naturally are very critical of the methods and accomplishments of collectivistic liberalism; collectivistic liberals who do not call themselves radicals heap abuse on their own position in the idiom of radicalism. Even where they have not yielded to the temptations of the fashionable radicalism, they see nothing but the flaws of their own society and complain that their program is not being realized. They are so concerned with innovation and the correction of shortcomings that the positive achievements of the institutions of a liberal society pass unnoticed and unacknowledged. The achievements are there but they are so taken for granted that they are not recognized. What has been accomplished, even if admitted, is thought to be insufficient.

The failures of Communist regimes are failures to live up to the vague promises of "genuine freedom," of "workers' rule," of greater material well-being which are contained implicitly and explicitly in the writings of Marx and Engels and their epigoni. They are the failures of Communist regimes to live up to the ideals of liberalism which they appropriated without acknowledgement. They are failures of "Soviet democracy" to be "a thousand times more democratic than bourgeois democracy." Communism was alleged to realize the ideals of liberalism, which could not be realized under capitalism. It has certainly not done so. The standpoint from which communism is criticized within the Communist regimes testifies to the vitality of liberal traditions, to the urge to discover them anew, and to the desire to reinstate them under conditions of harsh and brutal adversity.

The criticisms of liberalism that are made within liberal-democratic countries also testify to the vitality of liberal traditions. On the one side, collectivistic liberalism is criticized by a more austere autonomist liberalism which holds firmly to its central belief in the value of the private sphere of individual freedom and initiative, and which would confine the power of governments. There is practically no criticism of liberalism from a conservative position which would replace the rule of law by laws that deal differently with individuals in accordance with their lineage, that would establish a hierarchy of status and privilege in accordance with differences in lineage and affinity, that would make inheritance and prescription the decisive rule of society. There is no conservative criticism of liberalism which asserts as self-evident the rightness of tradition and authority. The critics of liberalism who call themselves conservatives and who are called "reactionaries" by radicals and collectivistic liberals are in fact liberals, more stringent and more faithful to the tradition of liberalism than the collectivistic liberals whom they criticize and who criticize them. For better or for worse, much that was valid in the conservative tradition has been put aside, together with what was ethically intolerable to the progressivist and individualistic attitudes of liberalism.

Collectivistic liberalism sees only autonomist liberalism as its enemy nowadays. It sees nothing inimical to its ideals in radicalism. It might disapprove lightly of the tactics of radicalism; it might say at times that radicalism goes a little too far. Insofar as it is uneasy in the presence of radicalism, it is because it regards radicalism as the keeper of its conscience and as the purer embodiment of those values which it most esteems.

9

Liberal politicians and theorists in the past assumed the moral rightness of a liberal regime. They seemed to believe that once it became established its merits would appear to be so great to all its beneficiaries that there would be no danger of its subversion from within. Locke was more realistic: he thought that there was a danger of subversion by atheists who did not feel bound by their sworn undertakings, although he did not seem to believe that they had an alternative regime which they would, in their infidelity, attempt to establish. Liberal politicians and theorists were negligent about the dangers to the liberal regime from subversion by those who would benefit from its toleration. Furthermore, contending as they did against mercantilist and absolutist regimes which resisted their replacement, liberals assumed that those who were responsible for governing a society would, as a matter of course, believe in its rightness and would not freely and voluntarily yield when pressed to change their fundamental arrangements.

But this is not wholly characteristic of the governing contemporary liberal regimes, and even less true is it of the intellectuals devoted to the collectivistic liberalism their regimes practice. In the United States, collectivistic liberals have become so devoted to the liberties integral to liberalism that they are apprehensive of any actions which might be needed to save it, particularly if those actions would involve disadvantages for radicals; they are indeed sympathetic with the carriers of ideas that are subversive of the liberal order and think that there is much that is right in their arguments. Partly, too, they are fearful of regressing into the tyrannical attitudes and practices of "McCarthyism."

The dangers to liberalism posed by the transformation of collectivistic liberalism into radicalism are not the same as the dangers which the Communists constituted in the liberal-democratic regime in Czechoslovakia in 1948 or as the Bolsheviks did in October 1917, or the armed *putschists* in any black African or Middle Eastern country of the last few decades. There is no danger in the United States for the time being that a group of armed revolutionaries—led by *The New York Review of Books*—will "seize power" through the commandeering of arsenals and garrisons, railway yards and airports, centers of communication, etc., or that nests of civil servants and soldiers coordinated with a revolutionary armed force under the leadership of a new revolutionary clique outside the government will announce that they are henceforward in charge of affairs.

The domestic safety of collectivistic liberalism today is in a far different position. Its instability lies within its own standpoint; it lies in the tendency of those who are powerful in it to slide unwittingly and without any sense of contradiction or inappropriateness toward a regime governed by the radical outlook. It lies in their acceptance of elements of the radical view as self-evidently correct. It has been said repeatedly, ever since Joseph Schumpeter wrote it in *Capitalism, Socialism and Democracy,* that intellectuals are the grave-diggers of the liberal order. The intellectuals are not alone in this grave-digging action. Many politicians, civil servants, and businessmen have joined them; they accept the extension of collectivistic liberalism into radicalism. The transformation by extension is very patchy and uneven; far from all collectivistic liberals have been swept into it. Some resist the transformation. Its progress is undramatic and unannounced. This makes its progress that much easier.

10

In the United States today, the political terrain is almost entirely divided between autonomist liberalism and collectivistic liberalism. The autonomist liberalism is not unalloyed. In most of its varieties it contains a definite admixture of genuine conservatism; it has also incorporated a modest amount of collectivistic liberalism. Among the varieties of autonomist liberals, there are few simon-pure "Manchesterians." Collectivistic liberalism has been making the run since the great depression of the 1930s. In the last decade of its advance, it has begun to turn toward radicalism, for which its proponents used to have a protective sympathy and which now has become an imitative sympathy. The autonomist liberals have allowed the designation of "liberal" to become the possession, nearly exclusively so, of the collectivistic liberals.

As a result, when we think of the outlook that is now called liberal in the United States, we think of a person who is hostile to capitalism, a strong advocate of civil liberties especially for radicals and revolutionaries, and who is critical of "machine politicians." He is very critical of the government but he automatically turns to governmental action to remedy every wrong which he sees in abundance in American society. He is in favor of larger welfare programs and favors rigorous, extensive, and penetrating governmental regulation of private business enterprise. He is for the "poor" against the "rich." He is nominally and selectively an "egalitarian." He is against "respectability" and the idea that some persons are better than others—although in practice he departs widely from this belief. He is for trade unions, favoring unions against employers, although he is discomfited by "bread and butter unionism," by gangsterism in unions, and by the lack of a sufficiently progressive outlook in union leadership. He favors the right of public employees to strike. He is critical of "law and order" which means the repression of criminals, and he favors penal arrangements only if they "rehabilitate" criminals. He is a "progressivist" who thinks that the new is better than the old and that scientific research is the proper instrument for continuous progress. He is a hedonist and, although critical of "materialistic values," is eager for the multiplied possession of material goods. He is strong for academic freedom including political agitation by academics within universities, favors "relevance" of academic studies but wants universities not to be "too involved with the present system"; he thinks that criticism of existing institutions should be one of the main functions of universities. He views with disdain the difference between "manliness" and "femininity" and would obliterate them and all differences between the sexes. He is against puritanism. He favors the free publication and sale of pornography. He is critical of advertising and favors public subsidy of television. He favors abortion on demand, free governmentally provided child-care centers and a national health service. He is critical of Communism but opposes others who are critical of Communists; he favors the Soviet Union and, even when critical of it, regards it as more often on the correct side in international politics than is the United States. He regards American foreign policy as unduly aggressive and as supporting reactionary regimes everywhere. He is critical of "patriotism," which he regards as "jingoism," but he is very sympathetic with the "nationalism" of the Third World.

The adherents of these beliefs have been so successful in establishing their hegemony in public opinion, particularly the opinion of the more educated classes of American society, that they have made the autonomist liberals think of themselves as "right-wing" or as conservatives. Collectivist liberals have become so ignorant of their own traditions that they think that they alone are "liberal" and that everyone else who does not share or enjoy their sympathies is a "reactionary" or "conservative." They are wrong in this belief, although they are right in seeing that there are significant differences between themselves and the autonomist liberals.

The autonomist liberal does indeed incorporate into his liberal outlook some important elements of conservatism. The Republican in the United States does indeed embody such a combination. He believes in the rightfulness of individual initiative and voluntary action and the abstention of the state from activity in the corresponding sphere. He is in favor of civil equality and of equality in the assessment of

achievement and personal merit. He believes in the rightfulness of a commensurate relationship between achievement
and reward. He believes in the desirability and necessity of
progress through exertion and technology and the application of science. He is a hedonist in that he believes in the
goodness of material possession, in the ownership of physical property, of ample supplies of food, physical conve-
niences, facilities in transportation, etc. He is what used to
be called materialistic. He believes in the rightness of popular sovereignty through representative government and the
separation of powers. He affirms the validity of the freedom
of intellectual expression—although in the past he has occasionally supported the restriction of the freedom of intellectual expression by radicals. He accepts the rightfulness of the
rule of law and hence, in the broader sense, the rightfulness
of law and order and the obligation of government to maintain it and of citizens to observe it. He believes that there is a
significant difference between criminality and lawfulness.
He believes in the virtue of civility, although in historical
fact, he has at times diverged in the direction of the protection and advancement of the interests of private business
enterprises when these have been disadvantageous to the rest
of society—for example, the privileges of tariffs and monopoly. He regards the Third World as backward rather than
as the locus of major moral and political values.

The preponderantly autonomist liberal elements are combined with certain elements of conservatism such as patriotism and local loyalties, piety, appreciation of the family
and of the virtues of manliness and femininity, an inclination
towards traditionality. Certain elements of conservatism are
excluded: deference of authority is greatly hedged about;
the evaluation of lineage is restricted. Traditionalism is likewise given a limited place. Deference and traditionalism have
tractive power but they are confined by the values of autonomist liberalism.

The puritanism which autonomist liberalism has carried
with it has made this outlook less open aesthetically, less
drawn towards the culture of Europe and other continents.

Its old cultural Anglophilia has yielded to its patriotism.

It must be emphasized that liberalism—although it is in some respects conservative in the only sense which makes sense—is for better or for worse "progressive." It is certainly not "reactionary," unless that term is used in the radical sense of being opposed to violent revolutionary replacement of existing government and the establishment of what radicals understand as a reign of complete equality.

The world is a far more complex thing than modern radicalism, with its naive contrast of "right" and "left," has ever dreamed.

11

Can collectivistic liberalism be saved from its degenerative potentialities? Can it renounce the sympathies—sometimes the sympathies of bad conscience, sometimes the sympathies which arise from the wish to be consistent and thoroughgoing, and sometimes the sympathies of a desire to be up-to-date—which have caused it to be extended and transformed into radicalism?

Every outlook can become an ideology, through the distortion of certain of its values toward extremes and through the neglect of others. In becoming such, it makes itself unwittingly into the protector and ally of movements of opinion, campaigns, and organizations which not only bring it into discredit but which deform it and endanger its continued existence. Conservatism and autonomist liberalism, too, have similar potentialities. There were European conservatives who thought, at least for a time, that Fascism and National Socialism were a form of conservatism appropriate to a time of crisis. Most of them were painfully disillusioned by the spuriousness of the conservatism of these movements once they attained state power. In the United States, there were conservative and liberal Republicans who tolerated and helped Senator Joseph McCarthy in his campaign of persecution in the decade that followed the Second World War. They had reservations about his vulgarity and harshness,

they thought that he "overdid things"; nonetheless they
thought that he and they were proper allies because they
had the same cause at heart. They were patriots, they were
against governmental dominance over economy and society,
and they were therefore opposed to Communism and Soviet
infiltration and expansion. Why, they might have asked
themselves, should they not support a politician who by and
large espoused the same values as themselves? It was true that
they also were attached to the toleration of divergent opinions, to the separation of powers, to the rule of law and
hence to the right to fair trial, and to the superiority of
representative institutions over plebiscitary rule. For the
time being, however, they were willing to suspend these
other beliefs and to give greater weight to these values which
McCarthy seemed to espouse. In the end the alliance was dis-
solved when they realized that McCarthy's procedures af-
fronted their other values and were not necessary to attain
the ends which they shared with him.

The attitude of one current of social-democratic opinion
toward Communism and to the Soviet Union in the period
between the wars, and even since then, has a certain similari-
ty to this. These social democrats—usually not in the leadership of their parties, except in Italy—believed that fundamentally, in what is most important, they and the Communists held the same ends: the abolition of private ownership
of the means of production as the indispensable precondition for realizing a reign of plenitude and freedom. The absence of political freedom in the Soviet Union they regarded
as transient, necessitated by conditions of emergency and the
"hostility of capitalist countries." The shortcomings of the
Soviet economy, where they were perceived and admitted,
they regarded as of the same transiency as the abrogation
of political freedom, when they did not deny them altogether as a fabrication of anti-Communist scholars and
journalists. They were so confident in the economic superiority and greater justice of a regime without private property in the means of production that they were willing, despite
the destruction of the elements of liberalism to which they

were attached, to place those elements in a secondary position. They were willing to suspend their concern for the liberal values which distinguished social democracy from Communism. Their unquestioning acceptance of traditional Marxian doctrine and the refusal of Marxists to acknowledge autonomist liberalism as one of their ancestors made them believe that there was a basic affinity between themselves and the Communists who declared themselves to be the sole heirs of true Marxism. They averted their minds from the affinities which bound them to liberalism.

So it is with many contemporary collectivistic liberals. They have slipped into a radical position because it seems to be only an extension of their liberal beliefs, and a more insistent demand for their more consistent application. Their long-standing prejudice in favor of the Russian revolution supports this complaisance.

Many of them, of the older generation which supported the New Deal, had been drawn into the fellow-traveling of the 1930s. Some are still under the impression that a country which has abolished private property in the means of production and established a "planned economy" to replace it must be on the right side of the movement of history. So it was with the older generation and those now in the fifth and sixth decades of their span of life. Those still younger found congeniality in the New Left bond and were spiritually formed by the student revolution of the 1960s. There is no sharp line separating them from radicalism.

Neither liberalism nor radicalism has been promulgated explicitly as a doctrine, and neither is advocated by a single organization such as a Communist party. Hence the boundaries are vague, and permeation of radicalism into collectivistic liberalism is easier. Many of the tenets of radicalism seem only more thoroughgoing, less qualified extensions and applications of collectivistic liberalism, just as the Marxism-Leninism of the Communists seemed in the 1920s to be a more thoroughgoing and less inhibited extension and application of the social-democratic version of Marxism. Like Communism, which annuls the ideals of social democracy by its "thoroughgoingness" and "unqualifiedness," so radicalism annuls the ideals of liberalism.

Can collective liberalism stop its slide toward radicalism? To do so will require that it become critical of those elements in its own outlook which have brought it where it is. It will have to renounce its beliefs in the omnicompetence of government and in the solubility of all problems by governmental action. It will have to renounce its belief that if any institution or activity is worthwhile, it should be conducted or at least subsidized by government. It will have to renounce its belief that every important decision in life falls within the political sphere; it will have to give up its belief in the primacy of the "political kingdom." It will have to reanimate its skepticism about the necessary beneficence and dependability of government authority and its capacity for self-restraint. It will have to reconcile itself to the limited capacities of human beings, individually or collectively, to govern their own lives and the lives of others in a wholly rational and scientific manner. It will have to recognize the value of traditions and the foolhardiness of the belief that every innovation is in itself a good thing. It will have to detach itself from its dogmatically unthinking belief in moral relativism. It will have to show more respect for traditional moral standards and traditional standards of taste. It will have to acknowledge that the care of the common good is not exhausted by the care of "the poor" or of particular ethnic groups, designated as "minorities." It will have to acquire and exercise more common sense and free itself from the doctrinaire application of formulae, such as "quotas," "racial balance," and from salvation by any recipes, such as "busing." It will have to recognize its closer affinity with the autonomist liberalism that is now wrongly called "conservatism," than with the radicalism towards which it has been moving. It will in fact have to learn something from traditional conservatism regarding the value of social order, patriotism, and locality. It will have to remind itself of the value of civil, intellectual and artistic and literary liberties which it enjoys. It will have to give up its belief that any government, party, or movement which calls itself "socialist" is automatically a good thing. It should draw a moral lesson from the courageous efforts of a few hardy souls in Communist countries who take great risks by seeking to establish there the liberties which have for a long time been well established and are relatively secure in the liberal-democratic countries.

None of these changes will require it to renounce its traditions of humanitarianism and of political democracy, or its commitment to the improvement of social arrangements. It will have to become, however, more aware of the limits of human powers and that every human action and every undertaking has costs that are economic and more than economic.

Autonomist liberalism must also renew itself. For one, it must see that there is more to its tradition than the market, crucially important though it is. It must broaden its interests and reassert with greater force its ethical foundations and its cultural interests. It must go beyond scoring easily made points through calling attention to the enormities of collectivistic liberalism at work. It must be careful not to forget the virtue of compassion simply because collectivistic liberals have become incontinent in its espousal. It must heighten its awareness of the ties which bind it on the one side to collectivistic liberalism and on the other to traditional conservatism. Incidentally, it must also cease being on the defensive and regarding itself as somewhat eccentric. It must leave behind the perception of itself as "right" on a continuum of "right" and left"; this is a construction of radicalism and collectivistic liberalism which confuses minds and darkens counsel.

The cause of liberalism is not a lost cause, but much reflection and many repairs are needed if it is not to become one.

Notes

1. I am aware of the unsatisfactoriness of this mode of designating that current of liberalism which continues the older liberal tradition. But to call it traditional liberalism would be misleading since collectivistic liberalism too has a venerable and effective tradition. To call it "anti-statist" would be negative as well as inelegant. The liberalism which I wish to designate is individualistic but also is attached to the free action, under law, of corporate bodies. "Pluralistic" liberalism has too many other overtones. Hence "autonomist liberalism," unattractive though the term sounds, corresponds most closely to the kind of liberalism I wish to designate.

2. It may be mentioned in passing that before the Second World War, when the universities had been severely constricted by the depression, heads of universities were adamant in refusing to seek the financial support of the federal government. They feared that it would lead to governmental intrusion into the affairs of the universities. After the war the universities accepted and then became dependent on the financial support of the federal government. They have since learned that the fears of their predecessors of the 1930s were far from groundless.

3. John Plamenatz, "Liberalism," in *Dictionary of the History of Ideas*, ed. Phillip Paul Wiener (New York: Charles Scribner's Sons, 1973), vol. 3, p. 52.

6

The Long Life
of Liberalism
Michael Mandelbaum

What is liberalism? On the evidence of the essays in this
volume it is not easy to say. Each author offers his own definition and each definition differs from the others. Each
author must fashion his own because there is no catechism,
no single authoritative document, no seminal thinker to
whom to refer. What is in question is a set of ideas, a series
of principles that have been firmly embedded in political
history. The life of liberalism has been experience, not logic—
or literature. So the study of liberalism is not an exercise in
textual exegesis. It is the scrutiny of ideas that men have
held, on which they have acted, and that have shaped the
history and institutions they have made.

Here liberalism differs from its two foremost historical
opponents, conservatism and socialism. Conservatism has
often been simply an attitude—a distaste for change, especially rapid change—rather than a coherent body of ideas. Where
there has been more to conservatism than this it has been
the defense of privilege, hierarchy, and other forms of
inequality. But conservatism has defended inequality not in

the abstract, but as it has been embodied in social institutions like the Church, the monarchy, and the aristocracy. Conservatives have argued that these were part of the natural order of things, since they had developed over many centuries, and that they gave society the blessings of order and tranquility. The conservative view of society has been an organic one, with each estate and class having its own part to play.

This version of conservatism has all but died out in the second half of the twentieth century. For it is the defense of the old regime. And the old regime is gone. This is so not only in the West, but all over the world. Scattered pockets of tradition do remain where industrial civilization has yet to appear, communities whose proclaimed social rules favor some of its members over others. But these are shrinking and disappearing. Inequality, of course, is still an important principle of social and political organization in many places. But it is called by other names, and justified in new ways undreamed of by conservatives.

Socialism is a term used more frequently in recent history than conservatism. Socialist slogans have been inscribed on the banners of parties and movements the world over. But socialism has not been a set of ideas intimately bound up with the practice of politics and government in the same way that liberalism has been. There is, it is true, a great corpus of socialist writing, socialist plans, socialist theory, criticism, and even party platforms that profess to be socialist. And there are states that claim to be organized according to the principles of socialism. But these states are divided—literally—into two camps and categories. The "socialist" states that are aligned with the greatest liberal power, the United States, are themselves, in essence, liberal societies. Those that are grouped around the Soviet Union are societies under authoritarian rule whose economies are managed by central direction; only political activity sponsored by the Communist party is legitimate, and an all-power planning authority sets quotas for investment and targets for production. Western socialism is liberalism adulterated with doses of welfare measures that vary in strength from country to country. In the East socialism is not, as Lenin proclaimed, electrification plus soviets. It is, rather, Pareto, or Djilas— or, under Stalin, Ivan the Terrible—plus Gosplan. Nor is this an unfamiliar combination. In ancient Egypt supreme political power resided with the pharaoh, and economic life was governed by edict. Without the modern means of transportation and communication the pharaoh's powers were less extensive than are the Communist party's. And the economic goals of ancient Egypt differed from those of its contemporary counterpart. The Soviet planning authority builds steel mills, not pyramids. But in broad outline the two political and economic systems resemble each other and are equally "socialist."[1]

Liberalism is the one true modern ideology. It is the work of no single theorist, the property of no particular group, but, unlike socialism and conservatism, it is carried in the hearts of citizens, written into the laws, and practiced in the everyday political life of existing, functioning political communities. Or at least liberalism is a far purer contemporary ideology, in this sense of the term, than the other two. Liberal societies are those whose three realms—political, economic, and, for want of a better word, cultural—are organized in distinctive ways that both resemble and reinforce each other.[2]

The heart of liberal society, from which it takes its name, is political liberty. Historically the enemy of liberty has been government. And so liberal states have built shelters, in the form of constitutions, to protect citizens from arbitrary and overbearing authority. In the modern era liberalism, as Giovanni Sartori notes in his essay, has meant constitutionalism.[3] Constitutions protect procedural liberties like freedom of speech and assembly and trial by jury. And they ordinarily guard another kind of freedom; the right of citizens to select their government. Democracy is a cardinal feature of political liberalism. This is not the direct democracy of the Athenian forum, or Rousseau's ideal republic where all participate in the single "general will," or the New England town meeting, in each of which citizens pass judgment on every issue that affects the community. It is representative democracy, in which citizens exercise control by proxy, at one remove. Liberal societies have developed an array of channels through which individual preferences can be expressed. Political parties and elections exist to select representatives. There are arenas for representation—parliaments, assemblies, and legislatures. And there are groups that stand between the citizen and the arena of representation, and outside the formal system of governance, and that also serve as channels for popular preferences. These are the secondary associations, whose special importance in the United States Tocqueville reported. The apparatus of representation, like the protection of individual liberties, is central to political liberalism.

Economic liberalism is the use of the market for carrying out three major tasks of any economy—investment, production, and distribution. The market is a decentralized system. Unlike an edict economy a market economy has many independent centers of decision—firms that produce goods and services and individuals who consume them. But each operates according to certain rules. And all these rules involve the assertion of maximal self-interest, defined as profit.[4] The market has the virtues of harmony and efficiency. The price system coordinates the activities of the millions of individual producers and consumers into a cohesive whole, as if an "invisible hand" were guiding them. And their selfish individual pursuits yield a greater volume of goods and services, at lower prices, than could come from a centrally planned and directed economic scheme.

The market has been called a "system of perfect liberty."[5] The individual is its basic unit. His desires reign supreme. The market offers an ongoing referendum on these desires. When they change producers adjust through the price system. The consumer bids up the price of what he wants and the producer, moved by self-interest, puts his resources into the making of it. Just as in political liberalism the citizen is the ultimate source of authority, so in the market system the consumer is sovereign. And just as a constitution protects the private citizen's political rights, so the market system places the wealth of a society in the hands of citizens, not government. Because the market system includes the private control of capital it is often called "capitalism."

Historically, political and economic liberalism have been associated. They are distinct, as Sartori notes.[6] And they have not always appeared together. Germany and Japan before 1945 had market economies without political liberty. But the saying "free markets make free men" has been true for Great Britain, France, and the United States. The relationship between political and economic liberalism has not been simple or direct.[7] But neither is it coincidental. Political liberty is essential for the smooth functioning of the market. Entrepreneurs must be free to accumulate funds and invest them as and where they choose. Labor must be free to move where the highest wages are available. The old regime was a straitjacket not just for political expression (and popular sovereignty) but for commercial activity. The merchant class, in struggling to be free of state-imposed restraints on commerce, often advanced the cause of political liberty as well.

Conversely, economic liberalism nurtures political freedom. In theory it is possible for a society whose economy is run by edict to grant its citizens a full panoply of political rights. In practice this is unlikely.[8] The governments of such societies have immense authority. The power to plan and supervise all economic activity is enormous, and it would be difficult to deny to a government vested with such power broad authority over political life as well.

A society is more than a mechanism for governing itself and a method for feeding, clothing, and sheltering its people. It has, as well, a "culture,"[9] a "spirit," an attitude toward itself and toward the future. The culture of traditional societies was expressed through religion. But liberalism disestablished religion. In its place came a sense of confidence and optimism, a determination to master the material world and a faith in the power of human reason. The spirit of liberalism has been the religion of progress.

That spirit has been embodied by science. The scientific method, with its rules of verification, puts into practice the faculty of reason. It is a test of truth. And the achievements of science are an ever-advancing measure of progress. To be sure not all the hopes for social improvement that liberals have held have been fulfilled. The kingdom of heaven perpetually fails to arrive on earth. Revolutions fail. But science has seldom been a source of disappointment. Scientists have learned more and more about our world, and ourselves. Their success has earned for science a place in liberal societies that has verged on the sacred.

Science has some signal features in common with political liberalism. It is democratic, a "career open to talents." The standard of admission to what has been called "the republic of science" is achievement, and achievement is the principal criterion for advancement in it. And the rules by which science operates resemble the ones that govern the market. Scientists, like producers, work separately. Although they know what their colleagues are doing they are, to some extent, in competition with them. But they also build on the achievements of others. And the work of every scientist must pass a kind of market test. It must win acceptance in the scientific community by meeting the standards of verification that are part of the scientific method just as a producer must find a demand for his product large enough to give him a profit. Without the stamp of approval of the community the scientist and the producer fail. If he succeeds the scientist may attract co-workers and disciples, and establish a center of research just as, with success, the producer will expand his firm. Finally, the tests for both scientific and market acceptance are disinterested ones. Research that meets the standards of verification passes into the body of shared, approved scientific knowledge, no matter from where or whom it comes. Similarly goods in the marketplace are evaluated according to the neutral standard of price.[10]

Science has been closely tied to political liberalism, for freedom of thought and inquiry are necessary conditions for the scientific enterprise. A scientist must be able to let his

mind wander and follow where it leads. And he must be able
to exchange ideas and information with his colleagues. In the
early modern period science flourished in the Protestant parts
of Europe, where thought and inquiry were freest.[11]

And science has, in turn, buttressed political liberalism.
The republic of science has two wings, both of which partake
of the spirit of progress. "Pure" science seeks to understand
nature. "Applied" science seeks to master it.[12] The fruit of
applied science is technology—the use of tools and machines
to perform mechanical tasks—and technology has transformed liberal societies (and some illiberal ones as well)
from largely agricultural communities with scattered commercial centers into the great urban industrial states of the
twentieth century. It has made the modern world.

There is a connection between technological advance and
the survival and prosperity of political liberalism. For technology spurred economic growth, growth produced affluence, and the affluence of liberal societies has shored up their
political institutions and practices by making social and economic mobility possible. By implication these are part of the
liberal program. The liberty it promises the citizen is not just
the freedom to speak his mind, but the freedom to rise as
high in society as his talents will take him. Economic growth
opened up social space into which men can rise. The American Declaration of Independence affirmed the inalienable
and universal rights of "life, liberty, and the pursuit of
happiness." Affluence sustained the third.[13] And it prevented
the kinds of gross disparities in wealth that marked traditional society, and that would not have easily coexisted with
the political equality that liberalism prescribes. The material
circumstances of the industrial worker's existence are closer
to the corporate executive's than the peasant's way of life
was to the lord's. Economic growth has given liberal societies
a steadily rising standard of living, and this has helped to prevent social conflict, especially conflict that might have arisen
from the unequal distribution of wealth that has persisted
in all of them, and has given all its members a stake in the
survival of liberal society. Not coincidentally liberal political

systems have taken root in Germany, Italy, and Japan in a period—the years following the Second World War—of unprecedented material prosperity.

In the middle of the chain that connects political liberalism with science stands the market. The system of independent centers of economic decision in liberal societies encouraged technological innovation. Individual entrepreneurs, hungry for profit, were willing to try new techniques of production. Since there were many producers many innovations were tested. Other societies where science prospered but where the state kept control of the economy did not translate the fruits of scientific endeavor into technological innovation geared to economic advance.[14]

Science has not been the exclusive property of liberalism. The socialist thought of the nineteenth century emphasized it. And the Eastern variant of socialism even today claims "scientific" status. It honors scientists above almost all others. But it does not permit them to practice science freely. The state keeps close watch over what they do. Soviet scientists do have some impressive achievements to their credit. But they have borrowed heavily from the liberal West, where almost all the major scientific discoveries since 1917 have been made. The heavy hand of the party and the state have handicapped Soviet science, especially by making it difficult to obtain what is available in the West as a matter of course—information. And on occasion Soviet science has been pushed backward. The baleful influence of the crackpot theories of Trofim Lysenko on genetics and agriculture is the outstanding example.[15]

The putative role of science in guiding public affairs in Eastern "socialist" societies has become a totem. It is a symbol used to justify the management of the economy by edict and the control of political life by a select few, because the older justifications, like contact with the Almighty, have lost their force.

Liberal societies have flourished in North America and Western Europe. The purest specimen is undoubtedly the United States. The first European settlers who came here found no old regime. There were no bastions of privilege to assault, only a vast and empty continent to fill. The debate about how to fill it, and how to govern it once filled, has taken place almost entirely within the boundaries of liberal assumptions.[16] There are two important exceptions. First, North America was not entirely empty when the Europeans arrived. Indians already lived there. But the Europeans came to regard the Indians as a natural barrier to be overcome and eliminated, like the frontier itself. And second, an illiberal political tradition arose in the thirteen southern states of the Old Confederacy. But the Civil War largely destroyed it.[17] The United States is the country most devoted to the principles of economic liberalism. Civil and criminal penalties for obstructing the free play of the market are written into the American legal code.[18] And some of the most important technological innovations have had American origins. Edison and Steinmetz were Americans. The telegraph, the telephone, the computer and transistor were first made in the United States.

Liberal society is 200 years old. Elements of liberalism can be traced much further back in history than that, of course. But two centuries ago the three aspects of liberalism came together, and their combination became self-sustaining for the first time. The defense of political liberty goes back to ancient Greece, and to the Magna Carta of 1296 and the Glorious Revolution of 1688 in England. But 1776 is a suitable starting point for modern political liberalism because it is the year of the birth of the United States, which was the first political community to design itself consciously as liberal, and to provide itself with the hallmark of liberalism, a constitution.

The roots of economic liberalism similarly reach beyond the eighteenth century. Market towns and mercantile communities were scattered throughout Europe and the Levant in medieval times. But in the "annus mirabilis," 1776, Adam Smith's book *The Wealth of Nations* appeared, and this was a turning point. For the book set down systematically, for the first time, the rules and practices of the market system.

And this made it possible for individuals to follow the rules, and for states to foster and enforce them.

Finally, 200 years ago is a convenient starting point for the scientific face of modern liberalism. For it was in the last quarter of the eighteenth century that the industrial revolution—the process of rapid technological innovation that led to sustained economic growth—gathered momentum in Great Britain, the nation where it began. In particular this period marks the swift expansion of the pioneering sector of the British economy in the industrial revolution, the textile industry, which paved the way for the enormous outputs of iron, steel, chemicals, and electronics that have followed in the last two centuries.

2

Two hundred years ago, and 100 years ago as well, the greatest challenge to liberalism came from the persisting inequalities of traditional society. But conservatism, like the Bastille that seemed in that feverish moment in 1789 to embody it, no longer stands. Only historical memories remain, like the plaque at the site of the long-dismembered French prison. Fifty and twenty-five years ago the greatest challenge came from militant illiberalism. Powerful states arose whose governing principles were radically at odds with liberal precepts, and who took it upon themselves to spread these principles and eradicate liberal ones. These states proposed to subject every human activity, from the cradle to the grave, to the control of the state, and so earned the title "totalitarian."

Well-wishers of liberal societies from Tocqueville to the present have judged it a difficult task to arouse such societies to protect themselves, since people who are devoted to private pursuits will be slow to join the common defense.[19] And the Western democracies did nod, fuss, and turn away during the 1930s while the threat of fascism was building. But they awoke in the 1940s to smash the Axis powers, and having smashed them converted them to liberal ways.

This was an astonishing missionary triumph—a triumph of both the book and the sword.

The vigilance of the liberal states carried over into the next decade, when Communism assumed the role of their arch-enemy. But as the two-hundredth anniversary of the beginning of modern liberalism arrived Communism seemed less menacing than it had loomed twenty or even ten years before. The Soviet Union had behaved less aggressively than had been feared in the early days of the cold war. Just how limited Soviet ambitions in international politics were certainly continued to be a matter of dispute. But the worry that the logic of Marxism-Leninism would drive the Soviets inexorably into a war against liberalism had abated. And Marxism-Leninism itself had become less radiantly attractive than liberals had once feared it was. The nations newly emerging from colonial rule had not been powerfully drawn to it. Many have come to be governed by authoritarian regimes, and some call themselves socialist. But it is not like-ly that these regimes would be appreciably different if Marx had never written, or if Lenin had never arrived at the Fin-land station. And the principles of Marxism-Leninism, such as they are, have little appeal even within the borders of the greatest state that claims to abide by them. They do not serve to enthuse and mobilize Soviet citizens,[20] who accept them the way the ruled accept the dictates of the rulers in other authoritarian societies, with the resignation of peasants facing a drought. If there is an Eastern threat to liberalism it comes from Russian arms, not from the Soviet example.

Political liberalism has weathered two centuries in mint condition. This is not the case for economic liberalism. Thomas Jefferson would find the American political system of the present day on the whole familiar. Adam Smith by contrast would discover that the British economy has changed considerably from the system that he described. Two great forces have moved liberal economies away from Smith's pure market of scattered small producers responding to the wishes of consumers through the price system.

The first is a nonliberal principle that citizens of liberal societies have embraced, leading to an "antinomy" as Edward Shils calls it,[21] or a conflict between liberals and liberalism. This is the principle of social and economic equality. Equality is not wholly compatible with individual liberty. If everyone can do as he pleases conspicuous differences among people are likely to arise. If, on the other hand, all must be equal, the freedom to be unequal must be restricted.

Egalitarian sentiment has taken root in liberal societies for two reasons: first, sympathy for the poor and downtrodden has nourished it. This sympathy is not properly speaking a part of liberalism. It descends from Christian compassion and charity and has been a central concern of those in the West who have identified themselves as socialists. But the indifference to the poor that the logic of liberalism prescribes—summed up by the (perhaps apocryphal) story of the social Darwinist sociologist who told his students with satisfaction that he had encountered a beggar on his way to class whom he had refused to assist on the grounds that the workings of the social "market" had placed the man in the gutter and so there he belonged—has never been wholly popular in Western societies, and it has become less so in the twentieth century. Second, the democratic political systems of liberal states have given the poor some power over the rich. They have been able to vote themselves some redistribution of wealth. In this sense political liberalism may be said to have carried within itself the seeds of the modification of its economic counterpart. The movement for equality has nowhere put all citizens on an equal economic footing. Often it has aimed not at leveling society so much as to bring its bottom layer up to some minimal plateau. The goal has been not strict equality but a universal minimum standard of welfare.

So liberalism as practiced in this century has split into two factions, which are divided according to their enthusiasm for diluting liberty with equality or welfare.[22] The "autonomist" liberals, as Shils calls them, favor as few hindrances to the working of the market as possible, no matter what the distribution of social wealth that results. The "collectivist" liberals believe that the government should intervene in the market to make the distribution of goods and services more equitable than it would be if only the market determined it.

Political debate in the Western liberal societies since 1945 has taken place between these two wings of liberalism over how far government intervention should go. The question divides the Democratic from the Republican Party in the United States, the Social Democratic Party from the Christian Democratic Union and the Christian Social Union in West Germany, the Labour party from the Conservatives in Great Britain, and the Social Democratic parties from their opponents in Scandinavia and the Benelux countries.[23] The issue at the heart of this ongoing debate is how much of one, liberty or equality, should be given up to promote the other. The collectivists have, on the whole, held the upper hand. Like the movement of a glacier the fraction of the social product that the government appropriates and redistributes has grown steadily larger.

The second great force that has modified the market system of Adam Smith has been the drive for efficiency. The purpose here has been not a different distribution of society's goods and services but a greater production of them. The drive for efficiency has taken three forms.[24]

The first was recognized by Adam Smith himself. Although he believed that government should, on the whole, stand aside from the working of the economy, it did, he thought, have the duty "of erecting and maintaining those public institutions and those public works which, though they may be in highest degree advantageous to a great society, are, however, of such a nature that the profit could never repay the expense to any individual or small number of individuals, and which it therefore cannot be expected that any individual or small number of individuals should erect or maintain."[25] These "public goods," which the government, not the market, must supply (and that the government must therefore tax its citizens to support), include roads, schools, police and fire protection, and national defense. Governments are also more and more taking responsibility for another kind of product that the market cannot adequately handle. This is the effluvia of industrial production, of which all members of society become consumers. Fresh air and clean water are increasingly becoming public goods that the government must intervene in the market to provide.

A second impulse for efficiency that has modified the economic society that Adam Smith knew comes not from the government but from the constituent parts of the market. This is the trend toward the growth and agglomeration of firms to the point that they dominate some sectors of the economy and can ignore market rules. They can set prices at artificially high levels, for instance, because no competitors exist to undercut them. There are several reasons for this drift toward what economists call "oligopoly." One is the fact that large firms can often produce more efficiently than small ones. Economists refer to the advantages of size as the "economies of scale." Abetting this is the desire of firms to maximize their revenues, which an oligopolistic position often permits them to do. It also gives them a measure of security that they do not enjoy in pure market conditions. Many enterprises, like many people, seek to be as certain as they can be of what the future will bring. Oligopoly increases their certainty by giving them some control over the future. A similar trend has, of course, long been at work in the labor market. Workers in liberal states have won the right of collective bargaining. With it they have pushed wages higher than they would be if each worker negotiated separately.

The third modification of the market for the sake of efficiency is the practice, begun in earnest in the 1930s, of government intervention to increase the overall level of economic output (and thus the level of employment as well). This practice is associated with the theories of John Maynard Keynes. Until Keynes the economy was regarded, as Adam Smith had described it, as a self-regulating institution. Like a gyroscope, if it leaned too far in one direction or another it would automatically put itself back upright. But in the

1930s it began to appear that, left to their own devices, the economies of the liberal states would topple over. Keynes showed why this could happen. Specifically, he showed why investment in a declining economy might not be sufficient to revive it. The necessary investment, he concluded, would have to come from the government. Adam Smith had cast the role of the state in economic affairs as that of a "night watchman," standing guard to make certain that nothing interferes with the glorious self-regulating precision of the market machinery. But since the 1930s the watchman has climbed further and further into the interstices of machinery, squirting oil into selected valves and joints to make it run more smoothly.[26]

By its two-hundredth birthday Adam Smith's free market of independent producers and sovereign consumers bound together through the price nexus with the night watchman standing by benevolently had metamorphosed into something quite different. The most striking difference was the new role of government, which took a direct part in a wide range of economic activities. Government had come to have a say in how much was invested, in what was produced, and in how what was produced was distributed. Economic decisions that had formerly been the purview of private citizens had fallen to the government. Citizens had made these decisions according to market rules—self-interest defined as profit. Governments made them on less consistent and more subjective grounds. The economy came to be governed less by standardized calculations and more by the interplay of power and policy that characterizes politics. But Adam Smith's economic system was not wholly eclipsed. Wide scope still remained for the relatively free play of market forces. A "public" economic sector, where choices were made politically, coexisted with a "private" sphere, where market rules still held sway. The pure market had evolved into the "mixed economy."

3

The mixed economy struck a balance between the domain of the government and the realm of the market. Those who make it their business to peer into the future of liberal society believe that the two will not remain in equilibrium, and predict that the forces that have modified the market system over the last century will, during the next one, overwhelm and submerge it. They foresee a transformation in the economic life of liberal states as broad as the shift from a pure market to a mixed economy—a transformation that, in sweeping away the remnants of economic liberalism, could cast the future of political liberalism into doubt as well.

The push for economic and social equality that has been under way for over a century will gain in strength. The list of goods and services to which each citizen is presumed entitled by right will lengthen to include such things as medical care, higher education, and housing. This is the forecast (among others) of Daniel Bell.[27] As the list grows, the government's writ over the economy will be extended and the allocation of more and more of the social product will pass from the decentralized, self-regulating, and more or less automatic mechanisms of the market to the more visible, less predictable, and potentially far more contentious political arena.[28]

The continuing quest for efficiency in the economies of liberal states will also, in Robert Heilbroner's view, diminish the vitality of the market. He believes that the economic machinery of the liberal states will suffer recurrent breakdowns, like local collapses and general recessions, which the government will be obliged to step in to try to repair. And it will become increasingly active in pursuit of the familiar goals of growth, high employment, and price stability. Keynes envisioned the government giving the economy an occasional prod when it tilted too far in one direction. Heilbroner thinks that it will become a permanent prop, without which the economy would tip over and collapse.[29]

The trend toward oligopoly also imperils the market. Some firms are becoming so large and powerful that they can act with considerable independence of the discipline of the price system and the wishes of the consumer. In John Kenneth Galbraith's view many firms have already wholly superseded the market. He divides the American economy into two sections; one in which enterprises still operate according to market procedures; the other, the "planning sector," which includes the 1,000 largest firms, where these procedures no longer apply at all. The size, the resources, the powers of persuasion and the links with the government of the firms in the planning sector give them effective autonomy from the considerations that Adam Smith deemed the supreme laws of economics. The leviathan of the planning sector, according to Galbraith, can not only fix prices and costs, as traditional oligopoly theory concedes, it can also "influence consumers, and organize the supply of materials and components, and mobilize its own savings and capital, and develop a strategy for handling labor, and influence the attitudes of the community and the actions of the state."[30] Galbraith foresees an increase in government control over the economy, not to dilute the power of the market further, but to assert public authority over the power that the market has already lost to the planning sector.

Bell worries about the decline of the market, for he does not believe that the political system for allocating the social product that will take its place can run smoothly and harmoniously without some overall concept of social welfare to guide it, and no such widely accepted concept presently exists. Galbraith welcomes the economic hegemony of the government, because this will better serve the "public purpose" than the present situation, in which officials of the planning sector, whom Galbraith calls the "technostructure," are in charge. Heilbroner has more neutral—or perhaps more mixed—feelings.

But all three agree that the market of *The Wealth of Nations* is in the process of withering away. If so a remarkable historical renewal is taking place. Surveying the liberal societies of the nineteenth century, Karl Marx, one of their severest critics, found their political institutions completely subservient to the wishes of the captains of their economies.

The state, in his famous phrase, was "the executive committee of the bourgeoisie." As the twenty-first century approaches the tables are turning. Business is becoming fused with government and, in Robert Heilbroner's words, "is apt to become more and more the civil service of the nation-state."[31]

This raises important questions about the future of liberalism. How will the social product be distributed? More specifically, how liberal will the means of production be? Will political liberalism be able to survive without its economic counterpart, which has complemented and buttressed it historically? These questions are particularly pressing when set against another, related forecast about the future of the economy of liberal society. This also comes most notably from Robert Heilbroner, and it fixes on the middle distance rather than the immediate future. Heilbroner predicts that environmental constraints will come to dominate economic activity. Resources will run short and the limits of the ecosphere's tolerance for the expansion of industrial output will be reached.[32] The vestiges of economic liberalism will disappear. The state will be in complete command of production and distribution. But it will preside over an economy that ceases to expand, that stagnates, that even begins to shrink. The cushion of growth on which political liberalism has rested will be gone. The worsening of economic conditions may necessitate the kind of retrenchment and sacrifice that only an authoritarian regime can impose. And if that occurs political liberalism will vanish.

The prospects for science, the third principal feature of modern liberalism, are scarcely so gloomy. But neither are they uniformly bright. For almost all of liberalism's 200 years the procedures of science have resembled the rules of Adam Smith's market. And society has respected the work of scientists while leaving them free to do it as they have seen fit. But as liberalism began its third century both the structure of science and its prestige have been called into question.

The structure of science has in fact changed in the last

twenty-five years. The scale of scientific enterprise has grown. This has been due in part to the requirements of research. As the frontiers of knowledge have been pushed forward, the task of pushing them further still has become more difficult. Scientific exploration has proved to be like drilling for oil; the deeper the penetration the more resistance there is to going on, and the greater the expense of overcoming this resistance. To take one dramatic example, at the beginning of this century Einstein could make historic advances in theoretical physics with a pencil and paper. Now theoretical physicists require for their work huge, elaborate particle accelerators that cost millions of dollars to construct.

Partly because of the mounting expense of scientific research governments have stepped in to help subsidize it. Since World War II governments have increasingly supplanted philanthropic foundations, universities, and business as the chief supports of science in the Western liberal societies. Not just the scale of the necessary financing has drawn governments to science; they have developed positive interests in the productivity of their scientific communities. For science has increasingly become the basis for national military power and economic prosperity, and the government is traditionally the guardian of the first and more and more the sponsor of the second. Still, even with the expanding role of government, the liberal core of science, freedom of inquiry, has remained intact—at least until recently.

But there are harbingers of change. The term "scientific responsibility" has come into common usage. It denotes the view that since scientific exploration has social consequences society should have a say in what and how scientists explore. Three scientific projects, and their effects, in particular have given rise to this view. Scientists have contributed to the fabrication of weapons of unprecedented destructive power. Scientific discoveries have laid the basis for industrial production that has proved to have toxic by-products; scientists are accorded part of the blame for pollution. And most recently refinements that scientists have made in the delicate art of genetic engineering threaten to put the fundamental alteration and even the creation of life itself within the realm of possibility.[33]

The alarm at the poisonous weeds that have sprouted in the garden of science has fed a broader, deeper disenchantment with the scientific enterprise in liberal societies. For whatever its achievements science does not satisfy the deepest longings of the human spirit. It does not solve, or even address, the profoundest mysteries of life. It does not offer the consolations of religion, which it has undercut but not fully replaced. Joseph Schumpeter thought that capitalism would die when society no longer believed in the values that underpinned it. He predicted that the entrepreneurial spirit would come to be regarded as crass and antisocial, and would fade away.[34] The disenchantment with science represents a similar crisis of faith. And it is not just a faith in science, but in all of liberalism that is in question. The cultural crisis of liberalism includes a preference for communal over individual social patterns, for the spontaneous expression of emotion over abstract thought, for the cultivation of inner tranquility and human relations over the pursuit of material gain, and for the acceptance and enjoyment of nature over the exploration and mastery of it.

Strains of this general dissatisfaction with liberalism have wafted through liberal societies for the past two centuries. But they became particularly pronounced in the latter part of the decade of the 1960s, and among the rising generation, the one born after the Second World War. In combination with the prospect that the market, the heart of economic liberalism, will soon be wholly swallowed up by government, and that the scientific market will also be hobbled by public authority, this challenge to the moral basis of liberal society portends a future for liberalism that is very uncertain indeed.

4

The appropriate assessment of liberalism's prospects is not, however, an epitaph, despite the challenges that it confronts.

Liberal society is resilient. Cultural liberalism will not be washed away by a tide of mysticism; even if Adam Smith's market disappears entirely it is not likely that an Eastern-style edict economy will replace it; and political liberty shows signs not only of surviving but of prospering. So the three faces of liberalism, or some version of them, promise to continue to complement and reinforce each other as the third century of modern liberalism begins.

The challenge to cultural liberalism seems on the wane. As it recedes in time, the tumult of the late 1960s appears more and more a passing event, the result of a fortuitous combination of circumstances. The disorders that broke out in all the liberal societies stemmed from the rise to maturity of a generation with a singular background. Its members were raised in affluence and in an atmosphere of admiration for the qualities of youth above all others, and they were fired with a sense of missionary righteousness, in the United States by the civil rights movement and throughout the liberal West by the revulsion against the American war in Indochina. This generation was angry at the injustices that its relatively innocent upbringing made especially unexpected and shocking, uneasy with the competition for place that followed from the numbers that the postwar baby boom produced (the events of 1968 in France began with protests against crowded conditions in the universities), and powerfully infected with the strain of romanticism that is a permanent feature of liberal society. But the blaze that these feelings kindled have died down as the rebels of the 1960s have grown older. The postwar generation differs from its predecessor, as all generations do. But it has not turned its back on all that its forebears, going back two centuries, have built and valued. And the generation that follows the rebels of the 1960s apparently has no revolutionary enthusiasm at all. Its members appear intent not on overturning liberal society but on joining it on the best terms that they can manage.

Although skepticism of science is probably greater now than at any time in this century science will continue to be practiced. But it cannot altogether evade the influence of the state. Scientific questions fall too emphatically into the public arena, the fruits of science touch too many people too directly for the scientific enterprise to return to the pristine circumstances of the prewar era. Proponents of total scientific independence, of "laissez-faire" science, are still to be found. But like the enthusiasts for a return to the pure market economy of Adam Smith their views are more a blend of religious conviction and nostalgia than a practical agenda.

Science is not fated, however, to fall under the tight government control that harnesses it in the authoritarian societies of eastern Europe and that has stunted its development outside the borders of the liberal world. The way the economies of liberal societies have developed offers a useful parallel: science may well follow the path that the economy took in the first three-quarters of this century. As in the past for the economy, in science there is a drift away from a simple market design. The scale of enterprises is growing and the government is seeking influence on the familiar grounds that what these enterprises do affects the society as a whole, that science like industrial production, has "externalities." But science may be expected to reach the same kind of compromise with public authority that the mixed economy represented, a compromise that leaves considerable room for the unfettered functioning of the scientific market. The government may decree a "war on cancer," but scientists will plot the lines of attack.

Another trend in the organization of science, which also corresponds to a development in the economic sphere of liberalism, offers further assurance that a compromise that permits its liberal core to survive will be struck. This is the increasing professional self-consciousness of scientists. They are following in the footsteps of doctors and lawyers in the United States who, faced with the demands for reform and public control in the early years of this century, declared that membership in these "learned professions" gave them both special rights and particular responsibilities. The professions of medicine and law, they asserted, are not only occupations, they are services as well. They involve special competence, which in turn requires special training to acquire. Because of this specialized character, they argued, laymen could not make competent medical and legal judgments: a patient could not prescribe treatment, nor a client try his own case. Full powers had to be given to the professional in these matters, and in related ones like deciding who shall practice and how much practitioners shall charge for their service. In return for these powers doctors and lawyers promised to regulate themselves strictly in the public interest.

Scientists appear to be moving in this direction. In response to public disquiet about their work they are setting up standards for their research, which they propose to police and enforce themselves. Societies of chemists, physicists, biologists, and engineers, and even those that include scientists of all kinds, like the American Association for the Advancement of Science, show signs of evolving from intellectual and social fraternities to guilds that set internal standards and pressure groups that lobby for professional interests.[35]

One of these interests is the maximum possible freedom from outside interference. And in return for the pledge of self-regulation, and because scientific competence is, after all, specialized and scientists, despite this spell of disenchantment, still have considerable prestige, they are likely to win considerable autonomy for science.

The prestige of scientists will remain high, for one reason, because their labors are likely to make an ever-larger contribution to economic prosperity. Limits to economic growth may loom ahead in the next century. But for the balance of this one and beyond growth will remain a prized goal of liberal—and other—societies. Growth depends increasingly upon innovation, and innovation, in turn, is becoming more and more closely linked to scientific research, rather than to the trial and error inventions of the nineteenth century. The growing importance of science in promoting growth does not necessarily mean that the liberal economic system, the market, will persist. Translating the achievements of science into economic terms might well come to be yet another of the responsibilities that government assumes. But there are indications that, contrary to the predictions of social seers, a revival of the market system is taking place.

In the United States there is widespread annoyance with the size of government. The "bureaucracy" has become a political villain, and aspiring political leaders now promise to do battle with it.[36] And some critics of American business are losing faith in the capacity of the government to bend large enterprises to the public interest, and speak of dusting of those ancient staples off liberal economic practice, the antitrust laws, to do so.[37] They are switching their hopes from regulation by the government to competition in the marketplace. There is a similar shift underway in the thinking about how to administer social equalization. The familiar approach has the government providing services to citizens who cannot purchase them in the market. It is being suggested, however, that the government simply give these citizens money and let them shop in the market for what they want like everybody else.

In the United Kingdom, the liberal society where government has, perhaps, gone furthest in usurping the prerogatives of the market, the Labour party, which has sponsored the advance of government control, has seen fit to lead its retreat, at least temporarily. Even these resolutely collectivist liberals have seemed sympathetic to the proposition, frequently advanced by their autonomist opponents, that without the incentives to work and to invest that the market supplies the economy will stagnate. There are, finally, predictions that enterprises of small and medium size, which are dominated by the market rather than vice-versa, will gain in importance in the economies of liberal states[38]—predictions that gain credibility from the ongoing expansion of the "service" sector of the economy, which is less susceptible to oligopoly than the manufacturing sphere.

Whether the steady drift away from the market will be halted or reversed remains very much to be seen. The portents of revival may turn out to be misleading. Market rules may cease entirely to govern the economies of liberal states.

But even if this occurs these economies will not be guided by wholly illiberal principles. Another parallel is instructive here, this one between economic and political liberalism. The development of the mixed economic system may proceed in a way comparable to the shift from direct to representative democracy.[39]

Economic decisions may come to be made centrally, and politically. But the process of decision is likely to entail bargaining among organized groups representing different interests. This already happens in the United States, where secondary associations have always been strongest. When Tocqueville observed them they were shelters for minority political views.[40] But in the twentieth century they have increasingly become vehicles for the advancement of particular economic interests. And more and more groups are now organizing themselves and pressing their claim upon the state. The precedent for the interplay of such groups is the way the U.S. Congress has traditionally distributed largesse in the form of public works projects—through "log-rolling" among its members. If the main pattern of economic decision becomes log-rolling, a shift will have taken place in liberal societies from a mixed to a corporate economy, in which the basic unit of decision will be the organized group.

This system would not be as democratic as the market, where the individual has had the power of decision over a very wide range of economic choices. The individual's power would be diluted, and those who are not organized would have very little power at all. But a corporate economy would be more democratic, and hence more faithful to liberal principles, than the edict economy, where a supreme authority responsible to no one except itself decides what will be produced and how it will be distributed. A corporate economy may also suffer, as Bell fears, from the absence of a principle of social welfare to guide its economic decisions.[41] In the past none was needed. By fragmenting these decisions the market made them effectively invisible. The result was unequal distribution, and because there was no central locus from which inequality flowed, and because the market mechanism itself commanded respect, inequality was tolerated. With the demise of the market and the centralization of distribution the various groups may clamor for ever-larger shares of the social product, and become angry when their aspirations are not met. This would make liberal society more disorderly than it has been in the past.

Another undesirable effect of the drift toward a corporate economy is already apparent: inflation. Lacking the philosophical basis and the political strength for resisting the claims of various corporate groups the state simply accedes to them. And being unable to pay for what it has promised out of what the economy produces it prints more money.[42] But it is not impossible that some concept of general welfare will arise, which includes some definition of the proper limits of corporate claims upon the state. The original thirteen American colonies decided that the advantages of unity outweighed the attractions of unfettered individual sovereignty. Corporate groups may similarly conclude that it is worth restraining their particular claims in order to achieve overall economic stability.

The survival of cultural and economic liberalism, even in modified form, depends in the end upon the strength of political liberalism. Science can only keep a measure of independence as long as a general commitment to freedom of inquiry and expression exists. The corporate economy will permit popular representation in economic decisions only so long as the political system that presides over economic decisions remains democratic. The fates of the second and third faces of modern liberalism are tied to the first. And this is why they may be expected to survive. For the prospects for political liberalism are bright. Its principles have taken deep root in the last two centuries. The force of belief and the force of habit behind liberalism give it the wherewithal to outlive the conditions in which it was born. Just as the Protestants of Max Weber's description developed habits of thrift and industry out of the conviction that these offered the way to salvation but worked just as hard even after their preoccupation with the next world had ebbed, so liberal values are likely to survive the drastic modification of the economic and cultural institutions with which they have been historically associated and that have helped to sustain them.

In fact, as economic liberalism is being eroded and cultural liberalism is in doubt, political liberalism is thriving. It is thriving especially in the United States. There its greatest triumph has been the civil rights movement, whose success has proven the fidelity of the greatest liberal state to its professed principles. The civil rights movement's goal was a quintessentially liberal one: to win full political rights—"the rights of Americans" they might be called in paraphrase of one of the slogans of the Revolution of 1776—for black citizens of the United States. The tactics that the civil rights movement used were deliberately designed to fall well within the boundaries of proper liberal conduct. Peaceful assembly and legislation were the mainstays. Even when they broke the law in protest against statutes that they considered unjust the soldiers of the movement did so openly, nonviolently, and in a way that affirmed their respect for the principle of the rule of the law, if not for every article of every legal code. And the battle for civil rights was won. Black Americans enjoy the same political liberties that their white neighbors have.[43] The Watergate affair of the 1970s, which wrenched the president himself from his pedestal, also affirmed liberal values. Mr. Nixon was pulled down in the name of restraining the authority of government and especially preserving the rights of citizens against it, and on the grounds that the sovereign does not have the right to lie, cheat, or steal.

In Europe, France and Italy harbor formidable native Communist parties, whose commitment to liberal principles are in doubt. It is more likely, however, that the French and Italian parties will either conform to these principles or remain in opposition than that either will take power and make the country over in the illiberal image of the eastern bloc. And liberty is beginning to flower in southern Europe. The political systems of Spain, Portugal, and Greece have all become markedly less authoritarian in the 1970s. It may be that political liberalism is following the path of economic growth southward, from the Protestant north of Europe to the Latin south to the Iberian Peninsula and then to the Balkans. These new recruits for the liberal camp lie, it is true, within the sphere of influence of the greatest liberal power, and the proximity of the United States and her allies has no doubt affected the political tendencies of neighboring nations. But they were within the American orbit for decades before their liberal inclinations began to appear.

Political liberalism has suffered its greatest recent setbacks in those parts of Asia and Africa that became independent of colonial rule after World War II, the nations of the Third World. In many of them the metropolitan country left, in the wake of its retreat, a series of liberal institutions that it had imported. In most these quickly collapsed and fell into disuse. But even in the Third World political liberalism is not extinct. 1977 was the year of democracy in the successor states to the British Empire in South Asia. The governments of Pakistan and Sri Lanka felt compelled at least to go through the motions of free elections.[44] And in India, the largest state on the subcontinent, the elections were so free that a government that had acted under emergency powers for two years, a Prime Minister who had held office for eleven, and a party that had ruled the country for thirty ever since independence, were soundly defeated.

The flower of liberty is in full bloom in North America and Western Europe. It is sprouting in the southern parts of Europe and poking through the soil in parts of Asia. And a few tendrils are even stirring below ground in Eastern Europe, where liberal values have never prospered. There are not many liberals in the Soviet bloc,[45] but there are enough to irritate mightily the regimes there. What does this mean? It would be too much to find in it a sweeping historical movement. Even the dramatic outcome of the Indian election and the courage of the Soviet dissidents do not make a worldwide libertarian imperative. But they do show that political liberalism—popular sovereignty and individual rights—still has considerable vitality. It is growing, not declining in attractiveness. Two hundred years after they first seized enough imaginations to be formally adopted as the basis for organizing and governing real societies the principles of liberalism remain robust. There is life left in liberalism.

Notes

1. See Robert Heilbroner, *The Worldly Philosophers*, 4th ed. (New York: Simon & Schuster, 1972), pp. 17-18.
2. This classification partly follows Daniel Bell's in *The Coming of Post-Industrial Society* (New York: Basic Books, 1973), p. 12.
3. See Giovanni Sartori, "The Relevance of Liberalism in Retrospect."
4. The basic market rule is that producers gear their output to the level at which the price received for a product equals its marginal cost of production. At that (theoretical) point supply and demand will be in balance.
5. The phrase is Adam Smith's. Cited in Robert Heilbroner, *The Worldly Philosophers*, p. 52.
6. Sartori, "The Relevance of Liberalism in Retrospect," p. 2 and *passim*.
7. Barrington Moore's superb study of the role of the landed upper classes in the origins of political liberalism traces the relationship for all three countries. In Britain the gentry pushed the peasantry off the land through the Enclosure Acts and took up commercial agriculture. It turned into a kind of merchant class and adopted a liberal political outlook. In France part of the gentry also took up commercial pursuits. But the peasantry remained on the land. They were needed to supply cheap labor. To keep them in harness the gentry retained its traditional privileges and its conservative political predispositions. It had the makings of an illiberal bourgeoisie, but was swept away by the revolution of 1789. (Germany suffered in the twentieth century from not having had such a revolution in the eighteenth or nineteenth. The rest of the world suffered also.) In the United States a politically liberal middle class grew up in the North. The southern plantation owners, however, like the French gentry, were capitalist but not liberal. The Civil War destroyed them. It was, in Moore's phrase, "the last bourgeois uprising"; the equivalent for American society of the French revolution. See Barrington Moore, *The Social Origins of Dictatorship and Democracy:*

Lord and Peasant in the Making of the Modern World (Boston: Beacon Press, 1967).

8. The occasions when liberal societies have moved deliberately toward edict economies are the exceptions that prove the rule. This has happened in wartime, when political liberties were also often curtailed, and when all national pursuits were in any case subordinated to the goal of victory.

9. The term here has a narrower meaning than the anthropologist's usage.

10. Goods are also evaluated according to quality in ideal market conditions, but in such conditions price presumably reflects quality.

11. Perhaps the most famous defense of freedom of expression is John Stuart Mill's essay *On Liberty*. Mill argues that the uninhibited circulation of ideas serves the interests of truth, since the test of truth is the ability to withstand criticism and the challenge of different views. This is precisely the logic of science.

12. For most of recorded history the two proceeded separately. Many of the important technical advances in the early years of the industrial revolution came from the workshops of "inspired tinkerers," who knew little basic science. But in recent years pure and applied science have drawn closer together. Today much of the technical innovation that occurs is tied directly to theoretical research. See Bell, *The Coming of Post-Industrial Society*, p. 20ff. David Landes notes that even for the post-World War II period a correlation between scientific activity, as measured by expenditures on research and development, and economic growth, is difficult to find. But he goes on to suggest reasons why the two have probably been associated, even though the association is difficult to demonstrate. David Landes, *The Unbound Prometheus: Technological Change 1750 to the Present* (Cambridge: Cambridge University Press, 1969), p. 520.

13. On this point see David Potter, *People of Plenty* (Chicago: University of Chicago Press, 1954), ch. 5.

14. See Landes, *Unbound Prometheus*, pp. 28-9.

15. The People's Republic of China seems to be following a similar pattern. Science there must "serve the people." Where the social usefulness of scientific inquiry is obvious Chinese science is relately sophisticated. Important work has been done, for example, in predicting earthquakes. But the criterion of social usefulness, as well as the requirement that everybody, including scientific specialists, take a turn at the peasant's round of life, has undoubtedly retarded Chinese science in other fields.

16. This is the well-known argument of Louis Hartz in *The Liberal*

Tradition in America (New York: Harcourt, Brace and World, 1955).

17. See note 7.

18. These are principally contained in the antitrust laws.

19. This was a preoccupation of John Kennedy's. See Henry Fairlie, *The Kennedy Promise* (New York: Dell Publishing Co., 1974).

20. Soviet citizens were enthused and mobilized during World War II, but by the cruelties of the German invaders and appeals to patriotic nationalism, not Marxism-Leninism.

21. See the chapter in this book by Edward Shils, "The Antinomies of Liberalism."

22. The concepts of equality and welfare have different political histories. But in the contemporary period they tend to merge, as what is regarded as the minimal level of acceptable welfare for every citizen rises higher and higher.

23. In the United States self-styled "conservatives" are on the whole autonomist liberals. But their preference does not always carry over into the political sphere. Many of them want the state to regulate things that classic liberalism insists it should avoid—pornography and the use of narcotics, for example. In the United Kingdom the Tory party is an amalgam, and not an entirely relaxed one, of autonomist liberals like Edward Heath and traditional conservatives like Harold Macmillan. These last are a dying breed. Their spiritual forebears, going back to the nineteenth century, supported many welfare measures on the grounds of noblesse oblige.

24. Greater efficiency of production can lead to greater equity of distribution. This is certainly true of the production of "public goods," like, for example, police protection. Without public police the rich would hire private security (as many in fact do) and the poor would have none at all. Another kind of efficiency, increased growth through government stimulation, has served as a substitute for redistribution, or so it is sometimes argued. As the total economic product expands so does the absolute size of each share. And this has the political consequence of overshadowing the fact that the inequality of the relative proportions of the product does not change.

25. Adam Smith, *The Wealth of Nations,* 1933 ed. (London: J. M. Dent and Sons), vol. 2, pp. 210-11. First published in 1776.

26. Robert Heilbroner has argued that the so-called Keynesian revolution of the 1930s was not the first episode of government intervention in the economy in the interests of economic growth. He cites two other periods of government involvement in the American economy, and they correspond to the two other variants of the drive for efficiency. The first came in the nineteenth century when the government

provided vital public goods, in particular the railroads, in support of the initial expansion of industrial production in the United States. The second came at the beginning of this century, when the federal government used its power to help regulate markets, to give firms the kind of security and predictability that they have sought through oligopolistic behavior. Robert Heilbroner, *Business Civilization in Decline* (New York: W. W. Norton, 1976), p. 22ff.

27. Bell, *The Coming of Post-Industrial Society,* p. 159, 282ff.

28. Bell calls this the shift from "economizing" to the "sociologizing" mode. He uses the term "sociologizing" because the basic unit of decision—the entity by and on behalf of whom the decision is being made—changes from the individual to the social group, and sometimes to society as a whole. He believes the growing importance of the "external" effects of economic activity, like pollution, will also expand the public sector of the economics of liberal states at the expense of the private. Bell, *The Coming of Post-Industrial Society,* p. 279ff.

29. This argument is to be found in Heilbroner, *Business Civilization in Decline,* especially p. 32ff.

30. John Kenneth Galbraith, *Economics and the Public Purpose* (Boston: Houghton Mifflin Co., 1973), p. 91. Galbraith's maximalist assessment of the power of the modern corporation, expressed most forcefully in this book, is not unanimously held within the economics fraternity, as Galbraith himself is one of the first to point out. The clearest example of it, and one that Galbraith liberally cites, is the defense industry. Because innovation is considered essential in modern weaponry and because the responsibility for innovation rests in large part with the firms, there is a sense in which the producer decides what the consumer, in this case the government, will buy. And the firms' numerous and close ties with the government give them inordinate influence over price as well. Galbraith's view of the American economy rests on the presumption that the defense industry is the norm that others are coming to resemble, not the exception.

31. Heilbroner, *Business Civilization in Decline,* p. 36.

32. Even allowing for "the invention of new extractive technologies, the development of synthetic chemistry, the discovery of means of disposing of vast mountains of tailings and wastes [and] the extension of capabilities for recycling materials," Heilbroner believes, growth at anything like the pace of the last thirty years cannot continue. And this is all apart from environmental considerations. Heilbroner, *Business Civilization in Decline,* p. 102ff. For a different outlook see Herman Kahn, *The Next 200 Years* (New York: William Morrow & Co., 1976).

33. See Stephen Toulmin, *New York Times* Op Ed, "DNA and the

Public Interest," 12 March 1977, p. 23.

34. Joseph Schumpeter, *Capitalism, Socialism, and Democracy,* 3rd ed. (New York: Harper & Row, 1975).

35. See John T. Edsall, "Scientific Freedom and Responsibility," in *Report of the AAAS Committee on Scientific Freedom and Responsibility* (Washington, D. C.: American Association for the Advancement of Science, 1975).

36. In 1976 in the state of Michigan a referendum was held on a proposal that government expenditure be limited to a specified fraction (8.3 percent) of the personal income of the state's residents. It was, however, defeated. See Milton Friedman, "After the Election," *Newsweek,* 15 November 1976, p. 100.

37. Galbraith, it should be noted, does not think that a revival of the antitrust laws is likely. Nor would this serve any useful purpose, in his view. What is required is to modify the market system where it presently exists, not to extend it to the "planning sector." Galbraith, *Economics and the Public Purpose,* ch. 21, especially pp. 215-17.

38. Andrew Shonfield, "Can Capitalism Survive Until 1999?" *Encounter* 47, no. 1 (January 1977):10-18; Norman Macrae, "The Coming Entrepreneurial Revolution: A Survey," *The Economist* 261, no. 6956 (25 December 1976):41-65.

39. The shift is as much theoretical as practical. There have been few truly direct democracies.

40. Alexis de Tocqueville, *Democracy in America,* vol. 1, paperback ed. (New York: Vintage Press, 1945), p. 198.

41. Bell, *The Coming of Post-Industrial Society,* p. 302ff.

42. See Samuel P. Huntington, "The United States," in *The Crisis of Democracy: Report on the Governability of Democracies to the Trilateral Commission* (New York: New York University Press, 1975), p. 103. New York City has suffered from this syndrome. Politically powerful groups pressed claims upon a government that could only meet them by the municipal equivalent of the national government's power of printing money—borrowing it. The city's enormous indebtedness triggered a fiscal crisis.

43. It cannot be said, however, that they have achieved social and economic parity with whites.

44. Just how free the Pakistani elections were remains a matter of considerable dispute in that country.

45. In no eastern bloc country are liberals close to taking power. And the further east the country, the fewer liberals it is likely to have. The Soviet Union, in this as in other things, is poorest.